Volume 15
SUN TRACKS
An American Indian Literary Series

Series Editor
Larry Evers

Editorial Committee
Vine Deloria, Jr.
N. Scott Momaday
Emory Sekaquaptewa
Leslie Marmon Silko
Ofelia Zepeda

Survival This Way

JOSEPH BRUCHAC

Survival This Way

*Interviews with
American Indian Poets*

*Sun Tracks and
The University of Arizona Press, Tucson*

THE UNIVERSITY OF ARIZONA PRESS

Copyright © 1987
The Arizona Board of Regents
All Rights Reserved

This book was set in 11 on 13 Linotron 202 Electra.
Manufactured in the U.S.A.

Library of Congress Cataloging-in-Publication Data

Bruchac, Joseph, 1942–
  Survival this way.

  (Sun tracks; v. 15)
  Bibliography: p.
  1. American poetry—Indian authors—History and
criticism. 2. Poets, American—20th century—Interviews.
3. Indians of North America—Interviews. 4. Indians of
North America in literature. 5. Poetry—Authorship.
l. Title. II. Series.
PS501.S85 vol. 15   811'.54'09897   87-16224
[PS153.I52]
ISBN 0-8165-1024-5 (alk. paper)

British Library Cataloguing in Publication data are available.

Contents

Preface to

Survival This Way

Interviews with
Native American Poets

Survival, I know how this way.
This way, I know.
It rains.
Mountains and canyons and plants
grow.
We travelled this way,
gauged our distance by stories
and loved our children.
We taught them
to love their births.
We told ourselves over and over
again, "We shall survive
this way."

So writes Simon J. Ortiz, contemporary Acoma Pueblo poet. His words are rooted in the southwestern landscape of his childhood and in the traditions of his people, yet they are words which might have been spoken by almost any Native American writer today, for it is apparent that, to the American Indian writer, poetry is a language of affirmation. Its central themes are neither the depiction of downtrodden peoples nor frustrated protests against the social and racial inequities of America past and present. Its strategies, instead, are primarily those of celebration and survival.

There are few myths as deeply ingrained in American literature and the popular consciousness of this nation (and, indeed, the Western world) as the myth of the Vanishing Redman. From before Fenimore Cooper, the major presence of the American Indian in the writings of non-Indians has been as one of two opposed, yet complementary, incarnations: the murdering redskin and the noble savage. These guises, of course, are two sides of the same coin—a currency unfortunately not yet devalued by overuse. Whether bloodthirsty beast or one of nature's noblemen, the Indian is one whose culture and bloodlines are, for better or worse, slowly and surely being eroded away by the powerful tide of white civilization. So goes the myth of the Vanishing Redman.

As one of Indian ancestry, I began in my teenage years to be suspicious of Native American stereotyping. Like most American children, I had grown up identifying with the cowboys, seldom making a connection between myself and those be-feathered and painted cretins who were afraid of the dark, panicked when their chiefs were killed, and fell like tenpins before John Wayne's infallible bullets. It was a great relief for me in 1969 to encounter Vine Deloria's discussions of that very stereotyping in *Custer Died for Your Sins: An Indian Manifesto*. Deloria, though, was not the first Native American writer to challenge stereotypes of his people in North America. There is a long tradition of American Indians as essayists, writers of autobiographies, poets, and novelists. Cherokee writer Geary Hobson has completed a study which documents the more than two hundred years of significant written literature among the

Cherokee people alone. Hopi writer Wendy Rose now has more than three thousand annotated entries in her bibliography of published writings by American Indians, stretching from 1772 to the present day.

However, it is only in the last two decades that a conscious assault has been made by a growing number of widely diverse American writers, all of Indian blood and from many different tribal traditions, on the assumption that the end of the "American Indian race" is inevitable. It was an assumption held by most whites and many Indians. As Louis Oliver, a Creek poet, told me when I interviewed him in his home in Tahlequah, Oklahoma, "We were always taught in the schools that the Indian was doomed to be absorbed into the American melting pot and that all of our old ways were only memories. Before I met some younger American Indian writers, I was just like that old ground hog. I had crawled in my hole and just accepted that I was forgotten." Now in his 80s, Oliver published his first book, *The Horned Snake*, in 1982. There were, of course, many Indian communities that never doubted their ability to survive as a people. The land-based Navajos, the Hopis, the Zunis, and many of the other Pueblo peoples are examples. But, until mid-century, the common assumption about Western Civilization in America was that the nation's movement was progressive, that tomorrow would be better than today, that being white was better than being Indian. The Nuclear Age put an end to that. Everyone knows that technological miracles have spawned not only the luxuries of electricity and indoor plumbing but also Hiroshima and the nuclear balance of terror, the pollution of air and water and the seemingly unsolvable social inequities of class and race which neither Lyndon Johnson's War on Poverty nor Nixon's program of "Bringing Us Together" solved. Today, as we question Pentagon budgets, drug-ridden classrooms, and PCB-filled streams, many of us ask if the secret of surviving may be found not in the dreams of the future but in the lessons of the past.

But what is the true American past? How far back does the past go in a "nation of immigrants"? One group of "Americans" has roots as deep as the rocks. They go back, at the very least, thirty thousand years. As descendants of those oldest "Americans," American Indian writers may be better equipped to speak of the American past and to draw from it lessons relating to survival.

Their very histories and, in fact, their continued survivals as peoples despite mixed bloodlines, lands sold and stolen, ancient customs outlawed or made impossible—point to the tenacity of their lifeways. That the most recent national census shows a doubling of the numbers of American Indians in only twenty years is an indication of that tenacity. It may also be seen as an indication of a growing pride in affirming one's Indianess, since past censuses may have contained many more Indian people than figures actually showed. "Passing for white" is easily done by many Native American people who have discovered that an Indian, even with a face like Geronimo's, can go unrecognized when he or she dresses and talks like the majority culture. "Invisibility" has been a survival tactic for at least four centuries in the Northeast. The Abenaki people of western Vermont, for example, endure into the present day by keeping a lower than low profile while still remaining "Indian."

When N. Scott Momaday's novel, *House Made of Dawn*, was published in 1968 and won the Pulitzer Prize in 1969, it opened the eyes of a new generation of Native American writers. We read the novel and heard the message of its powerful writing: a person caught between cultures can, despite the deepest of problems, find a way to survive, a road which circles out of the past, "The House Made of Dawn," and ends in the beginning of understanding. It is clear to most Native American readers that Momaday's main character in *House Made of Dawn*, Abel, runs toward healing at the end of the book, "running on the rise of a song." *House Made of Dawn* is a deeply poetic book—perhaps, in a way, an extended prose poem. The book is certainly realistic in its depiction of the difficulties of Indian life in the West. But it does not, as Charles Larson concludes in his *American Indian Fiction*, show us that "the Indian is a vanishing breed."

Paula Gunn Allen speaks for the reactions of many Native American writers to *House Made of Dawn*: "I wouldn't be

Survival This Way

writing now if Momaday hadn't done that book. I would have died." She continued: "It told me that I was sane—or if I was crazy at least fifty thousand people out there were just as nutty in exactly the same way I was, so it was okay. I was not all alone. It did that and it brought *my land* back to me. Part of what I was going through was land sickness—loss of land. It brings great grief to you not to be at home, and he brought it back because he's such a careful writer. I could read the passages and I had been there to the places that he describes. I knew every inch of what he was saying. It was that and the fact that he could write a novel about an 'Abel.'" Where a non-Indian critic saw a depiction of "a vanishing breed," Paula Gunn Allen and many other Native American writers have found the strength and inspiration to continue.

More and more, in response to destruction of both language and life, Native American poets have concerned themselves with the themes of survival. In this collection of interviews they talk about survival of the old ways, survival of individual Indian nations, personal survival, survival of Indian people as a whole, the survival of the natural world and, ultimately, of this planet, this biosphere, which is the greatest of the circles.

The following interviews, selected from more than forty such conducted over four years, all speak to central themes of continuance and renewal, even as they present diverse, talented, eloquent writers. Listening to them talk about their lives, the stories of family and traditions, the struggles to find their own voices, I feel that we hear a central chord of the song from which a truly American literature may now be growing. I hope this is so, for my experience in doing these interviews leads me to believe that this growing song is one of love for the people and the earth, for all living things. Sometimes joyous, sometimes painful, it is, I think, a song of honesty and hope, a song of surviving.

JOSEPH BRUCHAC

Survival This Way

I Climb the Mesas in My Dreams

An Interview with
PAULA GUNN ALLEN

With the publication of her essay "The Sacred Hoop," Paula
Gunn Allen established herself as one of the leading critics of
Native American literature. Her own accomplishments as a significant contemporary American Indian poet and fiction writer
are at least as strong as her critical reputation. Her most recent
books, a collection of poems entitled *Shadow Country* (UCLA
Native American Series, 1982), *The Sacred Hoop: Recovering
the Feminine in American Indian Traditions* (Beacon, 1986),
and a novel, *The Woman Who Owned the Shadows* (Spinsters
Ink, 1983) attest to her diversity.

Like the main characters in her novel and in the writings
of such other southwestern Indian writers as Silko and Moma-

day, she is of mixed ancestry. Her father, a former Lieutenant-Governor of New Mexico, is Lebanese. Her mother is Laguna Pueblo. Allen is related to two other writers from Laguna Pueblo: Carol Lee Sanchez is Paula's sister and Leslie Marmon Silko is a cousin.

Paula is a short woman who laughingly describes herself as overweight and out of shape. Both her intensity and her sense of humor come through in conversation, and her dark, piercing eyes suggest that very little of what goes on around her will go unnoticed. Our conversation took place in the small house which she was renting in 1983 in Berkeley with the poet Judy Grahn. The living room was dominated by a good-sized personal computer which she and Judy had pooled their resources to purchase. It contained in its memory disks both their poetry and a large critical study which Paula was then doing on Native American writing. We moved into Paula's study just off the main room and began the interview with her reading a poem of her choice.

Recuerdo

I have climbed into silence trying for clear air
and seen the peaks rising above me like the gods.
That is where they live, the old people say.
I used to hear them speak when I was a child
and we went to the mountain on a picnic
or to get wood. Shivering in the cold air then
I listened and I heard.

Lately I write, trying to combine sound and memory,
searching for that significance once heard and nearly lost.
It was within the tall pines, speaking.
There was one voice under the wind—something in it
that brought me to terror and to tears. I wanted
to cling to my mother so she could comfort me,
explain the sound and my fear, but I simply sat,
frozen, trying to feel as warm as the campfire,
the family voices around me suggested I should.

Now I climb the mesas in my dreams.
The mountain gods are still, and still I seek.
I finger peyote buttons and count the stalks of sweetsage
given me by a friend—obsessed with a memory
that will not die.
I stir wild honey into my carefully prepared cedar tea
and wait for meaning to arise,
to greet and comfort me.

Maybe this time I will not turn away.
Maybe I will ask instead what that sounding means.
Maybe I will find that exact hollow
where terror and comfort meet.
Tomorrow I will go back and climb the endless mesas
of my home. I will seek thistles drying in the wind,
pocket bright bits of obsidian and fragments
old potters left behind.

—Paula Gunn Allen

I Climb the Mesas

JB: In "Recuerdo," there are images of movement, of loss, and of searching, images I see in many of your poems. What is it that is lost or looked for?

ALLEN: A sense of being securely planted. A therapist once said to me, "You're balanced but not grounded." I'm balanced but, the thing is, I float. It's fairly easy to shove me by the shoulders and knock me over. It's not because I'm off balance; it's because I'm not grounded. That's my body's way of expressing what my poems also express. One of my most important, basic images is the road outside the house where I grew up, in Cubero. That tiny part of western Valencia County, New Mexico, where I grew up is absolutely primary to me. In moments of stress or when I'm dreaming, at a time when important changes are going on, or in visions, the first thing I'll get is the road, and then other things will be superimposed on it. The road is—do you go up to the hills and the mountains or do you go out to the highway, to the urban Western World?

JB: Mountains and the landscape of the Southwest appear often in your poetry. What do those mountains mean to you?

ALLEN: To me, they are the gods, just as it is saying in "Recuerdo." It's the mountains to the north and it's Mount Taylor. It just *sits there*. Of course, we're quite high in Cubero, we're at sixty-five hundred feet. But the mountain rises another eight thousand. So it's just there. It doesn't loom. It's there. It's a soft and lovely mountain, but when you get to that mountain it becomes a very frightening place. It is so powerful. It's not scary like "I'm going to get lost and never come back." It's scary like "Who lives here that I don't know?" It's not a sense of personal danger; it's a sense of overwhelming wilderness. My home is in that exact hollow which the poem talks about. I lived literally in a hollow. Most of the village was above us, and we lived in a little hollow. So the wind went over us rather than being on us all the time. To me it's like the hollow of a hand—and that's a Christian metaphor.

JB: There's a moving back and forth in some of your work between that Christian awareness and a more Indian sense of land and place. Is that a balance you're conscious of in your poems?

PAULA GUNN ALLEN

ALLEN: I seldom do it on purpose. It's implicit in my life, so it's implicit in my work. Sometimes I get in a dialogue between what the Church taught me, the nuns taught me, and what my mother taught me, what my experience growing up where I grew up taught me. Often you can't reconcile them. I can't reconcile them.

JB: What did your mother teach you?

ALLEN: My mother taught me several things. One is that reality is all important and reality meant paying attention to what was going on—the sunset, the birds. There's a bullsnake that lives under the house and that's my snake and we don't kill her. You take care of people and you take care of creatures because that's what you do and you don't do anything else. You don't lie because, if you lie, you'll get lost. You treat people as though they are real, even little tiny people. You don't trivialize them and act like they're idiots. Instead, you treat them as though they are perfectly intelligent beings. You remember that your mind is inviolably yours, that no one can have it, ever. So you act this way or that way, depending on what they want from you because that's not what is important. What's important is that they can't change your mind, which is a very Laguna thing. They're very stubborn people. She's got that stubbornness of, It's my mind and that's that!

JB: Laguna is important to you . . .

ALLEN: Laguna to me is where you go when you're going home. Laguna to me is where people are grounded. Laguna is Feast Day. What I remember about that, one of the first things I ever remember, is leaving Feast with my grandparents and looking out the back window of the car. It was dark and there were fires. Laguna is on a hill and you could see campfires on all the hills around it. Of course you can't see that anymore, but when I was little a lot of people traveled by wagon and that's what you could see. To me, that was the absolute essence of a perfect place to be. That was *it*.

JB: It's interesting that such a small pueblo as Laguna has produced so many writers: you, your sister Carol Lee Sanchez, Leslie Silko, Harold Littlebird, and others not yet as well known.

ALLEN: It's a crossroads. One of its fundamental values

from the time of its founding has been progressivism. They acted from between 1945 and 1979 or '80 as if they were going to be very conservative. But as the Pueblos go, they are the most "liberal." They've always been. That's because they weren't "Lagunas" to begin with. They were a polyglot people. They had to be liberal. So, when they started getting very rigid elements in the village, they threw them out. Ceremonially, that is—through a ceremonial "fight" they threw them out. The Lagunas have always valued learning. Most of the young people today hold college degrees. There's not a lot of illiteracy there. There's a very high standard of living, or at least there was until the mines closed last year or the year before. I understand the income dropped to some abysmal level and there's growing unemployment where there was full employment two years ago. *Full* and at very good wages. Anyway, they've always been like that. When the Bookmobile comes out to the Laguna villages, it doesn't get to half of them before it's empty. That's just how they are. Whether they're very traditional or very peripheral, it doesn't make any difference. They value knowledge and they value learning. It isn't that they value hustling and making it in the white man's world—they just value learning. I think that's what happened. I think that's why we get writers and artists who, in our own way, just value it. We just like to do it, so we do it.

JB: Certain anthropologists, such as Elsie Clew Parsons, have "written off" Laguna, saying it no longer has a kiva, it's no longer really a Pueblo. Parsons comes close to saying it's not even Indian. How do you respond to that point of view?

ALLEN: I usually laugh because it's such a limited point of view. But then I say, "Okay, why are people always looking *further back?*" They've got to find a utopia—the perfect place— and Indians always fail them. Indians are always *not quite* something or other, whatever the something or other is that they want. People will come up to you and say, "There aren't any Indians anymore. You know, Indians put Pampers on their babies! They watch T.V.!" And all of this means that Indians are not Indian to the white world which loves Indians and is looking for the lost noble savage or something like that. I will say

6   PAULA GUNN ALLEN

that Laguna has never been very good at noble savagery. But Parsons's work in itself indicates that they were so thoroughly primitive, so thoroughly wilderness people, that how she could write them off simply astonishes me.

My mountain is wilderness. Where Cubero is, is between civilization and wilderness; and the choice for me is: Which way do I go? The resolution for me is that I don't take either choice. I stay in the middle of both. I tend to value wilderness as an aesthetic and moral and personal value over civilization, though I can see civilization being useful for me personally. Nevertheless, I always judge the civilization in terms of the wilderness, rather than the other way around.

JB: And "primitive"?

ALLEN: Primitive means several things. Savage is a better word and I'd rather use savage. I censored myself when I started to say "savage" and thought, "I can't say *that.*" So I said "primitive," meaning uncluttered with alienating concepts such as secularized or industrialized or urbanized people are fraught with.

JB: Going back to that duality you mentioned between the lessons of your mother and the lessons of the Church—what were the lessons of the Church?

ALLEN: Do you know that poem of mine called "Resurrection: Easter Sunday"? Those are the lessons of the Church. The lessons of the Church are that everybody I love is a murderous, vicious, guilty creature, including myself. The only good person was killed and we killed him. What I'm supposed to do about that is be abjectly sorry and I'm supposed to worship a corpse. A very frightening reality to be raised in and I *was* raised in it.

JB: A lot of Indians were.

ALLEN: It's just overwhelming. It took me until I wrote that poem to make some kind of peace between the crucifixion and my own sense of innocence and my sense of my people's innocence. None of the people I know are going to crucify anybody, never mind Jesus Christ! But the Church, the nuns, and the images around you keep saying, "You're a murderer, you're a murderer, you're a murderer. You ought to be dead, you ought to be dead, you ought to be dead." And you ought to want to kill yourself.

JB: What have been the influences on your writing, both when you were beginning to write and at present?

ALLEN: I really wish I could tell you a lot about this, but I'm not really clear on them. I've always had an affinity for literacy, always. My aunts, my father's sisters, were just delighted by that. I would learn anything. They taught me "Mary had a little lamb," and "There was a little girl who had a little curl," and all those nursery rhymes. I would say anything. By the time I was two and a half they had me saying "The Gettysburg Address." In public. I was taken around here and there and shown to eighth graders who couldn't learn it. They'd put me up on the desk and have me recite it and say, "She can learn it. Why can't you?" So that's very early. That's an early influence. I read. From the day I could read, I read and read and read. I read anything and everything. I read the Hardy Boys and the Bobbsey Twins and *Anne of Green Gables* and Shakespeare, whatever there was to read. My mother had quite a collection of books—you've seen it—and I read my way through it. At school, whatever was in the library I read. I didn't like school. It was an uncomfortable place for me. So I would do my work real quick and then I'd hide a book in my notebook and I'd read. So, who knows what influences are working here?

More consciously, I fell in love with Gertrude Stein when I was in high school—ninth or tenth grade. My mother bought me everything she could find, everything that was available, and I read Stein and tried to copy her, tried to write like her. Then I gave up for a while. But the earliest work I ever wrote, which no one will ever see because I lost it, is noticeably Stein.

The other people that I was simply made for were the Romantic poets. Shelley, in particular, and Keats. If you look at my poem "Moonshot," it's Keats. It came to me as quite a shock last summer. I was listening to some dramatic readings and this man up on stage happened to be reading "Ode to a Nightingale." I had come in halfway through the performance, so I heard just the last half. I realized then that I had written "Moonshot" like a tangent to "Ode to a Nightingale." Even some of the images are the same except that they're skewed slightly. I was just stunned. I wasn't conscious of doing that, but that's what I did.

JB: What about current influences?

ALLEN: Among them the most important single influence on my work at present—and for the last couple of years—has been Judy Grahn. In her poetry she works for clarity and she works for ease of comprehensibility so that anybody walking into your reading can understand what you're saying and anybody who picks up the book can understand what you're saying. She's taught me a great deal about doing that and simplifying the structures that are so ridiculously obscure. Some of the changes you've noticed in my work come directly from studying her work as well as living with her. I wrote "Recuerdo," and "Los Angeles 1980" and "Laguna Ladies Luncheon" before I met her, so I was moving in that direction. But it's like she jumped it up. Adrienne Rich has also had a real influence on me and more recently Audre Lorde.

JB: When did you return again to writing after that earliest work influenced by Stein?

ALLEN: In college I happened to get into creative writing as a direct result of Bob Creeley's *For Love*. By accident I read the book, and I was absolutely thunderstruck. I thought he was a genius. I had fallen for this man Creeley hook, line, and sinker. The man who had loaned me the book told me, "Well, he's teaching here." This was in Albuquerque. He also told me I ought to get into Creeley's class. I said, "Who, me?" I had, by then, written five poems in my whole life and I was going to be a fiction writer or a nonfiction writer. I never thought about being a poet. Well, I went to see Bob and, of course, he let me in his class. I think I worked with him for about two years. He introduced me to Charles Olson, Allen Ginsberg—and Ginsberg has been a major model of mine. Olson has been a major model. Robert Duncan, Denise Levertov. Levertov was the first poet I ever saw read, and that was actually over twenty years ago. She was very important to me. Partly as a model, as a woman up there reading, partly because she knows how to end the poem more effectively than anybody I know. I could not end poems. I'm not good at ending things. So I studied her intensively to learn that. So, those are really the primary shaping people until 1965. About then I began to take it over for myself—and it took a long time to take it over for myself.

JB: There is often a certain kind of density, a layering of meaning in your poems. That reminds me very much of the Black Mountain School.

ALLEN: Well, they were really really important to me for the first two or three years I was trying to learn how to be a writer. It was Black Mountain all the way. I didn't pay attention to anyone else.

JB: But then in 1965 there was a change?

ALLEN: Yes, when I went up to Oregon. I finished my last year there and I took a lot of writing classes. Then I did an M.F.A. there. By that point I knew that I knew enough from other poets and that what I had to do now was find Paula. I didn't find Paula, although I did write several poems in that period where you can hear me. There are several in my book *The Blind Lion. The Blind Lion* covers that whole period, and here and there you can hear what's eventually going to be Paula. A transitional voice begins to show up. I was working with Ralph Salisbury who, at the time, was just as "white" as white could be as far as I knew. Now it turns out he's an Indian.

JB: Cherokee.

ALLEN: I'm really sorry I didn't know that at the time because I was dreadfully alone and dreadfully suicidal. There was absolutely nobody there. Luckily for me, Dick Wilson came up. He's an old friend, not the Dick Wilson of infamy, but another one from home, a Santee Sioux whom I'd known since my hippy days in Albuquerque. This was before there were hippies, but he and I and a number of other weirdos from Grants and Pruitt, New Mexico, were hippy types. He came up to Oregon to teach and probably saved my life. Dick's presence and Momaday's novel are probably what saved my life.

JB: *House Made of Dawn* has been very important to innumerable Indian writers, hasn't it?

ALLEN: I wouldn't be writing now if Momaday hadn't done that book. I would have died.

JB: What did it do for you?

ALLEN: It told me that I was sane—or if I was crazy at least fifty thousand people out there were just as nutty in exactly the same way I was, so it was okay. I was not all alone. It did that and it brought *my land* back to me. Eugene, Oregon is nothing like *Cubero*. Part of what I was going through was land sickness—loss of land. It brings great grief to you not to be at home, and he brought it back because he's such a careful writer. I could read the passages and I had been there to the places that he describes. I knew every inch of what he was saying. It was that and the fact that he could write a novel about an "Abel." An Abel with the same sickness that I had—or something like it—but Momaday had enough control over that sickness to write a book about it. That said to me, "You're okay. This is nothing to get all excited about." (laughs) This goes back to my mother: "Just be calm, stay cool, and everything will work out. You're not nuts, you're just different, but that doesn't make you nuts." It's taken me years and years to get over all of that, but if that line hadn't been thrown in my direction, I wouldn't be here now.

JB: There's a clear, storytelling quality to some of your recent poems, which I like very much. Do you think your work is now tending in that direction?

ALLEN: Yes, yes. As I get more control over what I do, as I'm less concerned about whether or not anybody understands me—and, more importantly, as I'm less concerned about whether or not anybody misunderstands me. Misunderstanding doesn't mean they're going to kill me. That's what it always meant to me, but I've begun to learn that they're not going to kill me. Laugh at me perhaps, but not kill me. So it's okay to take chances and you've noticed that. The work gets calmer and less dense and less obscure. It becomes easier and easier to say what it is I want to say.

You know, part of it was getting to be forty. Now you're forty you can say what's on your mind. Until then you weren't allowed to because you were just a child. Don't ask me where I got that, but I've known it all my life. I've always known that, once you were forty, then you got to speak up clearly.

JB: Isn't there generally a different idea about women aging, though, among American Indian people?

ALLEN: Sure. The young girls are the ones who are in a very, I don't know, *backwards* kind of position. You're supposed to be shy and gentle and careful—if you're a Laguna, anyway. But the older you get the more you come into your own and the more your stability increases and your knowledge and your sense of who you are and how things ought to go. Your sense of properness becomes more and more useful, not only to yourself but to the people around you. They're supposed to listen to you. It's like I knew all that. My mother has always made fun of people who dye their hair or who try to hide their wrinkles or in any way try to alter the fact of how old they are. To her, the older you get the better you are—and the better life is supposed to go for you. You're more valuable. And so, of course, I'm the same way. The first few white hairs I got, I was just so proud of them. I was scared to death somebody was going to take them away from me. I like having all this white hair. It makes my life easier. It's easy for me to go out now and talk, and it used to be excruciating. I attribute it to my white hair.

JB: That probably explains why some of the strongest people I know are Indian women over the age of forty.

ALLEN: Aren't they, though? In fact, some of them are downright terrifying.

JB: Yet within majority white culture, once you're over forty you either have to think of a facelift or doing something. . .

ALLEN: You think of ways to placate people so they won't punish you and they won't ignore you and they won't abandon you. That's what women in the dominant culture between the ages of about thirty-five and seventy-five do. Then they reach a point where it finally dawns on them that they're *old*. There's nothing they can do about it, they're still here and the hell with it.

JB: Why has majority white culture perpetrated this on women?

PAULA GUNN ALLEN

ALLEN: Old women are powerful. They really are powerful. That's not a culture perception, that's a fact. So, what you do with powerful people whom you don't wish to have powerful is you put a mind trick on the whole society. You convince them that those who have power do not have power. You do that by degrading them, trivializing them, disappearing them, and murdering them. They were murdered in great numbers toward the end of the Middle Ages. And that thing is kept up by talking about "old bags" and "old witches" and "old crones" and making fun of them, laughing, and saying, "Don't go near her—she's got the Evil Eye," which is what immigrant populations do. All those sorts of things instill in the minds of all people that old women are not powerful because, of course, they are. If they weren't really powerful, would it be necessary to do all we do to them? It wouldn't be.

JB: Isn't this one of the lessons now being learned by many women in the United States?

ALLEN: Finally.

JB: A lesson that American Indian women could have taught. . .

ALLEN: If non-Indians had bothered to pay attention. Yes. I think of old women not as grotesque and ugly, but as singular with vibrancy, alive just as the leaves get before they fall. That total brilliance of them. I wish that white women could see that in themselves and in their mothers and grandmothers and in aging women, in general. I wish they could see that incredible brilliance and fire that's so magnificent. Then they would think, "Well, these are the most beautiful of all." Of course—because old women are, they are *so* beautiful.

JB: Could you talk a bit about *Shadow Country?* I'm curious about the name.

ALLEN: It's "Shadow Country" because shadows are important. My novel explains a lot of this, by the way, because to me shadows are good, good places. Hollows, you know, have shadows in them.

JB: As in the hollow where your house was located in Cubero?

ALLEN: That's right. You see, it's cool there and, where

I come from, the sun can get so hot you can get sick from it. So the people who are always running around with their images of bright daylight give me a headache because bright daylight gives me a headache. I like the sun to shine, I like to be in the shade watching the sun shine, you see. A tree is so valuable out there in New Mexico because the tree gives shade. The mesas are valuable because the rocks give shade. So, shadow means that. Shadow also means the land of the dead. Where I come from the land of the dead isn't a terrible place, it's where the rain comes from. Rain clouds, oh the shadows they make are not to be believed. And they are the people coming back to bring the rain.

And shadow means it's not dark and it's not light. It's Cubero, as I said earlier in this interview, the wilderness on one hand and civilization on the other. That's where shadow land, the shadow country, is. It also means half-breed. Quite simple—neither dark nor light. It also means not really in focus, blurred. It has a whole bunch of meanings. So, when you look at "Que Cante Quetzal," which means "what do you sing, god?" because the quetzal bird is the god (actually the goddess, not the god), that's all the traditional, that's the wilderness and what's happened to the wilderness. It's both things. How I relate to wilderness and where the wilderness is—that's the first part. The second part, which is "Shadow Country," is going back and forth. It's really being in shadow country. Back and forth and back and forth. So you have such poems as "Los Angeles 1980" and "Words for a Bike-Riding, Osprey-Chasing, Wine-Drunk Squaw Man." I like that title better than the poem. (laughs) And you've got the poem "Shadow Country" itself which ends dark and light, side by side—and it's set in a bar. Bars are notorious for the fact that they're shadowy and dark, intimate and sexy and full of deviant kinds of folks. Nice people don't go there. They are the city's interface between wilderness and civilization, between fertile chaos and focusing structure. Everybody goes there to meet who they really want to meet. Everybody parties there and everybody puts on all their trips there and everybody lays all their crap on you there—and so

PAULA GUNN ALLEN

on. Another section of the book, "Recuerdo," means recovering. Going back, putting back together, assembling in another way. That section is really about the hollow where things meet, which side is which. The last section, "Medicine Song," is simply about women and about women as healing agents and happy-making agents. Just women. The way the book is made up I see "Medicine Song" as something akin to a resolution. It's really moving the whole song to another key, it's really the section that does the transposing. The next book, presumably, will actually be in the new key. I don't see "Medicine Song" as the solution but as a modulation.

JB: Song and singing seem very important to you and to your poetry.

ALLEN: Song structures are my favorite structures to work with. My sister Kathy is a musician. My mother and father are musicians. We had a lot of music in our house. When I was young, Kathy was studying at the Conservatory of Music in Cincinnati. We had this big upright piano that Pop had bought for Mother when they were first married, you know. It cost $15. Kathy used to sit at that thing and she'd play Chopin and Mozart and Rachmaninoff. Mozart, particularly, I loved. I was determined to write poetry that had as a structure what classical music, particularly Mozart, has as a structure. When I wrote "Los Angeles, 1980," I showed it to Kathy and she analyzed it musically. I was very astonished. I actually succeeded in doing what I had set out years and years and years before to do. That's the basic structure of what I write, that's really my . . . it's my notion. You set out a theme and then you do variations on the theme. You set out a tempo and you vary the tempo. In the end you bring them together like a watershed—not like an answer to the question, because there's never an answer to the question.

JB: I sometimes sense another music, an Indian sound.

ALLEN: I just noticed it. Yesterday I was reading a poem of Simon's in that article "First Languages: Perception and Expression." Well, he's got a little hunting song in there, and I'm saying the hunting song and I come to the refrain which is exactly Pueblo! The beat in it is exactly Pueblo. Particularly in my earlier work I would do that. I would wind up the ending so it would keep going and keep going and keep going—which is what they do. My poetry professors kept telling me to stop doing that. So now I write a truncated last line which is the exact opposite of what I want to write. My last line should be going, spread out like a fan. Left to myself, that's what they'd be.

JB: For me, music always ties in strongly to the world of the spirit. I find that world of the spirit very strongly present in your work as well. Could you talk a bit about your involvement with psychic phenomena in your personal life and your poetry?

ALLEN: Let me talk about my own personal involvement and then go on to the poetry. My own personal involvement is, of course, all my life. More specifically, as I've gotten older and older, I've become more centered in that particular world. It actually began as a conscious thing when I lived in Oregon. That was during the drug revolution, if you remember. I took some TCP one night and I was sitting out in the back yard. I was living on the MacKenzie River. God, it was beautiful! And I looked up and there were the trees—and I could see that the trees were people. So I started talking to the trees. Well, I knew that I could do that and I've always done it subliminally, but I had never before done it out loud, consciously. That was the first time and, of course, I didn't lose that sense ever. I don't do any drugs except nicotine and caffeine now. I can't take them. What they do is they put me to sleep. (laughs) It's an overload to my system. I'm naturally stoned a lot of the time and apparently I always have been. My youngest brother once commented that it wasn't until he started smoking dope that he understood what I was laughing at all the time. (laughs) Then he went, *"That's* why she acts like that." I always see the world from a corner, from a slant, so to speak. I think that's what it is. I know a lot about Western occult traditions and about Tibetan traditions and about Egyptian traditions. In other words, I've made it a real study, and I've devoted years to learning all these different traditions. I see the American Indian traditions as fitting quite easily into the worldwide traditions. I'm a very religious person. I always have been. Catholicism is terribly important to me because I'm a religious person. It was the politics of the Church that I couldn't abide . . . and their incredible stupidity about human beings . . . and what they would do. The viciousness! I knew perfectly well they knew what they were doing.

JB: Racism, sexism . . .

ALLEN: Colonialism—all of it. They had no excuse. If they paid any attention to Jesus, to the Master, they could never have done those things. I've read The New Testament. Even as it stands—and it's a flawed document—even as it stands there is no excuse for their behavior, absolutely none in the New Testament. So, that's just simply a part of my mind. I learned it from my grandparents, all of them. By the way, the Lebanese people are the same way. My Lebanese ancestors are the same way. My father is enormously psychic. His grand-mother was a fortune-teller in the sense that she could predict the future. She was clairvoyant. His grandfather just loved that sort of thing. He used to charm snakes and do that kind of thing. So it comes at me from both sides. It has its very bad side. I haven't worked . . . it's in *Coyote's Daylight Trip*, but its hovering around the edges. I haven't yet learned how to talk out loud, on purpose, about the terrible evilness of it. And it can be very evil. There is so much evil about it—I mean in the Indian systems as much as I mean in the white system. That's why it's called the occult, of course, because it can be devas-tatingly vicious when misused.

Adrienne Rich wrote me a letter recently, and what she said about *Shadow Country* is that what astonished her was that this poetry could have a clear spiritual presence without ever going into Romanticism and that idealistic sentimental crap that goddess-worship people tend to get into . . . and it never has to deny political realities, either. That she liked, and she kept reading it over and over because she hadn't seen anything like that before. Of course, it's common for Indian poets to do that. I think some white poets do it, but not the way Indians do. I've never seen anything which so clearly showed that as the

Third World Writers Conference in May 1982 in Sacramento. It was so clear it was almost funny. You could count on the Indians to get up there and do it every time. The more political and biased and radical the rhetoric of the other poets got, the more likely the Indians would choose not their most political poems but their most spirit-directed poems. And they kept doing it. It just cracked me up. Toward the end I was just walking around laughing. That's why I wrote that paper called, "This Wilderness in My Blood: The Spiritual Foundations of the Poetry of American Indian Women," because I saw so clearly that spring what the difference was between us. That's the paper Bo Schöler published in *Coyote Was Here*. I went through Wendy Rose's work and Linda Hogan's work, Joy Harjo's work, and my work and Carol Lee Sanchez's work and Mary Tall Mountains's work and we all do it differently. We all have a different approach to it, but we all do it. It is always there in the poetry. My poetry addresses it as I address anything that's going on in my life. It's not something I'm doing deliberately. It's just common mind work, and to me a poem is a recording of an event in the mind.

JB: How has your mixed-blood heritage affected your worldview or your poetry?

ALLEN: My poetry has a haunted sense to it and it has a sorrow and a grievingness in it that comes directly from being split, not in two but in twenty, and never being able to reconcile all the places that I am. I think of it as Wordsworth did when he said we come into this world "trailing clouds of glory," when he said nothing can bring back the hour when we saw "splendor in the grass and glory in the flower." We shall not weep but find strength in what remains behind. That poem—I was in college, I was a sophomore when I read it, and I just wept. I was completely, absolutely desolate because I thought he understood. He understood, of course, in his own way exactly what happens when your reality is so disordered that you can't ever make it whole, but you have the knowledge of what has happened, what has been done. There's a song that goes, "what have they done to my song?" For the longest time, I thought

PAULA GUNN ALLEN

that song said "what have they done to my *soul?*" That's the experience of the half-breed.

The other experience is that we have a mediational capacity that is not possessed by either of the sides. What we are able to do is bridge variant realities because everybody is pissed off at us and we are pissed off at ourselves. What we are able to do is move from flower to flower, so to speak, and get the pollen moved around among each of our traditions. Then we can plant back into them. You find that the writers from Laguna are all breeds and you find that Laguna is a breed Pueblo. It always has been, culturally speaking, not necessarily blood speaking. But even blood speaking, the people who formed the Laguna settlement were from several different Pueblos and they included some Navajo. They were mediational people. They were people who chose to live together and then to work out their differences. I think you can look at the Laguna people as a culture that has worked out this capacity to be a breed. Then we ourselves are not as estranged as we might be if we were, say, Hopi and having to deal with it or if we were Iroquois and had to deal with it, because our whole Pueblo is that way—whether they want to admit it or not. Most often, they do want to admit it.

JB: So this ties in to why there are so many American Indian writers of mixed blood? That dual vision leads them to mediate?

ALLEN: That's right and that, of course, is what a writer does. Ideally, what a writer does is talk to two perspectives. I don't know a writer who doesn't feel essentially alienated and that's what a breed is. It's fundamentally, "I'm not this and I'm not that and I am two of everything."

JB: If there is such a thing as a "Pan-Indian Consciousness," it seems it is being expressed by contemporary American Indian poets.

ALLEN: And artists and painters.

JB: Do you think that American Indian poets are too aware of each other these days? Our names keep turning up in each other's poems.

ALLEN: Not aware enough. We need a school and we need to have a very clearly developed sense of what that school is. We *are* a school. We really are a very special group of poets.

JB: That makes me think of the American Writers' Congress. I remember, after the American Indian writers session, people kept saying "You Indians all seem to know each other and to work so well together." Why is that?

ALLEN: We're strangers in a strange land, that's why. (laughs) We need each other. Our work is very unique and we need to recognize that. So that our names keep cropping up in each other's poems, our images keep cropping up in each other's poems, our understandings keep cropping up in each other's poems and articles and reviews and so forth is all to the good. What do you think the Imagists were doing? If we are to have the impact that I believe we all want to have, this is how you do it.

JB: What is it that is unique and important?

ALLEN: Our spiritual vision, our ability to be fundamentally practical *and* spiritual because Indian people *are* practical and spiritual. We don't horseshit around. We're not coy and cute. Occasionally we're difficult, but that's different. We don't believe in metaphor. Very few of us even understand what that term means in terms of what it means to the greater poetry community around us or to the critical establishment.

JB: Or surrealism?

ALLEN: Or surrealism, which is silly. We really have a *vision* that the Imagists attempted to get at, that they lied about where they got it. You know that. They got it from Native American tribal literature and then they pretended that they got it from the Chinese, and that is so much horse hockey. Pisses me off. But that's fine because we were the only ones who could do it. They couldn't do it, so I suppose it works out pretty well. Yeah. You know, we can transform American culture because that's what writers do.

JB: Paula, you've developed a reputation as critic, as poet, as prose writer. Are any of those genres more important to you or is this just an artificial division?

PAULA GUNN ALLEN

ALLEN: They're artificial divisions. I do each in itself, of course, but I suit the form to what it is I'm trying to do—to the purpose. So the novel—I couldn't do that in poems. What the novel does is what novels do and what the critical articles do is what criticism can do and what the poems do is what poems can do. My form is determined by my purpose, my point. They're all writing and that's what I'm doing. I'm a writer. It's like asking a seamstress if making dresses is somehow separate from making skirts and blouses. Sure, one has a waistband that's separate and in the others one part is connected to the other, but it's all sewing.

Talking with the Past

An Interview with
PETER BLUE CLOUD

It was a rainy day in California as I climbed into the Sierra foothills toward North San Juan. The creeks were rushing across the roads and, as I drove along the unpaved trails which led deeper into the hills, I had to stop several times to ask for directions. All of this land had been mined out once, and what looked like great stones to either side were piles of earth that had gone through the machines that extracted the gold. Second-growth evergreens were everywhere, but it was a land which had been wounded before and was now threatened with that same treatment again, for modern miners wanted to come back in to get out the gold that had been missed the first time. There was also something wild about this land, almost like a place soon after the first days of Creation. You could feel the presence of Coyote in these hills, hills also inhabited by pot-farmers, Zen Buddhists, poets such as Gary Snyder. It had been Peter Blue Cloud's home for more than a decade, despite his roots in the Northeast on the Canadian Mohawk Reserve at Caughnawauga. He was staying at the house of an artist friend, and the rain which surrounded the cabin as I arrived was re-placed by rain the next morning, obscuring sight of the moun-tains above us where snow was falling. All around the house were paintings and carvings he had been working on, and Peter spoke of the difficulty of surviving on the edge as an artist and writer, of his desire—which would later be satisfied—to return to the East Coast, to Mohawk Country. As we spoke, we were sometimes interrupted by Peter's two children, who were playing around the table where we sat. Peter would turn to them, gently answer their questions or help them with some-thing, and then turn back to the interview. Though not an old man, having been born in 1933 makes Peter Blue Cloud one of the elders of the current generation of Native American poets, and he began by reading a poem which reflected the length of his commitment to poetry and the Native American struggle, a poem about the takeover by Indians of Alcatraz in 1969.

Alcatraz

As lightning strikes the Golden Gate
and fire dances the city's streets,
a Navajo child whimpers the tide's pull
and Sioux and Cheyenne dance lowly the ground.

Tomorrow is breathing my shadow's heart
and a tribe is an island, and a tribe is an island,
and silhouettes are the Kachina dancers
of my beautiful people.

Heart and heaven and spirit
written in drum's life cycle
and a tribe is an island, forever,
forever we have been an island.

As we sleep our dreaming in eagles,
a tribe is an island
and a tribe is a people
    in the eternity of Coyote's mountain.

nov. 1969

—Peter Blue Cloud

JB: It's hard to believe it was fifteen years ago that you were part of the occupation of Alcatraz.

BLUE CLOUD: Yup, it sure is.

JB: Was your first book the anthology *Alcatraz is Not an Island?*

BLUE CLOUD: Yes, the history of the occupation and some of the prehistory of the area.

JB: As a writer and an Indian person, what was the meaning for you of that occupation?

BLUE CLOUD: I think we were trying to get the unity thing together. The idea of Indians of All Tribes is a very old idea. We haven't really been able to do it. Maybe A.I.M. is partly doing it now. But to get the Indians together once and for all, as one force. The Council of Elders now is, I think, the best step toward that. And A.I.M.,* too. I've never belonged to A.I.M. and I was sort of suspicious of it at the beginning, but I've just attended this meeting in San Francisco and met Bill Wapapa and Phillip Deer and I like what they're saying. This is not militant talk; it's talking of unity and getting with support groups—non-Indian support groups—talking to them so they will understand the problems.

JB: Your own poetry has a lot of pan-tribalism, things which come from many parts of the country, not just Mohawk traditions. How did that happen?

BLUE CLOUD: That's me. (laughs) That's a touch of Coyote. I've just figured out a while back that I've spent one-half plus one year of my life in California. So I've been longer in California or out West than I have back East. I've lived in the desert, Nevada. I've logged in British Columbia. I went to the Caribou. All up and down the coast. And I like the desert. The desert is great and I like the forest. I like the plains. I don't know, I just keep moving. I've stayed here quite a while. It's time to move on, but I kind of like it up here. The living is soft.

JB: What do you like about this part of northern California?

*The American Indian Movement.

BLUE CLOUD: Right here? My kids. Actually, that's what it is. I've got a family here. The climate's good. It gets a little too hot in the summer, but the winters—they wouldn't believe it back East. I mean, rain! If the original forest were here again, it would be beautiful.

JB: There are still a lot of trees outside, though. Redwoods? I noticed that, despite the clearcutting in the area, there are still some very beautiful trees.

BLUE CLOUD: There's Ponderosa pine, fir, and cedar. No redwoods, they stop at the coast. Yeah, imagine how this area used to have trees six, seven feet at the butt. People wonder why it's so dry and hot. They think it was always like that. It wasn't. I tell them this was a big huge forest, and even in the middle of summer it was nice and damp and had running water. But it was clearcut, probably three times, four times. Of all the trees you see, very few are original. We can still see stumps all over the place.

JB: When did you first start writing poetry?

BLUE CLOUD: You mean on paper? Well, my grandfather was a schoolteacher. He spoke perfectly good English. But in his house—I stayed with him as a kid—they wouldn't let me talk English. I had to talk Mohawk. But he turned me on to books, Shakespeare, when I was just a little kid—and the songs from the Longhouse. And stories. They have a rhythm unlike stories in English. You hear the songs, the repetition of the chants, and you begin thinking that way. I didn't start writing stuff down probably till I was thirteen. Then I was almost as good as Robert Service. Everything rhymed and I used meter. It had to be a perfect beat. I've written songs all the time. I've probably written a hundred songs in my life. Country music. All Indians across the country are listening to country music.

JB: Where were you first published?

BLUE CLOUD: *Akwesasne Notes*, I'm pretty sure. I had a few rejection slips, I tried to send stuff out in the late '50s and early '60s, but I knew I wasn't ready. I had a lot of stuff. I had books of stuff. At the time Alcatraz happened, I had my first one-man art show, too. So, I started feeling confident that I had something to say, communicate, to other people. I felt good about sending my stuff out, and *Akwesasne Notes* was intimate. Then, because of Alcatraz, a lot of Third World support papers reprinted my poems. Then I started getting requests to submit poems and I did. I just heard someone up here recently say publication is not important. I disagree! It feels damned good to be published. And it helps. I get a manuscript done and, if there's a chance of having it published, I continue on instead of thinking about that. I think of what's next.

JB: After being published by *Akwesasne Notes*, you began working with the paper. What year was that?

BLUE CLOUD: '75 and '76. Poetry Editor, supposedly. I got to do everything else. The mailing was my specialty. I could really wrap those bundles up fast. We had a good crew. We had fun. That mailing would last a week, sometimes. Day and night, we'd just switch off crews and keep laughing. I enjoyed all of it.

JB: What was it like as Poetry Editor with work coming in from people who were Indian or writing about Indian people all over the country?

BLUE CLOUD: It was nice. There was an awful lot of bad stuff you had to send back. Rarihokwats, the editor, always had a hard time rejecting things. I had to compose the first reject letter. I don't know what he did before that. I guess he just stashed the stuff and told them maybe he'd use it some day. I straightened out the files—nothing had ever been put alphabetically.

JB: Your own first book was *Turtle, Bear and Wolf*, published by Akwesasne Notes.

BLUE CLOUD: Yeah. Rarihokwats asked me while I was working, "Well, you want to do a book?" He'd just finished *Native Colours*.

JB: By Alex Jacobs, Karoniaktatie.

BLUE CLOUD: So Rarihokwats says, "You want to do a book? You got enough poems?" "Sure!" Actually most of them had been in *Notes* before. I was very excited, and I think it's the best book I've ever done.

JB: How did you put the book together? Was there any central theme or direction, any process of organization that you're conscious of in the book?

BLUE CLOUD: It happened with me working on *Notes* and it happened with me having been on Alcatraz. The movement was strong, the so-called "Indian Movement" was going good. So, that's the theme and I think in most of my poems I went back in time. I try to take it from way back.

JB: As in the Turtle poem, when you go back even before Creation?

BLUE CLOUD: We're back at our beginnings, where we should be. Before we make any move we should look back at where we came from so we don't step in the cow pad. (laughs) So, this is my favorite book, always will be. I think some day I'll get it reprinted if I can find a publisher.

JB: Had you thought about the fact, when you titled it, that those three are the clan animals of the Mohawk people?

BLUE CLOUD: I wrote "Bear" first and then I wrote "Wolf." I had a kind of suspicion what was happening, but I didn't mean it to. Actually I was going to call it after another poem: "For a Child," and Rarihokwats said, "Nah," and he suggested this title. He said, "After all, this is the theme." He said, "I know you put those poems in back, but that's the theme, isn't it, basically?" And I said, "Yeah." I thought it was too obvious, but it isn't. It works.

JB: Animals have always been very important in your work. I see them occurring again and again, especially Coyote.

BLUE CLOUD: Well, I've lived in cities but I've lived out in the country most of the time. And I see animals all the time, birds, fish. And usually they're much more interesting than people are to me. Just as trees are. I like the outdoors, what's happening there. The animals don't have a college degree and they're fine.

JB: There's a different relationship, it seems to me, between American Indian writers and animals and between other American writers and animals. The animals aren't just symbols or subject matter. They don't just stand for something and they're not regarded as inferior to people. Certainly in your work the animals are very magical, full of power.

BLUE CLOUD: Yes. Well, people are too. Like those guys that stand for the clans. They can be just a symbol of the clan, but they're more. As a matter of fact, I can look at Mohawks and tell you what clan they are because I sincerely believe they take on the characteristics of their clans. I can tell a Bear from a Turtle and I can tell a Wolf. If you live in the country and you're not a person from the city, you see all these animals and they mean something. They have personalities.

JB: How so?

BLUE CLOUD: You can recognize Bear by bulk, usually, slow moving. Turtle is slow moving, too, but a Bear person always seems to be bigger. I could describe a Wolf better. They're kind of slim, they move fast. They're not running, but their movements are fluid and swift and they don't talk. Bears talk quite a bit. The Wolf people just look opposite to a Bear. It's that fluid motion and no wasted movements. They look like a scout. The women included. I'm not just talking about the men. And the Turtles always strike me as more serious, thinking things out. But that might be just because I'm a Turtle.

JB: How about Coyote? Why is Coyote so important to you?

BLUE CLOUD: Because I started hearing about . . . well, I heard about Raven first. It was up on the West Coast in British Columbia. Then in southern British Columbia I started hearing about Coyote and in Oregon and in California. Wherever I'm living I always find out where the Indians are and go hang out. That's when I heard Coyote stories and calling people Coyote and kidding about Coyote. I got really curious, and I started hearing those stories. I thought they were the best thing. There's stories like that back home, but usually they use a person, an individual.

JB: I've heard some of those stories.

BLUE CLOUD: And with Coyote, you can cover any kind of ground—philosophy, history, make fun of current events. I got accused of being a sexist by a certain woman because of the way I write. I told her—not an Indian woman, a white woman—you go up to the Bear Dance and go into the kitchen where the old women are cooking and listen to them. You'll hear stories that I wouldn't dare write down, speaking of sex! I sat there having coffee once and one of the old ladies looked at me and said, "I bet that guy is listening to us." I said, "You got it, but I'm getting out of here!" (laughs)

JB: There's that quality to your Coyote stories in *Elderberry Flute Song*. That book includes most of the stories you've written about Coyote, doesn't it?

BLUE CLOUD: Yes. I like to think of them all as original works. Every once in a while I'll base something on some other story I've heard, but I put my own twist to it.

JB: That's one way your Coyote stories are different from much that's been collected by non-Indians and done by non-Indian poets who take stuff right out of the old Bureau of American Ethnology reports.

BLUE CLOUD: Yeah, "retranslations." I think I'll leave that subject alone. I think I summed up white shamans and people who write from translations out of the Smithsonian papers in a piece called "Coyote's Discourse on Power, Medicine, and Would-be Shamans." That was written for my friend, Coyote, up Round Valley way and for the people around here. I started getting a little bit pissed-off when I first moved here because of all these . . . there must have been a dozen poets within five miles of here. I mean published. Yeah, they were concentrating on being "very Indian" and it made me a little bit mad. Why aren't they writing about themselves and what the hell do they know about Chief Joseph or Sitting Bull? But they used them in every other line. A tribute, supposedly, but . . .

JB: The Coyote stories you've brought into being are new and they're old at the same time. They seem to me to be part of a continuing tradition.

BLUE CLOUD: I hope I'm doing that. I want to bring it into the contemporary scene. People are still doing the same stupid and good things that they were doing hundreds of years ago, so why not tell the same stories and just bring them up to today?

JB: I've noticed patterns of repetition in your stories and your poems from the very first things of yours I ever read. How conscious are you of those patterns of repeated words and lines, sounds and rhythms?

BLUE CLOUD: And meanings. It's not done consciously. I don't set out to do it on purpose, but the way I write it has to work that way. It's a chant. Most of my poems have a certain rhythm to them and, if it's a song or a chant, it has to go back to itself and repeat phrases. Even if the words are different, the beat is the same. I think it just goes back to chants, songs.

JB: What does repetition do?

BLUE CLOUD: Maybe re-emphasizes what I'm trying to say or just keeps that as a goal in your mind. If you have four lines in front of something, you have a chorus. And you keep going back to that chorus because each verse is written around that chorus, on both sides of it.

JB: Like the natural sounds you hear in the morning. You told me you like to wake up early in the morning because of those sounds.

BLUE CLOUD: Well, that's my time. 3:00 A.M. If I'm working at something hot at 3:00 A.M. then I'll work till 6:00 A.M. and then fix my breakfast. That's the only time I write. I might rework something during the day. But I cut myself off at 7:00 A.M., even if I'm really going at something. My mind is nice and clear at that time.

JB: What's the difference between a song and a chant?

BLUE CLOUD: I think a song can be a chant and a chant a song, but a chant, I guess, is more sacred and spoken. It's not sung. It's a spoken thing. A song can be lyrics, a story. Maybe my Coyote stories are songs. I like to think of them that way. Read them fast or read them slow, but they should have some kind of flow. Chant is something like "For a Child" or the one I read, "Alcatraz." Yeah, it's there, that line: "A tribe is an island, a tribe is an island." That's the refrain for the whole thing. That's the chant. That's like a prayer, that particular part. Many of them are like that. "Crazy Horse . . ." I even have it indented. That's the chorus. This poem is a song and a chant. The two verses and then the chant. But I don't really differentiate that much. I like to think I'm writing songs and chants rather than poems.

JB: Maurice Kenny says certain of his writings are chants, but he differentiates between a poem and a chant.

BLUE CLOUD: Each piece? You mean, he can tell? No, I don't do that. I might even change my mind about what I just told you. Now "Death Chant" with those lines, "buffalo, buffalo, buffalo, buffalo . . . ," that's a chant.

JB: When was that written and where were you then?

BLUE CLOUD: '71. San Francisco or Berkeley. I like to put notes down somewhere, where I wrote them. I remember I really produced the time I stayed for one year at Akwesasne and everything was about out here in California because it was still with me. Then I wrote my New York poems after I got back . . . well, I wrote a lot of them when I got back here. It takes a while to catch up with you.

JB: You wrote under a number of different names, didn't you?

BLUE CLOUD: Yeah. Coyote with a number 2 afterwards, Coyote 2, Owl's Child, Turtle's Son, Kaienwaktatsie.

JB: How did you happen to use those names?

BLUE CLOUD: You mean why? I hate to admit this, but I was editing a magazine and we were trying to get poetry and no one sent us any poetry. So I was using my stuff and another guy's stuff. Jerry Hill and Lydia Yellowbird, there were just the three of us around. So, when they ran out of material I took my own stuff and just started using different names. Besides, I was thinking at the time, *why am I publishing these poems? Is it for my ego or am I trying to say something?* I published some under my Indian name, too. It shouldn't matter who wrote it; if the message is there, it's important.

JB: What was the publication?

BLUE CLOUD: *Indian Magazine*, the same material which was in *Alcatraz is Not an Island*. But we did this one in Berkeley with a group of people. We did it for nothing. We hustled and everything and did all the work ourselves. It was a nice little publication and we gave it away. We took it to the Indian Unity Caravan and handed it out all over the place.

JB: Now all of your work is published under the name Blue Cloud, which is a translation of your Indian name, isn't it?

BLUE CLOUD: No, my Indian name is Aroniawenrate. "Blue Cloud" was a present given me by some Paiutes. They asked me my Indian name and I told them. They asked me what it meant, and the closest you can translate it is "Stepping Across the Sky." But then you have to say there's blue in there because of the first part, *Aronia*. *Aronia* is blue, so "Stepping Across the Blue Sky." Or it could be "Climbing up toward the Blue Sky," so they said, "Ah, *Blue Cloud*." That was twenty-five years ago, and I said "That's my name from now on." That's the name I took. That's not the Christian name I was given in a piece of paper. That one I buried.

JB: I think many people don't realize the difference Indian people see between their "legal" names and the name they're given in the Indian way.

BLUE CLOUD: I sort of resent my Christian name. I didn't ask for it. I kept the Peter because my grandfather had the exact same name. I hate to tell you what the rest of it is. It sounds very English or Welsh or something and it's embarrassing to hear it. But it was carried about three times through my grandfather's father and his father. But the name *Aroniawenrate* was carried maybe thirteen or fourteen times and that's much more meaningful to me. Besides, I'm not Welsh or English. I might have that blood in me, but I *am* Mohawk.

JB: Sometimes people don't understand how a person of mixed blood could call themselves Indian. Or they'll say there is no such thing as a full-blooded Indian anymore.

BLUE CLOUD: They wouldn't understand even if you explained it. I've explained it to people and they pretend to. Some do, I guess. The fact is that we adopted a lot of non-Indians in the old days. But when we adopted someone and they entered the clan, they became *us*.

JB: Just as people from other tribes were adopted and became whatever people they were adopted into.

BLUE CLOUD: I don't think white people understand. Not very many do. They say, "Well, you're still part white blood." How do you argue with it? Because I am. It's sort of like the anthropologists insisting that we come from Siberia. They still haven't proved it. I used to work with anthropologists. I worked there quite a while *with* them, not *for* them. But I suddenly realized why they wanted to put us back there—it was to justify the conquest of this continent.

JB: To say you came and then they came.

BLUE CLOUD: Yeah, *you came from there, too.* It's as simple as that. People say it can't be that we originated here, and it's because the Indians are still being taken. We have nothing left on this big continent and the white man knows it. So, he wants to put our roots back in Siberia or some other place.

JB: I've read some interesting, though disputed, research which indicates evidence of human activity on this continent as far as a million years ago.

BLUE CLOUD: I remember when it was only ten thousand years at the oldest. Then it went back to fifteen, to twenty. Now they have carbon-14 dates from Mexico seventy-eight thousand years ago. And that's young to 'em. That's not very old. I think it will go a lot further, but I can't see the importance of finding out. We know where we came from—we came from *here.* When I meet anthropologists, I always ask them, "What are you really doing? What is the real importance?" They say, "Well, we're putting out all this material that's going to be lost. We're helping people." The only help I see is if the anthropologist is working with the missionaries, translating language and the ways of the people so that missionaries can come in there and take them over and break apart their system because they know how to do it. The only *good* anthropology is maybe physical anthropology because that helps with medicine.

JB: It strikes me as interesting that the Iroquois were the first to be hit by the whole idea of anthropology. Lewis Henry Morgan's book in the mid-1800s on the League of the Iroquois is the start of modern ethnology. It seems that the Iroquois have been the subject of a great deal of anthropological scrutiny. Do you think there is any contribution that all these people have made who've written about the Iroquois?

BLUE CLOUD: No. It's for scholars and students who sit there and read. If someone wants a true understanding they might like Edmund Wilson, who was so impressed with what he found that he went out and talked to live people.

JB: *Apologies to the Iroquois*, which was published in 1960.

BLUE CLOUD: It's a damn good book. Aside from that, no. I see the church in control of my reservation and many others because the priest and minister can speak the language. They know how to deal with the people—supposedly they know how they think. But no, I think anthropology has always been used against the people it studies.

JB: Then when those people begin to speak for themselves they're accused of being half-breeds or acculturated.

BLUE CLOUD: Well, *they* can't talk. The anthropologists already wrote it all down. "Indian, keep your mouth shut!" I think that's the attitude. There are always white people there to tell us how it *should* be done. There were Third World groups saying, "Hey, you Indians don't have it together, man! You have to do it this way. You've got to fight and get really mad."

JB: Saying that you're too passive, you're too calm? There's a difference, though, between black militancy and the militancy of American Indian people.

BLUE CLOUD: Yeah, for sure. I don't know any other people like American Indians. I haven't met any.

JB: What is the difference?

BLUE CLOUD: I don't know. I don't really know. A lot of times I still see people who were beaten so damn bad that they're still recovering. (long silence as he draws in a breath and lets it slowly go) I know Indians have a different way of looking at things. Maybe even different than Africans or other people still living on their original lands. Maybe Australian Aborigines might be closer to Indians. But certainly there's a whole different way of looking at things around us.

JB: I've heard traditional people say that it's not our way to exclude someone. It's not our way to leave people out. We can't make those divisions and judgments because, if we do, we're defeating ourselves.

BLUE CLOUD: Well, yes. Talk about the most powerful country on earth here, this so-called United States government. A lot of it is based on the Six Nations, but they left out all the important parts like the Clan Mothers, like the Council of Elders, like the Chiefs who really are the chiefs and not erected by television or commercials. If they'd really chosen wise men to run the country and women to be behind them like Clan Mothers, really using that philosophy, maybe it would have worked.

JB: For example, if someone oversteps their bounds, the Clan Mothers remove them from office?

BLUE CLOUD: Yes, with a couple of warnings first.

JB: Among the Iroquois, women really had and still have power, don't they?

BLUE CLOUD: Yeah. The traditional women back home, if somebody asks about "women's liberation," they'll laugh. "If they lost it, it's their fault, not mine!" It's like the old women telling Coyote stories out here in California. They're not against their own sex, it's just the way things are. Yes, the Clan Mothers are very strong and necessary.

JB: The traditions of Iroquois oratory, the moral teachings such as The Great Law make me personally rank the Iroquois very high in terms of contributions to both government and philosophy for living human beings. How have those traditions affected you, personally?

BLUE CLOUD: Me? I guess I don't know. It's with me all the time. I'm not a great orator, that's for sure. I like to think I'm a fairly good poet, but that's certainly the tradition behind me. Those guys who got up and talked were talking behind the philosophy, and they knew the Clan Mothers were behind them watching. They were speaking for a clan and a tribe and a nation to other nations. What they said had to have meaning to everybody they were talking to and be of something important. They wouldn't just get up and tell a joke at a council meeting. This was business.

JB: As in Red Jacket's famous speech to the missionary?

BLUE CLOUD: Yes. Everything had to do with the people. "The people" means tomorrow. So, when you have elders and youngsters in a council, you're talking with the past and you're talking about tomorrow's children that aren't even born yet. That's what those men have to keep in mind. They know that the Clan Mothers are behind and listening to every word. If they make any mistakes, somebody stops it and corrects them. It isn't done very often, but it can be done. So, it's well thought out before it's presented so there are no mistakes when it is presented. One of the biggest words in Mohawk is *Orewa*, reason. *Reason* is the philosophy over everything. It's the meaning of the Longhouse, what they call "The Great Law of Peace." I don't call it the *Great* Law of Peace, but I'm not going to argue. The way I learned to talk Mohawk, my understanding is that "good" and "calm" are the words. Not "great." The Good Peace or the Calm Peace. And good and calm equal reason. You can't reason unless you are calm. You meditate with yourself and with others. Maybe you do verbal meditation. But in order to use reason, you have to be really calm, especially if it's a problem involving a lot of people and not just yourself. Now I can't remember the question. (laughs)

JB: I was asking how you feel about your role as a poet related to the Iroquois traditions.

BLUE CLOUD: Yes, well, okay, then what I just said—that's the way I feel. Even as a poet, I'm not speaking for the tribes. I'm speaking for myself—and I'm hoping I communicate some ideas to other people—but I think I have that behind me, the philosophy of the Six Nations.

JB: Your *White Corn Sister* poems are, as I understand it, part of a larger project which ties into what we were talking about.

BLUE CLOUD: Yes. I'm going to call it fictitious. It is based on the Six Nations, especially the Mohawk, but it's a fiction. It's my thinking, from what I have learned from the philosophy, about the way the people live, the history. I want to present it as an idea for other people to look at. Not as an anthropological paper, but as a poem, a play for voices. I want to write about when the whites came, the first treaties and how they were broken and Sullivan's March. I want to write a very long piece, an emotional piece. I want to make people cry if I can. I want to do that because I know what happened. Not just there, but that's an example of what happened to all Indian people. I want to be able to make non-Indians feel what happened, how it feels to have your children murdered and your cornfields burned and your houses burned down. Not to make anyone suffer or liking anyone to suffer, but I don't think the white people yet actually know what happened to the Indians. They know it historically on a piece of paper. The truth just started coming out a few years back. But I think they should know it a little bit further than that. They complimented us when they said, "You Indians are animals." Of course they didn't mean it that way. "You Indians are nothing but animals!" Of course we're nothing but animals!

JB: It's a compliment that way.

BLUE CLOUD: Isn't it wonderful? But not the way they say it! Well, they're starting to accept us as human beings. I don't want to rub anybody's face in it, anything like that. I just want to retell it, through my eyes now in 1980-something, how it feels. You were asking me before about the difference between Indians and other people. I still *feel it*. I can still see that first ship landing in 14-and-something. I was there! I fed them corn and gave them deer meat and showed them how to fish. I was there, I really was. And I'm still here tomorrow after I'm dead. Those kids (gestures at his children) are going to be running around, and they're going to be having kids of their own. No way am I going to let some second-rate actor from Hollywood blow up the whole world. Not if I can help it. What a country we have that puts idiots, actors, and fools in as presidents. When was the last good president? There wasn't one to begin with. I read up on these heroes, like Kennedy. I wasn't too sure about him, I never got into politics too much—I guess I was in my twenties, then. But I remember when he died and everybody was crying, he was a really great guy. So I started reading about him and he wasn't so damn great. He wasn't much better than the ones on either side of him. I can't remember their names. Yeah, I think the basic difference is that a lot of the Indians, most of the Indians I ever met, live in the past, in the present, and in the future. You have to. It's a continuous thing. And the future is just as important as the past because they all tie in. The circle. Going back to the circle. The whites in this country that I know, that I've met, they are straight people going along. They're walking a straight road. They don't think it ever curves. It just goes straight ahead, it never goes back to itself.

JB: Onward and upward?

BLUE CLOUD: Yeah! They build a house on the side of the road, live there, then buy a trailer and move on and leave that empty house. Indians leave a house, there's always somebody left there at that house. I've met white people who don't know who their great-grandparents were. "Oh, I think they were from Nebraska or Kansas." I know where all my great-grandparents are buried as far back as they'll let me remember. And it's very important to know. If somebody's bones are in a different place than they belong, I go over there and say hello once in a while. I don't believe in the Hereafter, but I believe in the spirit. Maybe the closest thing to that is *soul*. The gene pool. I believe that there is an essence in us, our own personal mystery, which is the power, which is the Creation. There is something in us that's alive, and when we die we don't die completely. There's something, maybe part of our mind, goes back to the gene pool, the mystery, the essence, back to Creation, and is passed on to other people. The good and the bad. I do that in Coyote, the good and the bad.

JB: Yes, you do. Very clearly.

BLUE CLOUD: I'm really getting stronger into that because I guess I've been studying people that I know here and there and trying to see that coming through. And it's there in everybody. It's fantastic.

JB: That's how I always think the old stories came about—by people paying attention, listening. Not just listening to what other people say, but to their dreams, also. That's a place where I see a difference in terms of Indian reality and white reality, the way dreams work for us.

BLUE CLOUD: Oh, yes. I wish we had dream doctors. We used to have them. We didn't need Freud. Can you imagine that there isn't one left, I don't think? I've never heard of one. With the Six Nations and with probably a lot of tribes we had these doctors who listened to your dreams. They thought about them and reasoned them out and then talked with you and did something. If it was a bad dream, it had a meaning for you. They'd try to explain it to make it work. They could even take evil and turn it inside out and make it work for you, sometimes. (long silence)

JB: I find myself listening to the silences between our words and wishing there was some way we could put that down on paper. Those silences are important, too.

BLUE CLOUD: It'd be easy. Just describe the silence of outside. You'd have to bring in the forest. (laughs) Yes, a lot of my poems start out with my creating a landscape. I don't mean to do it, but that's what sets me off, even if I know the subject of my poem has little to do with what's happening now, it has everything to do at the same time. So, I open up the poem describing what's happening outside. The sounds, the smells, and then lead into the poem. Setting the scene like a playwright.

JB: That's how it works in your verse plays, those poems from the different voices of Creation, the different voices of the animals, as in "Rattlesnake: A Dialogue of Creations."

BLUE CLOUD: Yes, I had the animals talking in that one. I've always wanted to do that on the radio. Maybe I'll get a chance.

JB: Why do you think the Mohawks have produced so many poets lately?

BLUE CLOUD: Lately? (laughs)

JB: I understand why you say that, but I mean why do you suppose there have been so many in recent years—yourself, Maurice Kenny, Rokwaho, Karoniaktatie. . .

BLUE CLOUD: I don't know. Let me think about this for a minute. Maybe they don't have as good orators as in old times. I don't think they do. I've listened at some of the councils. They're pretty good, but it gets repetitious after one meeting. They're not as eloquent as they used to be, so maybe we poets try to do that in poetry. Not to say a poet is an orator. He doesn't necessarily have to be.

JB: But the poets may be filling the gap?

BLUE CLOUD: Yeah. Maybe the gap is creating new songs and chants, telling new stories. There's not as many Mohawks sitting around a campfire at night. Most of the ones I know are sitting around a T.V. set in the living room. So, maybe the poets are by their campfire telling stories, old ones and new ones, making up some. Yes, there are quite a few Mohawk poets. That's good. A lot of other Indian poets, too. And there are new poets coming up, too, of course. That's great. The continuance. Yeah, I love that.

That Beat, That Pulse

An Interview with
DIANE BURNS

Diane Burns is one of the new generation of American Indian poets first published in the 1980s. Her book of poems, *Riding the One-Eyed Ford*, was brought out in the fall of 1981 by Contact/II Press and is now in its second printing. Anishinabe and Chemehuevi in ancestry, her years of life in New York City are reflected in the clothes she wears and the mod-to-punk style of her hair and her demeanor. A striking, slender young woman with long black hair, Diane makes heads turn when she enters rooms, and it might be easy for some not to take her seriously if they have not read her poetry—a poetry couched in language which blends the knowledge of the city streets with her deeply felt connection to her heritage.

The interview with Diane took place in the Turtle Museum in Niagara Falls, New York, where she and I had just judged a poetry contest for American Indian writers. As the interview began, the floor of the museum was taken over by a group of local black break dancers who had rented the museum space to practice for a competition. Somehow, it seemed like just the right atmosphere.

Big Fun

I don't care if you're married I still love you
I don't care if you're married
After the party's over
I will take you home in my One-Eyed Ford
Way yah hi yo, Way yah hi yo!

Modene!
the roller derby queen!
She's Anishinabe,
that means Human Being!
That's H for hungry!
and B for frijoles!
Frybread!
Tortillas!
Watermelon!
Pomona!
Take a sip of this
and a drag of that!
At the rancheria fiesta
It's tit for tat!
Low riders and Levis
go fist in glove!
Give it a little pat
a push or a shove
Move it or lose it!
Take straight or bruise it!
Everyone
has her fun
when the sun
is all done
We're all one
make a run
hide your gun
Hey!
I'm no nun!

'49 in the hills above
        Ventura

Them Okies gotta drum

I'm from Oklahoma
I got no one to call my own
if you will be my honey
I will be your sugar pie, way hi yah,
Way yah hey way yah hi yah!

We're gonna sing all night
bring your blanket
or
be that way then!

      —Diane Burns

JB: Music is very important to your writing, isn't it?

BURNS: Yeah, rhythm, y'know pulse, it's all in there. It's all everywhere.

JB: I notice in your poems a quality of rhythm that seems to combine both contemporary music and music from various Native American traditions. Is that consciously done on your part?

BURNS: Yeah, sure. I love music and I love those old saws, y'know, the old '49 songs. Yes, I love the old saws, I love the new old saws. I love the doo-wop stuff. I like a lot of things.

JB: You've been living in New York City for quite a while now?

BURNS: Yeah, ten years.

JB: How difficult is it as a writer of Native American ancestry to survive in the city atmosphere?

BURNS: It's rough, baby, it's rough. (laughs) It's tough, yeah. I don't know if being Native American has anything to do with it, but in terms of culture shock it's there. Like when I first went to New York I couldn't sleep for weeks because I kept hearing sirens and cars crashing and people screaming and dogs barking and guns going off. But after a few weeks I didn't hear it anymore.

JB: Is the blending of cultures in your work conscious?

BURNS: Well, I don't know if that's conscious or just a survival mechanism. Because, listen, my father's Chemehuevi and my mother's Anishinabe, Chippewa, and I grew up like in Sherman Institute at the time it was called Sherman Institute instead of Sherman Indian High School and there were other Indians all over there. But we also lived in this suburb near the barrio, so there were a lot of cultural things going on. Even up until college I still had words that I thought were English but they weren't.

JB: What words, for example?

BURNS: Well, different words, obscure words like . . . (laughs) I don't want to talk about the word I was just thinking of, but there are a lot of words I thought were English that were not.

JB: I'd like to hear more about the background you came from.

BURNS: As you know, the Chemehuevis are from California, toward Arizona and the desert. I mean real desert. When it rained everyone went outside because it was an occasion. My mother's from Wisconsin, and I grew up there also. There it's woods, lakes, it's really home to me though I spent a lot of time in California, too.

JB: I feel the presence of your Chippewa ancestry very strongly in certain of your poems such as "Gadoshkibos."

BURNS: My mother's family has been very supportive of me and what I'm trying to do. My uncles will tell me stories and my Grampa will tell me stories and sing songs to me, old songs, songs that were real old when he was a kid. They're great. And, of course, we've been there forever so we know everything. (laughs)

JB: When did you begin to write?

BURNS: I was always writing. I started a book when I was in grade school. I still have a copy of it someplace, the manuscript. In high school I wrote, and in college I started writing and getting paid for it. I started doing book reviews and newspaper articles and things like that. One day somebody called up the Indian Community House in New York and said, "Do you know any Indian writers? We need an Indian poet to read at this poetry reading." The only writer they could think of was me, so they gave them my number. They said they were going to give me fifty bucks for this poetry reading, so I said, "Okay, I'll write some poetry."

JB: What year was this?

BURNS: '78 or '79. I was just out of school. Class of '78.

JB: What school?

BURNS: Barnard. Yeah. Me, Joan Rivers, and Margaret Mead. I like to think I'm sort of midway between comedy and anthropology. (laughs)

JB: How did you choose Barnard or even end up in New York, for that matter?

BURNS: When I was sixteen I went to this sort of alternative school. It was in Scarsdale. (looks down toward the museum floor) Amazing. Everywhere I go there's break dancing.

JB: Break dancing at the Turtle Museum—somehow it seems appropriate for you, Diane. (laughter) So, after the school in Scarsdale you went to Barnard?

BURNS: I went to I.A.I.A.* first and then I went to Barnard. That's how I knew about Barnard to begin with, because I was in Scarsdale. There was a comic book store near Barnard that I really liked and that's the motivation. Besides, it was a good school and I could be in New York.

JB: Those poems you wrote for that poetry reading they invited you to do—were those the first you'd ever written?

BURNS: I won a prize for poetry when I was like five. I won a book titled "The Beat Poet." I still remember some of my poem. "A pencil can travel in any . . ." Well, I don't remember all of it, but it seems like yesterday. But, yeah, for that reading was the first time I wrote poetry seriously.

JB: What about "Big Fun," from which the title for your book *Riding the One-Eyed Ford* comes?

BURNS: I wanted to write something up-beat and something really fast that could be a lot of fun to read and a lot of fun to hear. That's what I wanted to do and "Big Fun" came out of it.

JB: Was that a memory of a specific '49 or a bunch of them lumped together?

BURNS: Sort of a montage '49. (laughs) I wish I could say '49er in French and then it would be a montage. Modene in the poem is my aunt.

Modene!
the roller derby queen!
She's Anishinabe,
 that means Human Being!
That's H for hungry!
and B for frijoles!
 Frybread!

*The Institute of American Indian Arts, a junior-college level program for Native Americans in Santa Fe.

Tortillas!
Watermelon!
Pomona!

You know? Sort of like this whole rancheria fiesta '49 kind of feeling to it that I like a lot. Yeah.

JB: What led to Maurice Kenny publishing your book?

BURNS: I was negotiating with another publisher at the time. On the publisher's suggestion I sent some poems to different magazines and one of them was *Contact/II*. I got a postcard right back saying they really liked them and they wanted more and they wanted to publish those. Through that I got a reading with Maurice Kenny and I met Josh Gosciak—the publishers of *Contact/II*. One thing led to another and now I've got a book from Contact II!

JB: Going back to family, you mentioned to me earlier today that your family is from the same part of the world as Louise Erdrich.

BURNS: Actually not. But my mother works in the boarding school system and Louise Erdrich's family also. Now they're from Turtle Mountain, I believe. It would have been the same town in North Dakota, Wahpeton. Which, incidentally, is the same Indian school that Dennis Banks and Floyd Westerman went to—and ran away from many times!

JB: Did you know the Erdrich family?

BURNS: No, you see I *really* hated Wahpeton. I ran away from there, too. I went to I.A.I.A., I went to this alternative school and to New York. I didn't want to spend a whole lot of time there. But my brothers, the family that's there, my one brother's like a mailman in Wapato, the postmaster or something. My other brother is president of the Native Americans at Dartmouth.

JB: What then do you think of as your roots?

BURNS: I really have to say that now I feel connected to Wisconsin and my family there. Yet I know I'm not a part of that life there. I'm only there once a year for two or three weeks. California—I go there maybe once every ten years. I don't call up people from grade school anymore. People are scattered. I've known people in New York a lot longer than people I think of as old friends.

JB: How have you been affected by your contact with other Indian writers?

BURNS: Oh, I've just had a ball with it, y'know. I just love the people, most of them. I haven't met anyone I've really disliked. I really enjoy the writers because there's a certain mind-link, I guess, and I love to like do what they call in New York "doin' the dozens." When you kind of insult each other. Writers do that but they do it in a different way, kind of a playing with words kind of dozens. I really enjoy that.

JB: Paula Gunn Allen said when I spoke with her that her life was saved by reading *House Made of Dawn*. She recognized then that she wasn't alone in her experiences and her feelings. Has anything like that happened to you in your contact with the work of other contemporary Indian writers?

BURNS: No. I'm really bad. I don't really read a lot. When I went to school I didn't study English, I studied political science. I have no idea what the great writers are about or even American Indian writers. I read people's books who I know, but I can't say that I've had that same sort of experience.

JB: Not a literary connection so much as a connection through writers as people you know?

BURNS: Right, because I didn't have any exposure to those people before I was writing myself. Y'know. And things happened real fast for me since I've started writing. I haven't had much of an education and I'm lazy.

JB: Do you feel then, that popular culture is as important as any influence in your work?

BURNS: Oh yeah! I live there, I live there. Everyone else lives there. I love the things that are stupid and trashy and tacky. I just love them because that's my connection with the rest of the world. (laughs) I feel I can eat in McDonald's and feel I'm one of this community or I can go to the Wax Museum here in Niagara Falls and feel good about that.

JB: I also sense that you come up with a stance—out of

this popular culture—which is critical of things which might not be noticed by the average person. For example, that refrain "the whites are crazy" in "Gadoshkibos."

BURNS: Well, I'm not a *part* of the popular culture really. We come from another culture which is in this one. It's like being in a movie. So I think I, of course, have a different viewpoint.

JB: That older culture which is important to you . . . you mentioned older relatives giving you stories, singing songs. Is that still happening?

BURNS: Oh yeah! Everytime I go home. My Grampa will tell me these wild stories about when he was little. My uncle will tell me incredible stories about people who used to live here and what happened on this corner and what happened over here by this tree and that rock. It's something. They're very supportive.

JB: You said that you haven't yet read *Love Medicine,* but what you've just said reminds me that in that novel there are wonderfully minute details about families, people, things in the past, things going on now, relationships built up in these small communities. You, too, find that community important, the Indian relatives, the extended family?

BURNS: Oh yes. I couldn't help but be there. It's me and I'm it.

JB: What sort of things are you doing with your work now?

BURNS: I'm really interested in the concept of conformity and nonconformity. You know, sometimes you feel you're really a freak, a weirdo, you're alienated, alone, and bizarre. Other times, the other side of that is that you're wonderful and unique and brilliant and positive, a marvel and a gem. These are two things. You can feel like an angel or a worm. This has to do with being part of things and not being part of things. I've really been exploring this in a novel and a short story that I've been writing. One of them deals with what happens when giant bunnies from Jupiter come and land on the earth on an Indian reservation. (laughs) Yeah, this has to do with aliens. I like the irony of the second invasion.

JB: What does the other one have to do with?

BURNS: It's about a culture in which drugs are *the* thing. Everyone does drugs. It's not unlike this society. The drugs are controlled by the government, not unlike, you know. Everyone is on drugs and this is an accepted part of the society. It has to do with the relationships of a number of people who are, like, revolutionary because they have pirates, thought pirates who begin this revolution. It's a long involved story but basically has to do with one person and good and evil.

JB: Although you tend to minimize your literary background, I know that you have done some teaching. You just recently did a workshop at St. Mark's.

BURNS: Yeah, that was a lot of fun. Bob Holman, who is co-director with Bernadette Meyer, called me up and asked me if I wanted to do it. I said, "Well, I don't know what to do." But somehow I developed something to teach. Yeah, and some good work came out of it. There were a lot of very talented people in the class, just fabulous. And we did a group reading at the end of the year titled "St. Mark's *on* The Bowery." But it was the first time I had been in a teaching sort of role. We studied a lot of right-brain left-brain creativity, exercises, stuff like that.

JB: Not long ago you were part of a radio program about Native American women writers, "The Key Is in Remembering." It seems as if there's a great deal of energy today among Native American women writers. Have you noticed that?

BURNS: Yeah, yeah. There's a lot of strong women's voices out there. There are also a lot of men writers, but the women seem to be more—well, I'm going to get myself in trouble here—but they've tapped into a more creative and individual persona. They've got their own voice, only more so. They're more on the cutting edge, more avant-garde.

JB: Why is this so?

BURNS: Well, I think in recent years women have had to deal beyond. In the '60s people were dealing with theoretical ideas and raising consciousness in the '70s. In the '80s the practical aspects of all of this are becoming more and more apparent to more and more people. As women living in America, of course we are affected by that. We also, as Native Americans, have this strong quality in our backgrounds, where women had their power in the society and in government in our own cultures. So these are not alien ideas to us.

JB: So in the '80s it is possible for a voice like Diane Burns to be heard, whereas it would not have been so ten or twenty years ago?

BURNS: Yes, I think so. I think so. I've seen B.I.A.*-published books from I.A.I.A., bits of poetry from students back then, and some of them are very wonderful considering the constraints there must have been at that time. There's good work in those little booklets. But you don't hear anything about the people who wrote in those things now.

JB: What has shaped you as a writer thus far?

BURNS: Well, I think I have a good ear sometimes. Not for everything, but for some things. I see a lot of performers, too. So I see a lot of different aspects to working in front of an audience—which I really enjoy. I would rather read poetry in front of an audience than almost anything else. I feel the most real when I am doing that because it is really expressing myself and what I am. By seeing a lot of performers I have so many more options to chose from. Like they say, "Steal from the best!" If I could kick over a mike like James Brown, why not?

JB: You're going to do some work with a band, aren't you?

BURNS: Yeah, right. I'm going to be working with Bobby Albertson who is with the Ray-Beats and formerly of the Bush Tetras, and Eric Lerner who was my student. We're going to be working in New York in May combining music and poetry. We'll see what happens with that. It's a positive direction to go to.

JB: Why do you think music and poetry are effective together?

BURNS: Because it's that beat, that pulse. Everything is. Even in the drums back home, it is all heartbeat, just pulse that's going through everything. Everyone is singing and dancing. It's a very primal kind of thing. It goes beyond just thinking

*The Bureau of Indian Affairs.

about it in your head. It goes right into your body. And your head just follows.

JB: You're talking about community, something that combines all of those heartbeats to make a unified experience?

BURNS: Yeah. But it's also about individuality too, because that's part of the community. Belonging and not belonging because, as American Indians, you always have this feeling of not belonging but you also have this feeling of belonging. As a woman it gets exaggerated. Living in New York it gets more exaggerated. Haves and have-nots.

JB: Do you think that this is something that will continue? This ability of Native American women to express themselves, of women in general to express themselves more freely. Or will there be a reversal of that trend?

BURNS: Hey, once Pandora's box is opened, forget it! (laughs) They're loose. They're loose, honey. No stoppin' us now.

JB: What it is that makes all these various writers so valuable?

BURNS: I believe that creativity is the force that propels everything. That's the energy of the universe. The more you feed it, the more there is to go around. I believe that what I am doing is as important as anything anyone else is doing. More than the President, certainly, more so than the president of UCLA! The more people can express themselves, the better things will be. I'm on a mission from God. Like the . . .

JB: Like the Blues Brothers?

BURNS: Right. (laughs)

JB: Actually, this ties into the old idea of the importance of ceremonies. When you do a ceremony, you're greasing the wheels of Creation.

BURNS: Maurice Kenny has an excellent way of saying it, too. He calls it "putting your stick into the fire." You put your stick into the community fire. Some people come by, they don't put their stick in.

JB: But you add to the heat and the flame. And sometimes a few sparks fly up, too?

BURNS: That's show biz!

That Beat, That Pulse   55

JB: What else has been important to you as a writer?

BURNS: Well, I could talk about how important it has been to me to be in New York City at this point in my life. It's where I can be seen by the most people, where I can have the most impact. It's my function to do this.

JB: You don't feel lost here, then? I've heard it said that being an Indian in New York is like being lost in a desert without water.

BURNS: Well, I can see why people would say that. New York is kind of out of the Indian centers network. It's real polyglot and there's a lot of friction here because of cultural differences. But, as an artist, I feel I'm more connected with new ideas and new thoughts than I could be anywhere else. If I were in North Dakota I wouldn't know who Verez was or who John Cage was. I'd just know what was coming in *Newsweek* magazine or *Time*. I always wanted to know. I always wanted to know it first, see it first, hear it first. (listens to music in background) Oooo, I love Prince. My cousin's in his movie.

JB: In *Purple Rain?*

BURNS: Yeah, it's wonderful.

JB: Any final thoughts?

BURNS: What should I talk about? Well, I could talk about yoga. I think I should be more healthy, well, everybody should be more healthy. But I'm particularly unhealthy. I do all the bad things. I smoke, uh, I smoke, eat sugar, caffeine. I'm going to take classes in yoga and clean up my act because I really feel the universe is telling me it's time to clean up. If it gets in the way, it's not worth keeping around.

As a Dakotah Woman

An Interview with
ELIZABETH COOK-LYNN

Elizabeth Cook-Lynn is a writer whose voice has only begun to be heard at a time when most other writers are already well established. As she says of herself, she truly came to writing in her forties and is still hesitant to call herself a poet. A member of the Crow Creek Sioux Tribe, she was raised on the reservation and is a fluent speaker of Dakotah. Her work reflects her connection to her people and she has been described by some critics as one of the most authentic of Native American "tribal" voices.

An Associate Professor of English at Eastern Washington State College, where she also edits *Wicazo Sa Review*, she is the author of two collections, *Then Badger Said This* (Ye Galleon Press) and *Seek The House of Relatives* (Blue Cloud Quarterly). The interview with Elizabeth Cook-Lynn was conducted over the phone.

At Dawn, Sitting in My Father's House

I.

I sit quietly
in the dawn; a small house in the Missouri breaks.
A coyote pads toward the timber, sleepless as I,
guilty and watchful. The birds are commenting on his
passing. Young Indian riders are here to take the old
man's gelding to be used as a pick-up horse at the
community rodeo. I feel fine. The sun rises.

II.

I see him
from the window; almost blind, he is on his hands and
knees gardening in the pale glow. A hawk, an early riser,
hoping for a careless rodent or blow snake, hangs in the wind-
current just behind the house; a signal the world is
right with itself.

I see him
from the days no longer new chopping at the hard-packed
earth, mindless of the dismal rain. I hold the seeds
cupped in my hands.

III.

The sunrise nearly finished
the old man's dog stays here waiting, waiting, whines
at the door, lonesome for the gentle man who lived here. I
get up and go outside and we take the small footpath to the
flat prairie above. We may pretend.

—Elizabeth Cook-Lynn

JB: I like that poem. The mood you've created is such a gentle and evocative one. The picture you give of the relationship with your father—though you don't speak directly about that—is a very strong one.

COOK-LYNN: Yes. I didn't know that for a long time, about my relationship to my father. It just seemed to be like all relationships are. I think that's one of the interesting things about being a poet, it leads you to discover things. The discovery of the relationship with my father is one of the marvelous things that has happened through the years. He's been dead now for five years, and I wrote this poem after his death but before I had really gone to this place. I think the poem does say a lot of things about my relationship with my father, who has turned out to be quite influential. I think the poem probably does some other things as well. You know, the Sun is, in Sioux mythology, a male figure. There are several ways to say "Sun." You can say *tunka-shina*, which is the actual word that you use for your blood grandfather. So, the Sun itself becomes a kind of father figure, symbolically speaking or metaphorically speaking—in the poem. This is one of those poems, too, that was just so easy to write. It was all right there. It's probably one of the poems that I've written most quickly and I don't know how to explain that, either. It's a positive poem, too. The Sun rises and so everything is all right, even though it is a poem about death.

JB: That is one of a number of things which strike me about this poem: the clarity and simplicity of statement, those very brief and direct sentences; the way the dawn comes into the poem and the sun is rising so that even though it is a poem about your father's death it is not pessimistic or negative.

COOK-LYNN: Yes, and that brings up, perhaps, some of the religious matters in the poem. We are talking about the dawn, after all, and there are many songs that one knows about *anpao wichakpe*, which is the morning star that comes then. There are lots of songs that are sung, religiously speaking. I happen to be doing some translation of some songs right now. I didn't have that in mind, I suppose, when I wrote the poem, but it does have that quality of singing to the dawn. Then there

ELIZABETH COOK-LYNN

is kind of a finished thing, too. The sun rises in the morning and that is the end. The sunrise is really finished. That's something I like about it. You know, so many times you write a poem and you're not satisfied and you just work at it and struggle with it so that it does seem complete. This one just was completed without any effort.

JB: There's a philosophical direction the poem takes— an attitude toward death, dying, and those who have died, which I see in American Indian writing in general.

COOK-LYNN: Death is certainly part of life. I think this poem affirms that cultural idea. It's not a poem that is in despair over this death. It is a poem that rather accepts it, I think, in that kind of way that American Indians have. It is not a poem that is filled with grief and loss. The narrator of the poem says, "I hold the seeds cupped in my hand." And when the hawk rises in the wind currents behind the house . . . there are so many things. And the sunrise itself finishing, that's a very positive sort of thing. It's odd, I suppose, that a Native American writer uses these kinds of things but very seldom knows about it until later. Until someone talks about it or pays particular attention to it. I was talking to Ray Young Bear one time, and he and I had just had some of our work discussed by Jim Ruppert. It was an essay called "The Oral Tradition and Six Native American Poets," something like that. Ray was saying, "I really like to read that because it makes so much more sense to me. It sort of explains to me what I'm doing and it clarifies it for me." I don't know if I ever told Jim that. I should have, probably. I felt the same way. I think there are a lot of poets, however, who *know* what they are doing. I think that Ray certainly does have a notion of many of those things. But I think that what he was saying was that when you talk about it, when you read some literary criticism, then it does clarify things you might not have thought about. I have the sense that *I* know less about what I'm doing as a poet than most people I talk to. So, it's an interesting process.

JB: When did you become a writer?

COOK-LYNN: The question of when you did become a writer is a question that I really don't know how to answer because I still don't consider myself a writer. Another friend of mine who is a writer said recently, "I finally got a passport and on it, where they asked occupation, I put down 'writer.' So now I'm a writer. It's on my passport." I said, "Well, I've never come to that conclusion." I think of myself in a lot of ways. I'm a teacher. I'm a mother. I'm a wife and a grandmother. I *am* a teacher. I do accept that. But when I talk of myself as a writer I don't know if I am. I very often say "I could have been a writer." (laughs) So I have this ambivalence, but I have been writing forever. As a kid I went to schools on the reservation, around Fort Thompson and Big Bend. When I first learned to read and write, I used to copy poems down—before I knew what poems were. I had these notebooks that I kept and I just copied them exactly as they were in the book. So I have the recognition that it was always an art which interested me, before I even knew what poetry was. I didn't write a lot of poetry when I was a child. I probably didn't write poetry until I was in college. I wrote stories, but I didn't do much of that until I was in college. My undergraduate degree is in Journalism, and I got that at South Dakota State College. It was then that I became very much interested. I wrote early things and published them then and after I was married. They were *terrible* things, and I don't know why anyone published them. Often quite emotional. So that's how I began, but I really didn't like anything I wrote until I got to be forty. Then I liked what I wrote. Then I really started publishing, and people started talking to me about what I was writing. Then I gave readings and so on. Isn't that odd?

JB: What led you to write poetry and fiction?

COOK-LYNN: I don't know. I haven't the foggiest notion about that. I just know that I have always been interested in writing and I have always been interested in language. I grew up, of course, in the midst of some very difficult times for reservation Indians. I was born and raised on the reservation. I married another Sioux from another reservation, the Cheyenne River Sioux Reservation, my first marriage. I'm sure that the whole notion of poetry and writing and those rather esoteric kinds of things were far from the influences in my life. I'm sure

ELIZABETH COOK-LYNN

that becoming a college professor wasn't even in the realm of possibility. So it's very strange how I managed to write and become a college professor and the editor of a magazine and all these things. I don't really know. But I *did* have a grandmother whose name was Eliza Renville. She was from the Sisseton Wahpeton Sioux Reservation up near the Canadian, North Dakota border. She wrote. She was a woman who seldom spoke English and so she wrote in Dakota language for some of the early Christian newspapers that came out of that part of the country. I was very close to that grandmother. I was with her quite a bit. She lived probably four miles from where we lived. I used to walk back and forth and we would talk and she was a writer. She was taught by the Presbyterian missionaries. There were Presbyterian missions in both North and South Dakota, and she and her family were very much involved in that. Her father and her grandfather helped put together one of the first Dakota dictionaries. Contemporary writers don't arise out of nowhere. They don't operate in a vacuum, they come out of some kind of tradition. So, even though I wasn't sure about all of that stuff and didn't know a lot of it, I think that must have been influential. I still have a lot of those newspapers that were published then. I suppose they started publishing them in something like 1850–60, and they went through to the 1930s. So there was a long tradition in that and my grandmother, even though she was really a *traditional* woman, became involved in that. Most of the time Christians thought that only men were people of importance, that her father and her brother were the important people. But somehow Eliza—I'm named after her, too—Eliza Renville did this. I read those newspapers every now and then. Of course she wrote about religious things. She also wrote about community things. And she also wrote about traditional things because there was a kind of a combination of Christianity with the old tradition that was still going on.

JB: So, you have both Dakota oral tradition and a relatively unknown Dakota literary tradition to back yourself up with?

COOK-LYNN: Yes. A lot of people don't think that there really is a Dakota literary tradition. A lot of people have no sense of that at all. But there is a kind of an interesting dual tradition there, and this was before very much work had been done concerning how to write down the language. I think she was writing at a time when people were just discovering how to do that. There's been a lot of criticism of that sort of thing lately in that the writing syllabary is pretty much oriented toward the English language rather than finding ways to do it like the Crees have done or as the Cherokees did back in the old days, where they invented their own alphabet. That didn't occur for the Sioux.

JB: This ties into a statement you made in *Wicazo Sa Review*: "Different poets concentrate in different ways and my own individual way of concentration generally comes from what I know as a Dakota woman." Can you expand on that?

COOK-LYNN: One of the things I worry about when I write poetry is whether I utilize the devices that one knows about poetry in the Western tradition. I think that I don't concentrate on a kind of lyric tradition that might come out of classical European poetry. When you concentrate on the lyric you are interested in emotion and then you are doing certain things. I would like to be able to do that, but that's not really my concentration. So, I concentrate more on the narrative. If you're concentrating on the narrative more than the lyric, then you're interested in the story, not the emotion. Then you're interested in characters and events. I think that's what I meant. And much of what I do in that rises out of the story or history. I'm not a really terribly religious person with access to all the rituals and all of that. So, I think I'm concentrating in different ways. Does that explain it?

JB: Yes. It also makes me think of your reference to a statement of Robert Penn Warren's: "short stories destroy poetry." Because of the way you use storytelling techniques in your poetry, I felt that you don't agree with him.

COOK-LYNN: Oh, yes. I think I don't agree with him. I think that they rise from the same thing. I think that they're both there. I've written a lot of poetry that is directly related to a story I've written. The poem may say something different, but it is certainly connected to the story.

JB: Your first book, *Then Badger Said This*, was published in 1978 and reissued in 1981. That book's structure is very interesting. You combine poetry, personal narrative, story, and essay. How did you happen to put it together that way?

COOK-LYNN: Well, of course the influence of Scott Momaday on Indian writers is just profound. I was trying, of course, to write the Sioux version of *The Way To Rainy Mountain*. I was trying to find out what I could discover in that volume about the Sioux tradition and what I know. So I started out to do that and I will be perfectly up front and open about that. People have said that *The Way To Rainy Mountain* and *Then Badger Said This* are similar in structure and I think that Elaine Jahner even wrote an essay in which, I believe (I haven't read it), she commented on the similarity of those two works. I happen to think that Scott Momaday discovered something terribly important when he did that, for all of us of specific tribal histories. He did it for himself, for a Kiowa, but I wanted to do it for myself, as a Sioux, in some important way. I don't know if I can say much more about that. But, of course, it fell into chaos and I ended up simply ending and putting a few poems in. The reason I called it *Then Badger Said This* was because the badger is not a terribly important figure in Sioux literature but he is *always there*. He comments on what people say. He sort of keeps the plot moving. Sometimes his observations are correct and sometimes they are not. But his basic function is to keep the plot moving. That's kind of how he operates in Sioux literature. So that's what I wanted to do with that. I wanted to keep the plot moving. Actually, I think you could use the devices that Momaday chose to use in there and you could explain a lot about the Yakimas and the Dakotas and the Hopi, all sorts of tribal perspectives could come out of that.

JB: You seem, like Momaday, to have done quite a successful job of blending various forms of narrative to produce an overall different texture and result.

COOK-LYNN: Well, I don't know that it was so much a classic quest on my part, as it is in his, clearly. Then he has the prologue and the epilogue also, which explain that. The essay "The Man Made of Words" goes along to explain it even further. I don't know that I was into it to that degree. However, I wanted to find out what the past has to do with the present, what oral tradition has to do with what you're doing today in literature. Things like that interest me. I think that more Indians who really come from some kind of a traditional background ought to try to use that form that he has put so clearly in front of us. It is more the Indian novel, you see, than *House Made of Dawn*. It does what a novel does, it gives you that worldview. That's the function of a novel. So I consider that the form of the Indian novel. I think it is fantastic.

JB: How would you describe that form?

COOK-LYNN: I don't really know. I don't know that I discovered that so much when I tried to utilize it. But I'm sure that you can see the possibilities in that form by looking at *Then Badger Said This*. Let's take a look at the one that starts on page 22:

> When the Dakotapi really lived as they wished, they thought it important to possess a significant tattoo mark. This enabled them to identify themselves for the grandmothers who stood on the ghost road entering the spirit world asking, "Grandchild, where is your tattoo?" If the Dakotah could not show them his mark, they pushed that one down an abyss and he never reached the spirit land.

That, of course, is myth. That's myth that everybody knows, I suppose. I'm not making it up and I'm not saying anything original. Any Dakotah who reads this simply knows it. Then, I talk about a particular man, LaDeaux. He dies and there is something in there that doesn't allow him to reach the spirit land. So, he has to have this ritual for that to occur. The father of the little girl sings the song, paints the man's face, and wraps him to get him ready for that journey. We never knew exactly what had happened to him. That comes from an actual death I knew as a child, I really did know Jack LaDeaux.

JB: Were you the little girl?

COOK-LYNN: Yes, I'm the little girl in the story and this is, of course, my father again. I don't want to make my father out to be a really traditional religious figure, because he wasn't.

He was just an ordinary man who didn't consider himself necessarily virtuous or religious. So that story is a personal matter I have to explore. I never did know why LaDeaux died, but there was something awful about it. Then the poem, which follows the story, gives some answers to that. I wrote the poem years later. In fact, I was leaving Seattle one time to drive across Montana to South Dakota. It was Sunday morning. I looked out of the window and there was this man standing there in his long gray coat and I thought for a moment I knew him. Then when I turned around and watched him I didn't know him. But I got to thinking what a terrible thing it must be, what terrible thing happened to this man that here he is now, probably drunk for days? The most terrible crime that can be committed in Sioux culture, in Dakotah culture, is to commit a crime against one's own relatives and against one's own brother. So I make that up, you see, and that gives me an explanation for why it is that LaDeaux found himself in the position of not being accepted into the spirit world. It also says something about the significance of myth and how it impacts one's own life. That's what I wanted to do when I put those three pieces together.

JB: Myth, then, impacts your life not just through the past but in an on-going way?

COOK-LYNN: Yes, it does. Yes, indeed it does. It explains many things for you. So, that's what I wanted to do. I wanted to use myth and personal history and poetry to discover a cultural value and to say what that value was in the very beginning and to say what it is now. That's what I was trying to do when I was doing this. I was so totally moved when I saw Momaday doing this in some important sort of way that I really didn't understand fully at the time—nor do I yet, probably. But I was for years trying to explain some of these things and then, when I saw how Momaday managed that, it was extremely useful. And I think it would be useful to a lot of Indians who are still significantly connected to the past.

JB: I'm struck, too, by the place where you've retold a story much like a story Momaday told. I'm thinking of the Sioux story of the boy in the lodge, which is very much like Momaday's now well-known parable of the arrow-maker.

COOK-LYNN: Yes, it is from the Dakotah literary tradition.

JB: But the message of your story seems a bit different from Momaday's.

COOK-LYNN: How so?

JB: In Momaday's story the enemy is recognized because he does not know the language. In your story, the owl speaks to the boy, Swan, and the connection to the natural world is the significant turning point.

COOK-LYNN: Yes, I thought of that at one time, but I sort of forgot about it. What do you make of that?

JB: It shows, to me, the way traditions cross boundaries throughout Native American cultures . . . and that there are different lessons which can be gained through almost the same stories.

COOK-LYNN: Yes, I think that both of those things are probably very true. You know that the Kiowas are very closely related to the Dakotahs, culturally speaking. In fact, we have a lot of stories that talk about the Kiowas, our traditional stories. I would imagine that is true of the Kiowas. They must have taken note of the Sioux . . . traditionally speaking. (laughs) Of course, the Sioux have a tendency to think how important they are. But I do remember some stories my Grampa used to tell, and they did mention the Kiowas particularly. And they were rather familial kinds of stories, almost like the stories that one tells about the Cheyenne. There's a lot of that kind of familial relationship in Sioux tradition. So, the Kiowas aren't terribly far removed, and I think that the story itself is in all of the Northern Plains and the Southern Plains literatures. It is a very common kind of story among groups that are similar. I suppose if you went to the Northwest or if you went to the East Coast, it wouldn't be there. So there is a kind of commonality, and perhaps that is why I was so terribly emotionally moved when I read Momaday back in the '60s.

JB: Would you regard Momaday as one of the major influences on your writing?

COOK-LYNN: Definitely—and I think Momaday is one of the major influences on almost any Indian writer that I know.

That's why I'm so disappointed in this new biography that's out on Momaday written by Matthias Schubnell, published by Oklahoma University Press. It says things that indicate Momaday's *real* contribution to literature is in common themes and common ground with people like Wallace Stegner and Georgia O'Keefe and five or six other western artists. Well, I think that is important to say about Momaday, that he *is* also effective in the western literary tradition. But the fact is that Momaday, almost single-handedly, made it possible for many of us to find out what it is we know and to express it.

JB: Yes, I think that book misses the point—as have a number of other critical studies which discuss Momaday. Are there certain things special to American Indian culture which you deliberately don't write about or only refer to in-directly?

COOK-LYNN: Oh, yes. I was thinking about that when I was talking about that thing from *Badger,* talking about the myths, the personal experience, and then the poem. I've got shoeboxes full of that stuff I don't publish and I feel it's an invasion—not only myself, but the people that I know, an inva-sion of the traditions which I don't really know that much about and I don't know that I should be talking about. So, yes, there is a lot of stuff I don't want to deal with. Sometimes I go ahead and do it anyway, but I'm not so happy about that. There is a story in *Then Badger Said This* about the woman and the little girl. I was talking to another Dakotah friend of mine, Beatrice Medicine, and she said, "Oh, that story is really good." And I said I was worried writing about that because I don't know anything at all about that thing I refer to in the story, the Elk Society, the male society that men used to have, societies that gave them power over women. I don't know a thing about that. But the fact is that I felt all right imagining it because I'm a woman anyway and a woman isn't supposed to know anything about that. (laughs) So I felt that would be all right. And maybe the Dakotahs who read it would say, "Well, she's a wom-an and she doesn't know." But I think there are two ways to approach that. One is that you don't know everything you need to know to explore it. The other thing is that perhaps it shouldn't be explored at all in the literary context—written and in English language.

I'm worried about a lot of the things I write. The trouble is you're expected to know absolutely everything. You're supposed to be this expert and you're supposed to have so much authority. The fact is I'm only a poet. I'm not an historian, I'm not a linguist, I'm not all these other things. I'm just a poet, and people have to understand that. Jim Ruppert also said in an article that of all the writers he knew I was the one who functioned as a tribal historian. I was appalled when I read it and I wrote to him jokingly and said, "Jim, really this is terrible." He said, "Well, I see that in your work." And I said, "But historians are supposed to be *right* about things. They're supposed to know. And besides that, historians are not self-appointed (in Sioux culture, at least) as poets are." But I think there is that worrisome feeling, and I've talked to Ray Young Bear who also expresses the same thing. I think a number of Indian poets worry about that. Even writing about my father intimately, or my mother or my daughter or my grandparents, I feel those also are invasions. The real trouble with being a poet is that you have to let people know you. I want to be a poet but I also want to be anonymous. (laughs)

JB: You mention the difference between men and women in Dakotah ritual life. I know some white feminist writers who—at one time, at least—would just hit the roof at the idea of women being excluded from things, at purely male ceremonials. But I sense a different feeling on your part. Can you explain that?

COOK-LYNN: Oh, yes. There has always been a kind of politeness toward one another. Politeness toward men because they're men and politeness toward women because they're women. You know, even in our language there are those distinctions. Women have different endings to words. They say things, they have words, vocabulary, that men don't use. The same is true on the other side. There are male kinds of things that women don't say. So I think there has always been the recognition of a kind of respect for one another as genders. Respect of gender. People, I think, have misinterpreted that and

have often said about Indian women that they are simply
beasts of burden following ten paces behind carrying all the
bundles. That is *not* the traditional perspective on feminine life.
I think maybe after Christianity came, after the world changed,
that things *have* occurred which American Indian women
might want to discuss in the feminist perspective. But I grew up,
perhaps in those times when Indian women were seen as
inferior. I was born in 1930 when women were having very
difficult times and Indians in general.

I think now that Indian women and men are going to
have to become familiar with one another in a contemporary
setting and discuss the things that have happened to us. You
know, there are a lot of Indian women writers now with very
strong voices. I think it is possible that different Indian cultures
will approach these matters in different ways. Many people
think that Sioux culture is very male-dominated, but I think
that taking note of that traditional respect of gender is a very
important thing to say. Whether or not that excludes men from
women's experiences and women from men's experiences, I
don't know. I tried to write about that—about an old couple
that used to come and visit my grandmother and grandfather.
They would come with a team and wagon and they would stay
for days. They came from Standing Rock. When it was time for
them to leave, she was the one who went out and caught the
horses and harnessed them. Then he would get in the wagon
and sit up there. She would hand him the reins and then get in
the back, with her blanket or shawl over her head and sit with
her back against his seat. Then they would leave. I never
thought anything of that. Their children were gone, and he was
old and very ill and couldn't catch the horses. She was younger than he was, his third wife, I would say. So she did it, and I
think that's the way things were and I didn't think of that as
being a detrimental thing to their relationship nor did I think of
it as a detrimental thing to her as a woman. I tried to write
about this but was not satisfied with it. However, I did not
perceive Lucy as being an inferior figure. This was just the way
it had to be done.

Whatever Is Really Yours

An Interview with
LOUISE ERDRICH

It was a sunny day in New Hampshire when Louise Erdrich
and her younger sister, Heidi Erdrich, a student in Creative
Writing at Dartmouth, met me at the airport. We drove to the
house her sister was subletting from Cleopatra Mathis, a poet
and teacher at Dartmouth. Louise and I sat out on the back
deck above a field where apple trees were swelling toward
blossom, two horses moved lazily about their corral, and we
could see the hills stretching off to the east. Louise is a striking
woman, slender with long brown hair. She is surprisingly mod-
est—even a bit shy—for one whose early accomplishments are
so impressive: a powerful first book of poetry from a major
publisher, a first novel which won critical acclaim, a National

Book Critics Circle Prize, and the Los Angeles Times Book Prize in 1985. But as we spoke, her voice was clear and her convictions as strong as those of any of the complex white, Indian, and mixed-blood characters who populate her work and her memories.

Indian Boarding School: The Runaways

Home's the place we head for in our sleep.
Boxcars stumbling north in dreams
don't wait for us. We catch them on the run.
The rails, old lacerations that we love,
shoot parallel across the face and break
just under Turtle Mountains. Riding scars
you can't get lost. Home is the place they cross.

The lame guard strikes a match and makes the dark
less tolerant. We watch through cracks in boards
as the land starts rolling, rolling till it hurts
to be here, cold in regulation clothes.
We know the sheriff's waiting at midrun
to take us back. His car is dumb and warm.
The highway doesn't rock, it only hums
like a wing of long insults. The worn-down welts
of ancient punishments lead back and forth.

All runaways wear dresses, long green ones,
the color you would think shame was. We scrub
the sidewalks down because it's shameful work.
Our brushes cut the stone in watered arcs
and in the soak frail outlines shiver clear
a moment, things us kids pressed on the dark
face before it hardened, pale, remembering
delicate old injuries, the spines of names and leaves.

—Louise Erdrich

JB: That poem is among the ones I like best of yours. It does two things I see as characteristic of your work—juxtaposes the two worlds and also hints at a natural unity which is broken yet hovering somewhere in the background. Why did you choose to read that particular poem?

ERDRICH: It might be something as simple as that the rhythm is something I like. Probably I chose it because I've been thinking about it on the way over here because it's the one I knew by heart and it started me back on remembering when it was written and the place where I grew up.

JB: I like the rhythm, but the subject matter, too, has a special meaning.

ERDRICH: It does, even though I never ran away. I was too chicken, too docile as a kid, but lots of other kids did. This, though, is a particular type of running away. It's running home; it's not running away from home. The kids who are talking in this poem are children who've been removed from their homes, their cultures, by the Bureau of Indian Affairs or by any sort of residential school or church school. Many kinds of schools were set up to take Indian children away from their culture and parents and loved ones and re-acculturate them. So, it is about the hopelessness of a child in that kind of situation. There is no escape. The sheriff is always waiting at mid-run to take you back. It's a refrain and it's certainly the way things were for a long time. I guess now that the boarding schools have finally started serving a positive purpose, the current Administration wants to cut them. They're finally schools that can take in children who have nowhere else to go. They do serve some purpose, but naturally they are threatened. It's just a damn shame.

JB: It seems to me, too, to be a metaphor for the things that are happening with American Indian writing and culture in general. People have been dragged into the twentieth century, European/American culture and frame of mind and running away from that means running not away, but back.

ERDRICH: Yes, running home. That's true. I have a very mixed background and *my* culture is certainly one that

LOUISE ERDRICH

includes German and French and Chippewa. When I look back, running home might be going back to the butcher shop. I really don't control the subject matter, it just takes me. I believe that a poet or a fiction writer is something like a medium at a seance who lets the voices speak. Of course, a person has to study and develop technical expertise. But a writer can't control subject and background. If he or she is true to what's happening, the story will take over. It was, in fact, hard for me to do that when stories started being written that had to do with the Chippewa side of the family because I just didn't feel comfortable with it for a long time. I didn't know what to make of it being so strong. It took a while to be comfortable and just say, "I'm not going to fight it." "Runaways" is one of the first poems that came out of letting go and just letting my own background or dreams surface on the page.

JB: In my own case, being of mixed ancestry, I'm sometimes surprised how strongly those voices speak from that small percentage of my ancestry which is American Indian. That seems to be true of many other mixed-blood writers of your age and my age, that for some reason that's the strongest and most insistent voice.

ERDRICH: I think that's because that is the part of you that is culturally different. When you live in the mainstream and you know that you're not quite, not really there, you listen for a voice to direct you. I think, besides that, you also are a member of another nation. It gives you a strange feeling, this dual citizenship. So, in a way it isn't surprising that's so strong. As a kid I grew up not thinking twice about it, everybody knowing you were a mixed-blood in town. You would go to the reservation to visit sometimes and sometimes you'd go to your other family. It really was the kind of thing you just took for granted.

JB: One reason I like *Jacklight* so much is that it does deal with both sides of your family—the sections in the butcher shop are very real. They're no less strong than the sections which take place on the Turtle Mountain Reservation. When did you first begin to write, to write poetry or to write anything?

ERDRICH: Well, my Dad used to pay me. Ever so often he'd pay me a nickel for a story. So I started a long time ago. Both my Mom and Dad were encouraging, incredibly encouraging. I had that kind of childhood where I didn't feel art was something strange. I felt that it was good for you to do it. I kept it up little by little until I got out of college and decided, this great romantic urge, that I was going to be a writer no matter what it cost. I told myself I would sacrifice all to be a writer. I really didn't sacrifice a lot, though. (laughs) I took a lot of weird jobs which were good for the writing. I worked at anything I could get and just tried to keep going until I could support myself through writing or get some kind of grant. Just live off this or that as you go along. I think I turned out to be tremendously lucky. Once I married Michael, we began to work together on fiction. Then it began to be a full-time job. It's a great thing, a miracle for a writer to be able to just *write*.

JB: That's something seldom talked about, those persons who enable you to be a writer. It's very hard when you're on your own to devote yourself completely to writing, even part-time.

ERDRICH: Michael and I are truly collaborators in all aspects of writing and life. It's very hard to separate the writing and the family life and Michael and I as people. He's also a novelist and has just finished his first novel. It's called A *Yellow Raft in Blue Water* and it's in the voices of three women; a young girl, her mother, and the grandmother speak. Very beautiful—and unusual, intriguing, interesting for a man to write in women's voices. I think it is because he was raised only by women.

JB: The male voices in *Love Medicine* are very strong and legitimate. The book ends with a male voice.

ERDRICH: Yes. I don't know why that is, but they just seem to be. You don't choose this. It just comes and grabs and you have to follow it.

JB: In one of your poems, *Turtle Mountain Reservation*, I notice how strong your grandfather is, how strong his voice is. A storytelling voice, a voice connnected to the past in such ways that some people may think him a little crazy—in the poem Ira thinks he is nuts. I wonder if that voice of your grandfather's has made you appreciate more and relate more to the voices of your male characters?

ERDRICH: He's kind of a legend in our family. He is funny, he's charming, he's interesting. He, for many years, was a very strong figure in my life. I guess I idolized him. A very intelligent man. He was a Wobbly and worked up and down the wheat fields in North Dakota and Kansas. He saw a lot of the world. He did a lot of things in his life and was always very outspoken. Politically he was kind of a right-winger sometimes, people might say. I think he gave Tricia Nixon an Anishinabe name, for publicity. I always loved him and when you love someone you try to listen to them. Their voice then comes through.

JB: His voice is a combination of voices, too. He can both be in the Bingo Parlor and then speaking old Chippewa words that no one but he remembers.

ERDRICH: I think this is true of a lot of our older people. People who aren't familiar with Indians go out to visit and they can't believe that there's somebody sitting in a lawn chair who's an Indian. It's kind of incomprehensible that there's this ability to take in non-Indian culture and be comfortable in both worlds. I recently came from Manitoulin Island, a beautiful place. People are quite traditional and keep a lot of the old, particularly the very old crafts. There is a great quill-work revival. I don't know if you're familiar with the kind of quill-working done up in Ontario, but this is really the center for it. But people live, even there, incorporating any sort of non-Indian thing into their lives to live comfortably. That's one of the strengths of Indian culture, that you pick and choose and keep and discard. But it is sometimes hard because you want some of the security of the way things were. It's not as easy to find the old as it is to find the new.

JB: In the poem "Whooping Cranes," legend-time and modern times come together, when an abandoned boy turns into a whooping crane. There's a sort of cross-fertilization of past and present in legend.

ERDRICH: And natural history. The cranes cross over the Turtle Mountains on their way down to Aransas, Texas. We always used to hear how they'd see the cranes pass over. No more, though. I don't know if they still fly that way or not.

JB: In some of Leslie Silko's work you see that mixing of times. Someone may go out in a pickup truck and meet a figure out of myth.

ERDRICH: Don't you, when you go on Indian land, feel that there's more possibility, that there is a whole other world besides the one you can see and that you're very close to it?

JB: Very definitely. Crossing the border of a reservation is always entering another world, an older and more complicated world. How do you feel when you go back to Turtle Mountain?

ERDRICH: I feel so comfortable. I really do. I even feel that way being in North Dakota. I really like that openness. But there's a kind of feeling at Turtle Mountain—I guess just *comfortable* is the word to describe it. There are also places there which are very mysterious to me. I don't know why. I feel they must have some significance. Turtle Mountain is an interesting place. It hasn't been continuously inhabited by the Turtle Mountain Band. It was one of those nice grassy, game-rich places that everybody wanted. So it was Sioux, it was Mitchiff, it was Chippewa. They are a soft, rolling group of hills, not very high, little hills—not like these (gestures toward mountains)— and there were parts that my grandfather would point out. The shapes were called this or that because they resembled a beaver or whatever kind of animal. He even incorporated the highways into the shapes because some of them got their tails cut off. (laughs) Even that people can deal with. Not always, though. There are many places that are certainly of religious significance that can never be restored or replaced, so I don't want to make light of it.

JB: As in the Four Corners area.

ERDRICH: Yes, I was thinking of Black Mesa. In the case of those hills at Turtle Mountain, there was that resilience because they were places which had a name, but not places— such as Black Mesa—much more vital to a culture and a re- ligion. Catholicism is very important up there at Turtle

LOUISE ERDRICH

Mountain. When you go up there, you go to Church! My grandfather has had a real mixture of old time and church religion—which is another way of incorporating. He would do pipe ceremonies for ordinations and things like that. He just had a grasp on both realities, in both religions.

JB: I see that very much in your work. A lake may have a mythological being in it which still affects people's lives while the Catholic Church up on the hill is affecting them in a totally different way. Or you may have someone worrying about being drafted into the army at the same time he's trying to figure out how to make up love medicine—in a time when old ways of doing things have been forgotten. It seems similar, in a way, to Leslie Silko's *Ceremony,* where there is a need to make up new ceremonies because the old ones aren't working for the new problems, incorporating all kinds of things like phone books from different cities.

ERDRICH: You may be right. I never thought about the similarity. This "love medicine" is all through the book, but it backfires on the boy who tries it out because he's kind of inept. It's funny what happens until it becomes tragic. But, if there is *any* ceremony which goes across the board and is practiced by lots and lots of tribal people, it is having a sense of humor about things and laughing. But that's not really what you're saying.

JB: Maybe—maybe no.

ERDRICH: Who knows? (laughs) Anyway, I don't deal much with religion except Catholicism. Although Ojibway traditional religion is flourishing, I don't feel comfortable discussing it. I guess I have my beefs about Catholicism. Although you never change once you're raised a Catholic—you've got that. You've got that symbolism, that guilt, you've got the whole works and you can't really change that. That's easy to talk about because you have to exorcise it somehow. That's why there's a lot of Catholicism in both books.

JB: The second poem in *Jacklight* is called "A Love Medicine."

ERDRICH: I was sort of making that poem up as a love medicine, as a sort of healing love poem. So, I suppose there are all kinds of love and ways to use poetry and that was what I tried to do with it.

JB: There are several things I see in *Jacklight*. One is an urge toward healing, a desire to ameliorate the pain, create something more balanced, even if it means facing difficult realities. Was that a conscious theme?

ERDRICH: I don't think any of it was very conscious. Poetry is a different process for me than writing fiction. Very little of what happens in poetry is conscious, it's a great surprise. I don't write poetry anymore. I've in some ways lost that ability. I've made my unconscious so conscious through repeated writing of stories that I don't seem to have this urge to let certain feelings build until they turn into a poem.

JB: Another theme I see strongly in *Jacklight*, and in all of your writing, is the theme of strong women who become more than what they seem to be. Transformations take place— in some cases, mythic transformations.

ERDRICH: That is true of women I have known. We are taught to present a demure face to the world and yet there is a kind of wild energy behind it in many women that *is* transformational energy, and not only transforming to them but to other people. When, in some of the poems, it takes the form of becoming an animal, that I feel is a symbolic transformation, the moment when a woman allows herself to act out of her own power. The one I'm thinking of is the bear poem.

JB: That's a really wonderful four-part poem.

ERDRICH: Oh, I'm so glad! But, you know, she's realizing her power. She's realizing she can say "No," which is something women are not taught to do, and that she can hit the sky like a truck if she wants. Yes, it's transformational. It goes through all of the work I've been doing lately. Part of it is having three daughters, I think, and having sisters. I have an urgent reason for thinking about women attuned to their power and their honest nature, not the socialized nature and the embarrassed nature and the nature that says, "I can't possibly accomplish this." Whatever happens to many young girls. It happens to boys, too. It happens to men, no question. In the book there are men—maybe not so much in the poetry, but in the

the fiction—like Lipsha, who begin to realize that they are truly strong and touch into their own strength. I think it's a process of knowing who you are. There's a quest for one's own background in a lot of this work. It's hard not to realize what you're doing. And you say, "Funny thing, I have so many characters who are trying to search out their true background. What can this mean?" One of the characteristics of being a mixed-blood is searching. You look back and say, "Who am I from?" You must question. You must make certain choices. You're able to. And it's a blessing and it's a curse. All of our searches involve trying to discover where we are from.

JB: It makes me think of Jim Welch's wonderful scene in *Winter in the Blood* when that old man turns out to be his true grandfather.

ERDRICH: Oh yes, yes. Certainly.

JB: In that same light, there's a similarity there with Leslie Silko, though I don't mean to imply that you've copied anything of hers.

ERDRICH: No, no, that didn't even enter my head. She's working out of a whole different tribal background. She was a discovery for me in a particular way I don't think any other writer will ever be. I'm very attached to her work.

JB: You don't write poetry now because you feel the conscious effort of writing prose makes it less available?

ERDRICH: It sands away the unconscious. (laughs) You know, there's really not much down there. But what really sands away the unconscious is getting up in the middle of night to rock your baby to sleep. When you live in isolation—I notice this whenever I leave—I dream poems. But when you get up at all hours feeding babies, you just don't have that kind of experience, you're just not able to let your unconscious work for you. However, I don't miss it. I'd rather have the kids than the tortured unconscious. Also, I have a very practical way of working. I just sit down and Michael works in one room and I work in the other and we just sit there as long as we can. I really have got more and more mundane about my work habits. There are times when I'm up at 4:30 and I feel like something extremely strange is about to happen—whether it's writing or not. Maybe

I'm just crazy. But I sit down and, if something is there, it will be written. Usually, though, after the kids are taken care of, I try to write and very few poems come that way. Almost none. I maybe have three now since *Jacklight*, which I don't think I'll ever publish. Those poems now seem *so personal*. I just don't know if I can put them in a book again! (laughs)

JB: I think you're tapping, though, the same sources for your prose that you've tapped for your poetry, even though the method may be different. I think the depth of experience, the types of metaphor, and the direction it goes are all on the same road.

ERDRICH: I'm connected to the poems because you feel so protective toward your first outpourings. You want them to have some kind of continuity in their life. I think that is probably true. You can see the themes that were being worked with in *Jacklight* go on into the writing in other ways. The poem you mentioned, "Family Reunion," turns into part of "Crown of Thorns" once it goes into the fiction. A lot of them do that. The next book, which is *The Beet Queen*, takes place in that sort of butcher shop world and incorporates people who are and are not in those poems. It's a very different book but also one which I think flows naturally out of both *Jacklight* and *Love Medicine*.

JB: What years did you write the poems in *Jacklight?*

ERDRICH: All through '77 and '78. Then, once it was accepted to be published I wrote a few extra ones. I was so thrilled to be finally published. The manuscript went everywhere and I thought it would never be published. Then it was, and I was given this great boost. So I wrote some of the ones I really like, like the one about the bear and about living with Michael and the children, because I was so happy. I guess it was surprising. I thought I would live my whole life without being published and I wouldn't care, but as it turned out I was *really* happy.

JB: When did you begin writing with Michael?

ERDRICH: Once we were married. In '81. We began by just talking about the work, back and forth, reading it. He always—right at first before I got to know him—was the person I would go to with problems. I'd say, "Michael, should I get into teaching, should I quit writing? What should I do?" And he said to me, "Look, there's only one thing to do. Throw yourself into your work. Don't take any more jobs." And I did it. I just tried what he said. (laughs) At times I found myself in some unpleasant monetary predicaments. But I've been lucky. I think it is because we started working together. He had ideas for the whole structure of *Love Medicine* that became the book. We worked on it very intensely and closely, and I do the same with his work. We exchange this role of being the . . . there isn't even a word for it. We're collaborators, but we're also individual writers. One person sits down and writes the drafts. I sit down and write it by myself or he does, but there's so much more that bears on the crucial moment of writing. You know it, you've talked the plot over, you've discussed the characters. You've really come to some kind of an understanding that you wouldn't have done alone. I really think neither of us would write what we do unless we were together.

JB: Didn't the genesis of *Love Medicine*, "The World's Greatest Fisherman," come about that way. Michael saw the announcement of the Chicago Prize. . .

ERDRICH: Yes. Michael was flat on his back, sick, and he said, "Look, you've got to enter this! Get in there, write it!" And I did, brought it in and out to him, changed it around, together we finished it.

JB: You have such a strong narrative line in all your work and stories seem so important to you, stories told by your characters in the poems, the stories of the poems themselves and then the structure of story in *Love Medicine*, which is, in fact, many stories linked together. What is story to you?

ERDRICH: Everybody in my whole family is a story-teller, whether a liar or a storyteller (laughs)—whatever. When I think what's a story, I can hear somebody in my family, my Dad or my Mom or my Grandma, telling it. There's something particularly strong about a *told story*. You know your listener's right there, you've got to keep him hooked—or her. So, you use all those little lures: "And then . . . ," "So the next day . . . ," etc. There are some very nuts-and-bolts things about storytelling. It also is something you can't really put your finger on.

Why do you follow it? I know if there is a story. Then I just can't wait to get back to it and write it. Sometimes there isn't one, and I just don't want to sit down and force it. You must find that, too, because you tell a lot of stories.

JB: Yes, there's something about a story that tells itself.

ERDRICH: The story starts to take over if it is good. You begin telling, you get a bunch of situation characters, everything together, but if it's good, you let the story tell itself. You don't control the story.

The Story of All Our Survival

An Interview with
JOY HARJO

This interview took place on December 2, 1982, in Santa Fe,
New Mexico, where Joy Harjo was living while a student in a
post-graduate film-making program at the College of Santa Fe.
Although the interview was done before the publication of her
new book of poems, *She Had Some Horses* (Thunder's Mouth
Press), a proof copy of the book had just arrived in the mail and
we made reference to it during the interview.

The living room of the rented house in which we talked
was one of those open "modern" living rooms typical of contemporary southwestern architecture. It was dominated by a
painting on the wall of a group of horses—the same painting

which became the cover design for her book—and a large stereo with reggae tapes piled on top of it.

I began by asking Joy if there was a poem she would like to start off with. The one she chose came out of her recent experience of teaching a workshop in an Alaskan prison.

Anchorage

This city is made of stone, of blood, and fish,
There are Chugatch Mountains to the east
and whale and seal to the west.
It hasn't always been this way, because glaciers
who are ice ghosts create oceans, carve earth
and shape this city here, by the sound.
They swim backwards in time.

Once a storm of boiling earth cracked open
the streets, threw open the town.
It's quiet now, but underneath the concrete
is the cooking earth,
                            and above that, air
which is another ocean, where spirits we can't see
are dancing   joking   getting full
on roasted caribou, and the praying
goes on, extends out.

Nora and I go walking down 4th Avenue
and know it is all happening.
On a park bench we see someone's Athabascan
grandmother, folded up, smelling like 200 years
of blood and piss, her eyes closed against some
unimagined darkness, where she is buried in an ache
in which nothing makes
                            sense.

We keep on breathing, walking, but softer now,
the clouds whirling in the air above us.
What can we say that would make us understand
better than we do already?
Except to speak of her home and claim her
as our own history, and know that our dreams
don't end here, two blocks away from the ocean
where our hearts still batter away at the muddy shore.

And I think of the 6th Avenue jail, of mostly Native
and Black men, where Henry told about being shot at
eight times outside a liquor store in L.A., but when
the car sped away he was surprised he was alive,
no bullet holes, man, and eight cartridges strewn
on the sidewalk
                all around him.

Everyone laughed at the impossibility of it,
but also the truth. Because who would believe
the fantastic and terrible story of all of our survival
those who were never meant
                        to survive?

—Joy Harjo

JB: I'm glad you started with that poem, Joy. Those last few lines, the "story of all of our survival,/those who were never meant to survive," are pretty much the theme I see as central in contemporary American Indian poetry: the idea of survival. What are you saying in this poem about survival?

HARJO: I see it almost like a joke, the story about Henry in the poem I just read. You know, he was real dry when he was talking about standing out there and all those bullet holes and he's lying on the ground and he thought for sure he'd been killed but he was alive and telling the story and everybody laughed because they thought he was bullshitting. And it's like a big joke that any of us are here because they tried so hard to make sure we weren't, you know, either kill our spirits, move us from one place to another, try to take our minds and to take our hearts.

JB: That poem has many stories tied into it, stories of people that you know, stories of women, stories of things that you remember. Storytelling seems to run through and even structure much of the work by American Indian poets. Is that true for you?

HARJO: I rely mostly on contemporary stories. Even though the older ones are like shadows or are there dancing right behind them, I know that the contemporary stories, what goes on now, will be those incorporated into those older stories or become a part of that. It's all still happening. A lot of contemporary American native writers consciously go back into the very old traditions, and I think I do a lot unconsciously. I don't think I'm that good of a storyteller in that sense, but it's something that I'm learning. I love to hear them and use them in my own ways.

JB: If there's an image of the American Indian writer that many people, who are not very knowledgeable about what an American Indian writer is, have, it is of what I call jokingly the Beads and Feathers School, nineteenth-century "noble savages." The poetry in this new book of yours is not Beads and Feathers, yet to me it's very recognizably from an American Indian consciousness. What is that consciousness?

HARJO: I suppose it has to do with a way of believing or sensing things. The world is not disconnected or separate but whole. All persons are still their own entity but not separate from everything else—something that I don't think is necessarily just Native American, on this particular continent, or only on this planet. All people are originally tribal, but Europeans seem to feel separated from that, or they've forgotten it. If European people look into their own history, their own people were tribal societies to begin with and they got away from it. That's called "civilization."

JB: Leslie Silko and Geary Hobson have both attacked the phenomenon of "The White Shaman," the Anglo poet who writes versions of American Indian poems. What are your thoughts on that?

HARJO: I agree with them. It's a matter of respect to say, "I'm borrowing this from this place," or "I'm stealing this from here," or "I'm making my own poem out of this," but the white shamans don't do that. They take something and say it's theirs or they take the consciousness and say it's theirs, or try to steal the spirit. On one hand, anybody can do what they want but they pay the consequences. You do have to have that certain respect, and you do have to regard where things come from and to whom they belong.

JB: Origins are very important in your work. Where things came from, where you came from. The title of your first book is *The Last Song*, and you ended it with "oklahoma will be the last song/I'll ever sing." Is it not true that you have in your work a very strong sense of yourself as a person from a place which informs you as a writer?

HARJO: I suppose. But the older I get the more I realize it's caused a great deal of polarity within myself. I recognized my roots, but at the same time there's a lot of pain involved with going back. I've thought about it many times, like why I travel, why I'm always the wanderer in my family. One of the most beloved members of my family died just recently, my aunt Lois Harjo. She always stayed in Oklahoma, and I've jokingly said the reason I'm always traveling is so that Andrew Jackson's troops don't find me. You know, they moved my particular family from Alabama to Oklahoma, and so I always figure I stay one step ahead so they can't find me.

JB: Some American Indian writers—you and Barney Bush, for example—are the epitome, for me, of the poets who are always on the move, going from one place to another. Yet I still find a very strong sense in your work and in Barney's that you are centered in place. You are not nomads. There's a difference between your moving around and the way people in Anglo society are continually moving, always leaving something behind.

HARJO: Oh, it's because in their sense they're always moving to get away from their mothers. They don't want to be from here or there. It's a rootlessness. But there will always be place and family and roots.

JB: Those are things which you come back to in your work: those connections to family, to memory. A poem of yours is called "Remember." I think that's very important. The idea of remembering is central, isn't it, in the work of many, many American Indian writers?

HARJO: The way I see remembering, just the nature of the word, has to do with going back. But I see it in another way, too. I see it as occurring, not just going back, but occurring right now, and also future occurrence so that you can remember things in a way that makes what occurs now beautiful. I don't see it as going back and dredging up all kinds of crap or all kinds of past romance. People are people, whatever era, whoever they are, they're people.

JB: In other words, memory is alive for you. You're not just engaged in a reverie—like the old man sitting by the fire and going back over those things in the past. Memory is a living and strong force which affects the future.

HARJO: Sure. People often forget that everything they say, everything they do, think, feel, dream, has effect, which to me is being Indian, knowing that. That's part of what I call "being Indian" or "tribal consciousness."

JB: You also talk in your poems about the importance of

saying things, *speaking*. What is *speaking* for you? What I'm asking, really, is for you to define words I see being used by American Indian writers very differently than most people use them. *Song* is one of those words. *Memory* is one of those words. *Speaking* is one of those words.

HARJO: It comes out of the sense of not being able to speak. I still have a sense of not being able to say things well. I think much of the problem is with the English language; it's a very materialistic and a very subject-oriented language. I don't know Creek, but I know a few words and I am familiar with other tribal languages more so than I am my own. What I've noticed is that the center of tribal languages often has nothing to do with things, objects, but contains a more spiritual sense of the world. Maybe that's why I write poetry, because it's one way I can speak. Writing poetry enables me to speak of things that are more difficult to speak of in "normal" conversations.

JB: I have a feeling that what many American Indian writers are attempting is to bring a new dimension, a new depth to English by returning a spiritual sense to something which has become, as you said, very materialistic and very scientific. German used to be described as the language of science. Today, English is the language of science throughout the world.

HARJO: I've often wondered why we were all born into this time and this place and why certain things happen the way they do, and sometimes I have to believe it's for those reasons, to learn new ways of looking at things . . . not necessarily new, none of this is really new.

JB: Even without the old language to say some of the things that were there in that old language?

HARJO: Which is always right there beneath the surface, especially right here in North America, which is an Indian continent.

JB: That ties into something I wanted to ask you, related to the whole question of the half-breed, the person who is of mixed blood. So many contemporary American Indian writers are people who have come from a mixed parentage. Does that mean a separation or isolation or something else?

HARJO: Well, it means trouble. I've gone through stages

with it. I've gone through the stage where I hated everybody who wasn't Indian, which meant part of myself. I went through a really violent kind of stage with that. And then I've gone through in-between stages and I've come to a point where I realize that we are who we are, and I realize in a way that you have to believe that you're special to be born like that because why would anybody give you such a hard burden like that unless they knew you could come through with it, unless with it came some special kind of vision to help you get through it all and to help others through it because in a way you do see two sides but you also see there are more than two sides. It's like this, living is like a diamond or how they cut really fine stones. There are not just two sides but there are so many and they all make up a whole. No, I've gone through a lot with it. I've talked to Linda Hogan, Lajuana, Leslie, a lot of other people about it, and everybody's probably been through similar stages with it.

JB: Then there is that point where you come to realize that this is still Indian land, despite people who say, "Well, if you're only half-breed, why do you identify so strongly with Indian ancestry?"

HARJO: Well, you can't not. I'm sure everybody's thought about it. I've thought about saying, "Hell, no, I don't have a drop of Indian blood in me. I'm not Indian, don't talk to me." Yeah, I've thought of doing that. But then I would be harassed even more. Everybody would come up to me and ask me why am I ashamed. But you just can't do it. And it also means that you have a responsibility being born into that, and I think some of us realize it much more than others. It's given to you, this responsibility, and you can't shake it off, you can't deny it. Otherwise you live in misery.

JB: Barney Bush has spoken about the idea of being tested.

HARJO: Sure.

JB: Being tested from all kinds of directions at the same time. I especially feel that testing in some of your poems. A tension exists there. It seems to reach a point where it ought to break into violence and yet it doesn't. Why don't they go into violence as some of the poems of the Black American writers do? For example, Amiri Baraka's?

HARJO: I don't know. I see where they could. There're always effective ways to deal with violence. There are ways to temper it. I just read this really neat quote by Gandhi. He's talking about anger and he says, "I have learned through bitter experience the one supreme lesson to conserve my anger, and as heat conserved is transmitted into energy, even so our anger, controlled, can be transmitted into power which can move the world." It seems that the Native American experience has often been bitter. Horrible things have happened over and over. I like to think that bitter experience can be used to move the world, and if we can see that and work toward that instead of killing each other and hurting each other through all the ways that we have done it . . .

JB: The world, not just Indian people, but the world.

HARJO: Sure, because we're not separate. We're all in this together. It's a realization I came to after dealing with the whole half-breed question. I realized that I'm not separate from myself either, and neither are Indian people separate from the rest of the world. I've talked with James Welch and other writers about being categorized as Indian writers. We're writers, artists. We're human beings and ultimately, when it's all together, there won't be these categories. There won't be these categories of male/female and ultimately we will be accepted for what we are and not divided.

JB: To connect, to celebrate, and also to understand. I think that there's a process of understanding that's going on right now in the United States and throughout the world. In fact, sometimes I think people in Europe are further ahead of many of the people in the United States in terms of listening to what writers such as the American Indian writers are saying and understanding what their messages can mean.

HARJO: I suppose. I was in Holland a few years ago reading. I remember riding on a train and talking with a woman from Indonesia, and she told about how Indonesians are treated in Holland. I knew they were welcoming the American

Indians and tribal people from all over, but they didn't realize that these Indonesians are tribal, too, you know. It's like during the Longest Walk when everybody was in D.C. And Carter wouldn't see the people, he said, because he had been out on some human rights mission involving the rest of the world.

JB: Joy, I'd like to ask some questions that deal very specifically with your newest book of poetry, the one that's just about to be published, *She Had Some Horses*. Horses occur again and again in your writing. Why?

HARJO: I see them as very sensitive and finely tuned spirits of the psyche. There's this strength running through them.

JB: The idea of strength also seems to fit your images of women. Women in your poems are not like the women I've seen in poems by quite a few Anglo writers. They seem to be different.

HARJO: I think they're different. I think they reach an androgynous kind of spirit where they are very strong people. They're very strong people, and yet to be strong does not mean to be male, to be strong does not mean to lose femininity, which is what the dominant culture has taught. They're human beings.

JB: I like that. A woman or a man simply being a human being in a poem has not been very possible in the United States in poetry. Instead, the sexes are divided into stereotypes.

HARJO: It's time to break all the stereotypes. The major principle of this universe, this earth, is polarity. Sometimes I think that it doesn't have to be, but the level that earth is, it is. You have to deal with it. I'm not saying it has to be that way— but this x-rated video game where Custer rapes an Indian woman—and then you have all these wonderful things going on in terms of consciousness. Such a split.

JB: Ironic. It's like the old maxim that there wouldn't be angels without devils.

HARJO: Or, again, like Gandhi's saying that bitter experiences can turn into a power that can move the world.

JB: You're saying that things which are not properly used have destructive potential but then when they're used in the right way they become creative. Even those things which seem to be curses we can turn into blessings.

HARJO: You always have to believe you can do that.

JB: Another question about your images or themes . . . Noni Daylight. I've gotten to know and like her in your poems. Who is Noni Daylight, and how did she come to your poems?

HARJO: In the beginning she became another way for me to speak. She left me and went into one of Barney's poems. I haven't seen her since. (laughter) Which poem was it? It was in his latest book. I remember when Barney showed me that poem, he was staying with me one Christmas and I looked at it and said, "Oh, there she is." She left and I really haven't written any poems about her since. It's like she was a good friend who was there at a time in my life and she's gone on.

JB: When did you start writing poetry?

HARJO: When I was at the University of New Mexico. Probably right around the time Rainy was born.

JB: So you started relatively late in life—compared to some people.

HARJO: Yeah, I never had a burning desire to write until rather recently. I always wanted to be an artist. When I was a little kid I was always drawing, and many of my relatives were pretty good artists. My favorite aunt, the one I spoke of earlier, was a very good artist. That's what I always did and it wasn't until much later that I got started, even interested, in writing.

JB: What do you think created that interest?

HARJO: Reading poetry and hearing that there was such a thing as Indians writing and hearing people read and talk, then writing down my own things.

JB: Who were the people who were your influences at that time?

HARJO: Simon Ortiz, Leslie Silko, Flannery O'Connor. The Black writers have always influenced me, also African writers, 'cause here was another way of seeing language and another way of using it that wasn't white European male.

JB: Seeing that freedom of expression?

HARJO: Sure. And I always loved James Wright. He was always one of my favorite poets. He has a beautiful sense of America. Pablo Neruda is also someone whose work I appreciate, learned from. . . .

JB: Neruda speaks about writing a poetry of the impurity of the body, rather than a "pure" poetry. A poetry as broad as the earth is broad, bringing all things into it. I can see that feeling in your work.

HARJO: Yeah, for sure.

JB: What's the landscape of your poems?

HARJO: The landscape of them? It's between a woman and all the places I've ever been. It's like the core of Oklahoma and New Mexico.

JB: Traveling seems to be a really major force in your writing. Movement, continual movement. I think I see a sort of motion through your new book. Is there a structure you had in mind when you put it together?

HARJO: I had a hard time with this book for a long time. I could not put it together right. So a friend of mine, Brenda Peterson, who is a fine novelist and a very good editor, volunteered. She did an excellent job, and what I like about it is that the first poem in the first section is called "Call it Fear." It was an older poem. And the last section which is only one poem is called "I Give You Back," which has to do with giving back that fear.

JB: The way it's arranged makes the book almost like an exorcism, too.

HARJO: It is . . .

JB: So it's not just another one of these cases where "poetry makes nothing happen."

HARJO: No, I don't believe that or I wouldn't do it. I know that it does have effect and it does make things happen.

JB: What does poetry do?

HARJO: I've had all kinds of experiences that verify how things happen and how certain words or certain things make particular events happen. There's a poem that's in the new manuscript about an eagle who circled over us four times at Salt River Reservation. I went home and wrote an eagle poem for that eagle and took it back and gave it to the people who were there and one of the women took it outside the next morning to read it, and the eagle came back. You know, that kind of thing that happens. So I realize writing can help change the world. I'm aware of the power of language which isn't meaningless words . . . Sound is an extension of all, and sound is spirit, motion.

JB: Yes, sound is spirit.

HARJO: And realizing that everything also does, not just me, but anything that anybody says, it does go out at a certain level that it's put out and does make change in the world.

JB: What about political poetry? Or do you think of your poetry as nonpolitical?

HARJO: No, I think it's very political. But, yeah, I look at a lot of other people's poems, like June Jordan, Carolyn Forché, Audre Lorde—I love their work. It's very political. Political means great movers. To me, you can define political in a number of ways. But I would hope it was in the sense that it does help move and change consciousness in terms of how different peoples and cultures are seen, evolve.

JB: That's great. Who do you like right now among contemporary writers? I'm not just thinking in terms of the American Indian writers, although maybe we could start with them. Who do you feel are the important people among Native American writers?

HARJO: Well, I think everybody is. I don't want to mention certain people so that other people aren't mentioned.

JB: That makes me think of what someone said to me at the American Writer's Congress. You remember that panel discussion?

HARJO: Yeah, I remember that panel.

JB: There were more of us than there were in the audience.

HARJO: We had a good time.

JB: It was great. But one person came up to me afterwards and said they couldn't understand why we all seemed to know each other and like each other.

HARJO: That's because everybody else is busy hating each other, I guess. Trying to do each other in . . . That doesn't mean, however, that there's none of that going on in our community!

JB: Why is there such a sense of community? Even when people get angry at each other or gossip about each other, there's a lot of that.

HARJO: Oh, I know, I was gonna ask you what you heard. (laughter)

JB: Yet there does seem to be a sense of community among the people who are Indian writers today.

HARJO: I suppose because the struggles are very familiar, places we've all been. It's very familiar and we feel closer. But at the same time I really can't help but think that at some point it will all be this way, the community will be a world community, and not just here.

JB: Do you notice that tendency in contemporary American writing?

HARJO: Yes, I do. I do more listening than I do reading about what's going on . . . I call it feeling from the air, like air waves. I see other people opening and turning to more communal things, especially among women.

JB: That's a good point. Could you say a few words about that?

HARJO: The strongest writing that's going on in the United States today is women's writing. It's like they're tunneling into themselves, into histories and roots. And again, I think maybe that has to do with the polarity of earth. In order to get to those roots, in order to have that vision, you keep going outward to see you have to have that, to be able to go back the other way. You have to have those roots. And it seems like they're recognizing that, whereas other writing doesn't often feel it has a center to work from.

JB: I like the fact that you dedicated your book, partially, to Meridel Le Sueur.

HARJO: She does recognize who she is, what she is from, and there is no separation. You know, she's been going at it a long time, has faced much opposition, and has kept on talking and speaking in such a beautiful and lyrical voice.

JB: F. Scott Fitzgerald said there are no second acts in American lives. But Le Sueur's life and writing seem to prove Fitzgerald wrong.

HARJO: She's really had a lot of influence on me in terms of being a woman who speaks as a woman and has been often criticized for it, and in the past she could not get her books published because she kept to her particular viewpoint and was sympathetic to certain unpopular viewpoints.

JB: And has influenced a lot of other women, too.

HARJO: Definitely.

JB: To begin writing at a point when most people would say your career is all set. You're a housewife, you're this, you're that, you're something else, you're not a writer. To begin to write at an age when most men have already been writing for ten or fifteen years . . .

HARJO: Well, I always knew I wanted to do something. When I was a kid I always used to draw, paint. I even had pieces at Philbrook Art Center, in a children's art show. I always knew I wanted to be some kind of artist . . . and here I am, writing.

JB: One last question. Your Native American ancestry is Creek. How do you deal with that particular ancestry in your poetry? Does that affect you as it has some other Indian writers?

HARJO: From the time I was a kid I knew I was Creek. But I was raised in an urban setting and in a broken family . . . It all influenced me. I was born into it and since then I've gone back and I'm very connected to the place, to relatives, and to those stories. They always recognize me. My father who was not always there but his presence always was—certainly the stories about him were!

JB: But you're not artificially going back and, say, pulling Creek words out of a dictionary?

HARJO: No, I mean that's who I've always been.

JB: Yeah, you don't have to do that. There's no need to *prove* that ancestry.

HARJO: No, they know who I am. They know my aunt Lois. You could sit down and talk with her, she knew who everybody was and who's related to who, you know, all of them, and they all know who everybody is. They'll say, "Oh, so you're so 'n' so's daughter." And they watch you real close, especially if you have white blood in you. Bad. (laughter) So in a way, I suppose, the whole half-breed thing gives you this incredible responsibility but it also gives you a little bit more freedom than anyone because you have an excuse for your craziness.

JB: That's nice.

HARJO: Of course, you realize it is because, oh, you're an Indian like Linda says, but it's the white blood that makes you that way. (laughter)

JB: I like that.

HARJO: And you also always have to have a sense of humor about it all.

JB: Yes, a sense of humor is right. We didn't talk about that, did we?

HARJO: I mean it's like that poem, "Anchorage," I remember that one jail. I went in there three times and the place would get more and more packed each time I came in because we would sit around and tell stories and—it was all men—and talk and laugh and they didn't want me to go because nobody allowed them to speak. We would all be crying at the end, and I remember when Henry told the story, yeah, you know, we were just laughing at him and saying, you know, you're full of crap, yet the story was really true. We all knew it was absolutely true and it was so sad that it had to be so funny.

The Whirlwind Is a Mirror

An Interview with
LANCE HENSON

Few Native American writers are as deeply involved with the
traditional and ceremonial practices of their people as is Lance
Henson. A member of the Cheyenne Dog Soldier Society, he
has taken part in the Sun Dance for more than seven years
and hosts the local chapter of the Native American Church.
Henson has chosen to earn a living, sometimes a marginal one,
from his writing and occasional workshops in the Oklahoma
Schools. He lives with his wife Pat and his two children, Christian and John David, in the house where he was raised by his
grandparents on traditional Cheyenne lands near Calumet,
Oklahoma.

A veteran of Vietnam and a devoted student of the martial
arts, the animal with which he identifies most is the badger.

Like the badger he is capable of holding stubbornly to the things he believes in, even when confronted by those seemingly more powerful than he. The Cheyenne, he sometimes says, were never a large people. They had to know both how to live in peace and how to fight.

My interview with Lance took place while we were taking part in a literary festival in Haskell, Kansas, honoring the one-hundredth anniversary of the famous Indian Junior College. As we sat in a motel room, surrounded by the typical fixtures of roadside America, his words took us to a place older and realer than the plastic and glass and cinderblock walls.

hi vo di das so

whirlwinds of light

the earths open hand is spinning them

a whirlwind is an ancestor
returned to look at you

a whirlwind is a red spider the white
man calls dust devil
because the white man said it
it became so

a whirlwind is the mirror of the great mystery
caught in the eye of a startled rabbit

whirlwinds of light

the earths open hand is spinning them

—Lance Henson

JB: Within your poetry I often find a deep connection to the old ways and a positive, nurturing relationship to the earth. What led you to that?

HENSON: I was raised by grandparents who instilled the idea of renewal through ceremony, and one of the ways I pay them back for it is by attempting to renew through ceremony the ways they taught me. I think my poetry attempts to reflect an homage. It is one of the ways I try to pay back the life that was given me through them.

JB: Can you tell me more about your grandparents?

HENSON: I was raised by Bob and Bertha Cook in Calumet, Oklahoma. They were a couple who were childless who realized that there were people in their family and in their extended family, children who needed homes. I was the last of five young men they chose to raise, and consequently I came to own their property. They were both involved very heavily in Cheyenne ceremonial ways. My grandmother, Bertha, was a tipi maker and carried a bundle that only women are supposed to carry and see. My grandfather was active through most of his adult life in the Native American Church and kept the grounds for Chapter Number One of the Native American Church in Oklahoma.

JB: I've visited that house which is your grandparents' house, the house that you still live in. It's a very important place to you, isn't it?

HENSON: Everybody's home should be the center of the world. It is there that children are raised and there that the important things in life occur. When you are blessed and given a home—as you understand—where you know that the walls and the floors and the door have a life invested in them which is invested in you, then there's a certain attachment which goes beyond a house and a person living in a house. It really becomes a part of your life force.

JB: Images of the Cheyenne lands, and references to Cheyenne history and culture are found in almost every poem of yours I've ever read. In some cases they are very direct references, in other cases they are oblique, just barely hinted at.

How do you think someone relates to that poetry if they don't know Cheyenne culture?

HENSON: I think the poems themselves are evocative enough to start an interest. For anyone who takes an interest in Native American life, for those people who know something about the Cheyennes, the interest is even more strengthened. The Cheyenne, like all other tribal peoples, are an entity unto themselves, regardless of what the dominant culture or any other culture puts on them. We must harken back to the idea of ceremony and how ceremonies sustain us. I think the Cheyenne way is a model for people looking at "tribes" and how they operate. I'm talking specifically about the ceremonial ways and not the political ways.

JB: What are the roots of your poetry?

HENSON: They are quite varied. I've taken my influence from a lot of writers, surrealists, Spanish poets, Oriental poets, a few American poets, fused with the things I've learned as a Native American, as a Cheyenne. Perhaps just as a life focuses its presence into daily life through many influences, so a poem goes, so a poet goes.

JB: How did school affect your development as a writer?

HENSON: School helped very little. Experience strengthens a writer. Formal education may have a lot to do with how a person looks at himself in relation to the world around him, but I think poets especially are people who are going to be poets and if they don't become poets they probably become outlaws of some other kind.

JB: Are you saying also that there is no particular teacher or person you would regard as a teacher who is a poet?

HENSON: No, I wouldn't. I'm influenced by good poetry, wherever it is, wherever I can find it. (laughs)

JB: Let's go back to that statement of yours about outlaws. What is an outlaw? How is a poet an outlaw?

HENSON: This country allows for very little creativity in its educational process, and those people who have moved education ahead have all been considered outlaws. Poetry is revolutionary. It must be to survive. It has to establish new boundaries and, while it may torture whoever is writing it to jump off bridges and look for ways to do themselves in, it must still move forward. We're talking about the writing itself. When it begins to stalemate or move backwards, whoever is writing can become self-destructive.

JB: When did you begin to think of yourself as a writer? When, also, did you begin to start writing poetry?

HENSON: I was a freshman in college in 1969. I had been a freshman three other times in Oklahoma and lied that I had flunked out of those other courses—this was before I went into the Marines. That was a particular point in my life where I had to start gathering some things together to survive by, and writing seemed to be one way to say how I felt about people and, especially, the particular time that 1969 was in this country. Writing poems became a vehicle for me to say those things.

JB: Earlier you mentioned the importance of ceremony and the way Cheyenne culture has maintained, more so than many other Native American cultures, almost all of the ceremonies. Those ceremonies are also very important to you as a person. Without asking you to talk about anything you shouldn't speak about, what can you say about your relationship to the ceremonies of the Cheyenne?

HENSON: Ceremonies have a way of lifting simplicity and grace to a level of understanding that's ultimate—perception circles back: the way a child understands life, the way a mother understands life . . . and a father and a grandfather and a grandmother and, I might even be so courageous to say, the way an animal or a tree or some of the natural forces view their relationship in this grand mystery called life. I have participated to a point that I can begin to accept the world as it is and go on with whatever life has given me and find in life the means to say back what I have seen. The ceremonies have offered me that and that has been enough and that is all I ask for. There is no greater thing one can learn than to reach out and help and to allow people to help you: to love and be loved by someone who cares enough to do that.

JB: This is really at the basis of the ceremonies, isn't it? What you are doing is not just for yourself but for the help and health of all the people and other things around you?

HENSON: It is never for one's self and anybody who enters those ceremonies finds that out very quickly—because it hurts. (laughs) It is painful and shakes your perceptions of the world to a point that you must begin to understand. If you can't do that, then your experience will lead you back to whatever stalemated you as a child and kept you from being open to the world. In that way I think ritual has its main power, in showing all of us how mortal we are, yet how we can be in touch with all the really powerful things around us at the same time. It's a very uplifting feeling.

JB: Do you think it is fair to say that the necessity for engaging in ceremony goes throughout a person's life? There is never a pinnacle of knowledge reached where one can say, "I know enough and I don't need it anymore."

HENSON: I believe the reverse is true. I believe the more one learns, the less one knows. The only thing that really matters when you understand your life in terms like that is one day at a time, one moment at a time, and trying to stay sane in those times.

JB: The image of the whirlwind, in that poem you chose to read, is a very strong image. That whirlwind is very important, isn't it, in a lot of ways?

HENSON: The whirlwind is a mirror, a microcosmic reflection of the universe. A recent scientific find has been that the source of our solar system is a great light, the sun, which functions as a power that turns the solar system. The Cheyennes knew that when they first began the Sun Dance, but scientists have just discovered it. When the Cheyennes practice their ceremonies they are "greasing the Great Wheel." That's the way it is described to participants.

JB: That whirlwind is also calm within its center, though things can be very confusing when you are out on the edges of it.

HENSON: And aren't we all out on the edges of it? (laughs)

The Whirlwind Is a Mirror

JB: Yes. How do you feel that the Cheyenne have been treated in literature?

HENSON: I don't think we've been treated at all. I can't think of a time when we've been more than mentioned in passing. I look forward to the time when someone, hopefully Cheyenne, is able to sit down and labor over the things that make a Cheyenne whatever he or she is, because the dynamics of it are something that maybe can't be spoken of today.

JB: I have seen, since your earliest poems, words in Cheyenne appear in your work. Recently, whole lines and even poems have been written in Cheyenne. What are the advantages to you in using that language?

HENSON: I am able to see clearly the distinction between Cheyenne and English. They are still far apart. There is so much power in Cheyenne, even written in English letters. When translated into English, the English pales in comparison to the Cheyenne. Anyone who hears Cheyenne and then hears the English translation will see that.

JB: You told me once about a certain poem which you wrote in Cheyenne. When you showed it to some elders, they felt it was more than a poem.

HENSON: I have written some poems that were not publishable because I was dealing with symbols that are very private to the Cheyenne. I was told that, while they were good pieces of writing and good poems, they were not to be published.

JB: They were like prayers?

HENSON: All poems are prayers when they work. These poems were *power* poems. While I might not have known I was writing them when I wrote them, I was very quickly shown and told not to send them out.

JB: Why use English?

HENSON: The Cheyenne quit fighting not because they were defeated but because they were dominated by an enemy who killed their women and children, even after they had killed their leaders. English is a *good* language, just as to a warrior the soldiers who fought the Cheyenne were *good* soldiers. English is an enemy, but it's the way we communicate. That conflict is something I haven't resolved yet. I don't know if I can.

JB: Language can be a weapon too, then?

HENSON: Most definitely it's a weapon. That's why writers' heads hit the chopping blocks first in any revolution.

JB: This leads to the idea of the warrior. In majority culture it seems there are often misunderstandings about what it means to be a warrior. You are a member of a Cheyenne Warrior Society and you have been a warrior, at war, in the forces of the United States military. You've also studied the martial arts. How does that tie in to poetry or to a life in a world where war is seen as an evil or a negative force by many?

HENSON: The strongest warriors I know are children and women. Certain animals exemplify warrior ways. There are few ways the human spirit can stand up and one of the ways it can, if it has a warrior culture, is by being a warrior. I'm not really sure I consider myself a warrior.

JB: What about the idea of Trickster? I find that occurring in your poetry and the poetry of almost every Native American writer. Who is Trickster to you and why is this so important in Native American literature?

HENSON: We are born out of a perfect state to be here and to be here is to endure the weight of gravity and, quite frankly, we need somebody here that doesn't happen to, to remind us that this place, after all, isn't real. It isn't the real place, but it is a place, and while we are here we must endure it. If we can do it with a certain levity, we can laugh at ourselves and have fun, then we have served a purpose here. The whole idea of the Trickster has its origin somewhere deep in the human psyche and its meanings are clear. All you have to do is read one Trickster story, or hear one, or know one, and the meaning of why they're here is immediately upon you.

JB: I have often quoted a statement of yours that Trickster is one who "fights the monsters during the day and gets drunk with them after dark."

HENSON: I think that's still true and truer even today more than ever. I would like to see now the whole idea of

Trickster taken into the public schools. We are at a real crossroads with education in this country. Even educators don't know where they are going.

JB: It might be healthier to have a situation in which whenever someone makes a mistake they are simply recognized as human, as opposed to being condemned for it?

HENSON: Absolutely.

JB: Perhaps, then, we need the possibility for failure which is recognized in Native American cultures? Is that one of the reasons why Trickster is so popular among Native American writers, because the image of failure has been placed so strongly upon Indians?

HENSON: I have only failed when I have dealt with the dominant culture. I have never failed as an Indian and the dominant culture is set up so that you fail. You are never good enough. As long as you have an overseer or a boss, you're never good enough.

JB: I have heard it said by some critics that you handle the short poem as well as anyone writing in English. Why have you chosen to write such short poems?

HENSON: I think brevity is one way to acknowledge strength and one way to acknowledge and pay homage to the Great Silence we came out of. I like to see all that white space around my work. Like drops of rain on a lake.

JB: Whenever you read your poems aloud, your introductions are often like poems or short stories in themselves. Have you considered casting any of the material you speak in your introductions in the form of stories or sketches?

HENSON: I think my wife, Pat, is going to transcribe those stories and type them up. I have no interest in doing that, but she does. I have been asked more than once to do something like that and to publish them.

JB: It seems as if you're working within the oral tradition when you do that. It might be a natural step for those to be transcribed and made a part of the available body of your work.

HENSON: At the present time I don't consider the stories as important as the poems. I'll let someone else do that.

LANCE HENSON

JB: Going further, there are also stories behind and hidden within your poems. What is said and left unsaid in your poetry and also in much of the poetry by other Native American writers?

HENSON: I think what is said is certainly a response out of the experience, to the experiences that made the poem. That's what I start with. Then I pare the work down so that what is left is a reflection of images that are the—how shall I say it?—what floats to the top, on the surface of experience.

JB: Then it may be both a way to filter experience and avoid disclosing those things which should not be disclosed? I heard a term used once by a California Indian medicine woman, "some things are not for innocent ears."

HENSON: I would change that to say the *untrained* ear, the *unknowing* ear. It isn't your fault if you don't have a culture which teaches you the things that many Indian cultures teach you. It may be your problem, but it isn't your fault. While a lot goes unsaid in the writing of many Native Americans, I think there's enough there for anyone interested to find, both positive and negative. I think what is being published today is just a glimpse of what can be published tomorrow because there is a growing awareness in Indian Country that dominant culture and government wish for what we do to cease. We will not cease, even if they terminate us as people. You can't terminate a people. You can do it on paper, but you can't terminate their hearts. You can't terminate their beliefs.

JB: There are many images of darkness, light, and shadow in your work. How do those images come to you and work their way into the poetry?

HENSON: In a recent interview I did I was asked if I was a mystic. (laughter) After much laughter ensued, even by the person who asked me, I responded by saying No, I wasn't a mystic, but I think the natural landscape influences of my given and chosen life reflect images that seem magic or mystical to some. To me they are simply part of my life. I happen to like houses that are lit only by the sun during the day, dark furniture. And it is that dark time that allows for things to settle, to calm down, to become settled. I write most of my poems at night. I think the majority of the poets I read do, because it is a time when the children are asleep or you can find a spot in the house where it is quiet. I also like to deal with the relationship between growing darkness and growing light, the dusk and the dawn, those times when there is a chance to see transition.

JB: Images of waking and sleeping also seem implicit in your work.

HENSON: That's a hard one to try and talk about. Again, participation in ceremonies shows you that the two have overlapping boundaries and time often suspends itself so that it is dark in the middle of the day and light in the middle of the night. One can go so far dealing with the human spirit to see those things.

JB: It seems to me that dream experience is a very real thing within your writing. Why is this so?

HENSON: The dream is a connection, another transitional time. An example would be light coming into the world at dawn. In dreams we sometimes can see resemblances of where we really came from, whether we can explain it or not. I think that happens in every culture.

JB: You've spoken of power dreams, also. What is power?

HENSON: Starting your chain saw with one pull. (laughter)

JB: As Peter Blue Cloud put it in his poem. I know it is a misused term these days, perhaps in part because of all the romantic images Carlos Castaneda has conjured up and which we all have to deal with these days when we deal with Native American writing.

HENSON: Power is a responsibility, as knowledge is. That's something the dominant culture doesn't understand. Power and knowledge are forces that depend on the holder and too many times both are used in ways that only enhance the holder's own balance. Knowledge means responsibility to tribal people. When you gain knowledge, you must use it for the betterment of your people. When you cease to do that, you are causing harm to your tribe and yourself.

The idea of being a writer is in this culture a very romanticized picture. A writer talking about writing is perhaps only as content as a thief among thieves talking about stealing. I think it is important to stress that, if one makes it as a writer when one happens to be Native American, one of the ways to cut one's self off from one's roots is to not give something back.

JB: Then you feel that now we have a generation of successful Native American writers, those people—such as Momaday, Silko, and Welch—need to "pay something back" to the people in the community?

HENSON: There are so many ways a writer of such status can help, and I'm not talking about monetary things. There are just certain ways writers who make it are obligated to give something back in some form for what has happened to them. I have been chided in Oklahoma for doing readings below the fee some people would have set. That is silly to me when in Oklahoma an artist is paid very little to do his craft. It's unethical not to give something back when you've been rewarded richly.

JB: Where do you see yourself going as a writer and what directions do you perceive for Native American literature in the years to come?

HENSON: I will continue to write and continue to strive to grow old. As for what I see in the future for Native American writing, I don't often say beyond what I hope to do or attempt to do. I would only hope that more Native Americans write down what they know—however little they think it is, however unimportant they think it is—because we have children who want to know. There are children in some tribes who want desperately to know their histories and their backgrounds and we owe them, we owe them our being responsible enough to give. I also think there will be another small series of revolutions by Native Americans in this country because of the way this country is treating us. The genocide didn't stop when all the peace treaties were signed. It only began stronger and that's just the way things are.

JB: And the writing will be part of those revolutions?

HENSON: Absolutely.

To Take Care of Life

An Interview with
LINDA HOGAN

Although she often speaks softly in conversation, Linda
Hogan's voice is both eloquent and strong in poems and stories
which draw much of their power from the landscapes of southern Oklahoma and Colorado, where she grew up. Her connections to family and her commitments to speaking of her people
and for the earth are constant threads running through the four
volumes of her poetry published thus far, *Calling Myself Home*
(Greenfield Review Press, 1978), *Daughters, I Love You* (Research Center for Women, 1981), *Eclipse* (UCLA, American
Indian Studies Center, 1983) and *Seeing Through The Sun*
(University of Massachusetts Press, 1985).

    This interview was done while Linda was at the Yaddo
Artists' Colony on a residency fellowship.

Man in the Moon

He's the man who climbs his barn
to look down on the fields,
the man leading his horse from the barn
that finally fell down.

When I'm quiet he speaks:
we're like the spider
we weave new beds around us
when old ones are swept away.

When I see too much
I follow his advice
and close my worn-out eye.

Yesterday he was poor
but tomorrow he says his house
will fill up with silver
the white flesh will fatten on his frame.

Old man, window in a sky
full of holes
I am like you
putting on a new white shirt
to drive away on the fine roads.

       —Linda Hogan

JB: What first influenced you to begin writing poetry, Linda?

HOGAN: I wasn't a reader. I didn't have a very good education. I was working as a teacher's aide with orthopedically handicapped students when I began to write poems on my lunch hour. In those early poems I tried to integrate my background with how I was living at the time. I was living in Washington, D.C., a sort of suburban kind of life, and I had a great deal of difficulty just trying to put the early life of moving back and forth between rural Oklahoma and working-class Denver together with that one.

At the time, I wasn't around an Indian community. I was married and was only with working-class white people and two friends from Venezuela. The poetry writing was very important to me. It was a way of trying to define who I was in an environment that felt foreign. I realize now that writing had everything to do with my life and my survival.

Before I did *Calling Myself Home*, I had one poem, a long one, with an abundance of material in it. It finally became the whole book. But I didn't know how to write. I had never read a contemporary poem. I discovered Rexroth shortly after that and I was really excited about him. It was the first contemporary poetry I read, and it was alive for me. It became a kind of model for how I wanted to write. Finally, in 1975, I went back to school and took a creative writing class.

JB: Who were your teachers?

HOGAN: My first writing teacher was Rod Jellema at the University of Maryland. He was kind enough to allow me to take a class from him even though I did not have an educational background appropriate to that level. It was an advanced creative writing class. I felt very lucky. He was a very gentle teacher. He didn't criticize me in the way other teachers sometimes do, nor did he laugh at the work as I've heard professors do.

I was working on what finally came to be in *Calling Myself Home*. As I said, it was basically a long poem. I didn't know how to separate it out or how to make connections. Later I went to school at the University of Colorado and then I quit writing on *Calling Myself Home* for a while because it was very uncomfortable writing about such subject matter in university classrooms. And people were not open to it. Because I was writing about Indians and I didn't "look" like their notion of an Indian, they reacted with hostility. I had always looked Indian to other Indians so this was confusing, but as I said, I was not intellectually prepared for a university life, nor was I as strong and resistant as I could have been. My intellect was still strong. I believed in fairness, equality, caring between fellow sharers in life—even students.

But when I began to BE a writer, was when I decided those connections did not exist in academe, which is much like big business in that way. I began to look for my own ideas, for critical work in books, and rejected what I heard in class. I found my own teachers.

Looking for my own definitions saved me. It has in all areas of my life. I am going my own way and doing it, I find miraculously, with many others. Working writers. Minority writers. People who are writing because they have to. People were, as I said, very critical at the University of Colorado until Alan Dugan came along. Alan Dugan was very good. Later Ed Dorn came and he is wonderful. I like to count him among my friends now. Alan Dugan taught me that we must write about our *real* lives.

JB: It has been said by a number of writers, including the German poet Rilke, that childhood and memory are of vital importance to a writer. Your first book, *Calling Myself Home*, has a great deal to do with memory and childhood. You first began writing those poems while in Washington, D.C. Why do you think you wrote those poems?

HOGAN: Well, I think the split between the two cultures in my life became a growing abyss and they were what I did to heal it; weave it back together. I think life would have been impossible for me psychologically had I not found some way to help myself return and see things. It's very difficult when you come from a family that has little privilege and when your people are used to horse-wagon life and have not had any luxury. Then suddenly you are a working-to-middle-class person driving around on freeways. And you are Indian and could pass for white. Go to powwows and to the opera with equal ease.

I think it is called dissonance. One life does not fit neatly into the other always. Creative work is a way to order it.

But there is a life deep inside me that always asserts itself. It is the dark and damp, the wet imagery of my beginnings. Return. A sort of deep structure to myself, the framework. It insists on being written and refuses to give me peace unless I follow its urges. Then the earth opens and a memory comes out and says Write this. Or an old person says, "Tell this: people need to know." Or the creatures of the planet emerge beautiful and breathing—and who could omit them in all their grace?

I search for the words that will speak the feelings inside my body and hope they touch those feelings in others. At the same time it is a celebration and sacred song given back to those of whom I speak, especially the animals who are made stronger by our acknowledgment of them.

JB: How did you make that leap in your life from the background of your childhood to that sudden middle-class existence?

HOGAN: There are several ways. I always wanted an "enriched" life. Not meaning money, but a life that held joys, ideas, activities that hadn't been available. I went alone to California when I was young, thinking that would open my world. It didn't. I worked two jobs, one as a nurse's aide in L.A., just to get by financially. The pay was low. But I went to adult education at night and later to Junior College. I still wasn't very realistic. So later I thought it would help when I married someone with a good education.

That is embarrassing now, but I remember when I got married, somebody said "Why don't you go to school and get a graduate degree?" I thought *I don't need to do that* because I was going to marry someone with a degree. Now, of course, I realize that was a very false way of thinking.

In those days, it seemed a way for women to bridge the gap into middle class. What I realize now is that I married someone who was also working class, and we were not ever able to make a change, either of us. Now I am more politically aware and I think of class constantly and what it means to come from privilege or not to. But I seldom think about it in terms of "making it." I see now that all people have their own routes of stagnation, and it doesn't matter if they have money or other opportunities. The U.S. is organized socially and politically and economically in ways to keep people without vibrance or energy. To keep them working hard, thinking they will "make it" if they work harder, all at the expense of their real lives.

JB: I recall a statement you made in a radio interview. You said you used to think—I'm paraphrasing—that you felt crazy because you didn't see things the way other people saw them. Then one day you suddenly realized it was just that you were Indian.

HOGAN: Yes. Actually that's a real interesting quote because it's gotten around a lot and it's different every time. I was having a conversation with a woman, Carol Hunter, and we were both in Chicago at the same time on fellowships at the Newberry Library. We were talking about our earlier experiences, and she was talking about how she had thought she was crazy and one day was visiting with her mother out in the chicken coop and suddenly realized she was very sane, except that she was an Osage Indian and would never think like the others. Paula Gunn Allen put it in an interview. It turned out a little bit different. But I liked it anyway, so I left it. This goes back to what you asked earlier about making that leap. Another thing that I think really helped me to make that leap was that I just went unconscious for a long time. I think that might look very crazy. I was an unconscious person. I did not read. I went to work and did what I was supposed to do and I didn't think about anything. I could not think. That was a survival technique, I suppose. I was a very emotional person because people seemed strange to me, as in Diane Burns's poem "Gadoshkibos"—"The whites are crazy." I had a lot of feeling but I did not have the language for putting anything into words. I could not put my feelings or emotions into any kind of words or context. I couldn't see what was happening to me or what had happened to my family culturally or politically because I did not have the language. When Carol said that I knew what

　　　　　LINDA HOGAN

she meant. My own particular circumstance guaranteed that I'd never feel normal or manage to fit into mainstream life. Until a person knows that, from the mind, they feel crazy. Now I see there's no need to fit. You know, it's not that Indians are different from the dominant culture. We are the same with the same needs and loves and heartaches. It's just that most Indians know time and space well enough from the heart to know that life is for living. Because we are short in our span here and we are not the most significant of lives on earth. We share the planet with plants and animals equal to ourselves, and we are small in the universe. So the daily strivings fall into place. I feel that poetry is a process of uncovering our real knowledge. To manipulate the language merely via the intellect takes away the strength of the poem.

JB: There are certain consistent images or points of reference for you in that first book of yours. First of all, I notice the importance of old people, especially old women. Why is this so?

HOGAN: My grandmother was a big influence in my life; my father's mother. I loved her very much and she loved me very much. I felt comfortable with her when I was a child. She never criticized. I felt very close to all the old people around there. I still do. When I go home I always look up all the oldtimers. I'm very fond of old folks, people who've lived a long time and seen a lot, who wear their lives on their faces. I believe I can learn from them.

JB: Your grandmother is the one who made that wonderful comment about the tobacco, isn't she? "Tobacco has more medicine than stones and knives/against your enemies."

HOGAN: In the poem, yes. My grandmother's name was Lucy Bradford Young Henderson. She went to the Bloomfield Chickasaw Girls' School. She was trained there to be a lady— they taught violin there. It was like a finishing school for Indian girls. They had big plans about what they were going to do with all the Indians in that part of the country and they were "civilizing" everyone. No more "Indian problem." So, she learned to play the violin and she could play classical music. She learned how to play the piano and she learned how to have good manners. Then she spent the rest of her life living in small rural places with outhouses and selling eggs in town. It was not because they didn't work hard, but because of policies that allowed for the removal of every single thing my grandparents created for themselves. It was very interesting the way that the white religious groups perceived what they were doing for the Indian people and what they actually were doing. Lucy Bradford Young Henderson. In reality they were breaking apart the culture and undermining the people's lives. It occurs to me that my grandmother and I had reverse experiences in our lives. Her father was Granville Walker Young, a métis who managed to get himself on the Chickasaw legislature. Her mother was a Chickasaw who descended from Winchester Colbert, a chief. My grandmother, a caretaker of the people, came from these people, these two worlds.

JB: How do you feel about your grandmother's life, her having gone through that experience of westernization, then to go back and live in a very unwestern way?

HOGAN: There are probably some people who would think that was a horrible life for her. But she didn't ever think that. It was very comfortable for her. My grandparents lived in a very traditional Indian lifestyle in Oklahoma. I said that once before in an interview in Ardmore and one of my cousins said, "You make it sound like they live in a tipi." Because of the stereotypes about what is traditional and so on, young people often face lives of denial. Maybe any life of resistance to mainstream culture is traditional Indian. At one point my Chickasaw grandfather, who was Charles Colbert Henderson, had homesteaded and they'd built up a large herd of cattle and horses. They were very well-to-do people then, but they lost it all and were very poor. I don't believe my grandmother ever complained when they had to move from one place to another. She had some kind of inner center that other people don't seem to have. She always knew that nothing material in the world would ever belong to her. That the government or other agencies could come in and take whatever they wanted, whenever they wanted. Our allotment land is now the Ardmore Airport. My father shows me where there was once a pond, where the blackland pasture was. It was land-swindled, I guess you'd say.

You know, you hear about white people who have their places condemned, like the families near bomb-test sites in White Sands, or about the demise of family farms. People believe they are secure and *own* their land, their houses. American history shows us that is never true. White people are shocked when their homes are taken away. It's unjust. But Indians have known that in their DNA. This government has broken over 300 treaties. Why believe them?

When I look back on it, I think my grandparents, as gentle as my grandmother was, were both very angry at the government. But they never let it out. One of the things that leads me to believe that is that on their tombstones they didn't acknowledge that they had been born in the state of Oklahoma. They were born *and died* in Indian territory. And they died in the 1960s.

JB: What did you learn in your childhood from your Chickasaw father and grandmother and grandfather?

HOGAN: I could bring out specific incidents but I think basically I've learned "qualities." Perhaps the answer to this question is "I learned everything," because I saw that there is a better and alternative way to exist in the world, better ways to love, to take care of life. I'm not saying it's been easy or good, but it hasn't been impossible either. Maybe some of the things that are not very positive in my life I've learned from them. Unlike my grandmother, I have a lot of fear. I don't assume good things will eventually happen. When I went to New York City, it surprised me how, if you have some money there, you can have anything you want. I didn't even know what I wanted. That's one thing that has affected me a great deal, that I never had many choices. I never thought about what I wanted. I haven't learned how to want something.

JB: And that may be because you've learned that you really cannot have anything material which might not be taken away from you, by government or by circumstances?

HOGAN: Or somebody else. That really is a hard question—what you learn. It is like asking what you learn from the experience of being an American Indian, which is a very big question because I don't know what I would learn if I weren't who I am.

JB: Can you think of a story out of your childhood which taught you something you feel was of use to you?

HOGAN: A lot of our stories were anti-greed stories of people who were going after something, got messed over or lost it or got ridiculed or made fun of. I never heard Coyote stories but I think you could take this as a southern Indian equivalent of Coyote. People would go out in the world to get something and do something great, and they'd be bragging around, or after someone's money. Then someone or something would sneak up on them and ambush them, and they'd fall flat. A person who is Indian and considered stupid by whites outsmarts whites, and they don't even notice because they're so quick in their lives they're already on to something else. My uncle told me one of these. He was working at a grain and feed. Out of nowhere a rich white woman arrives, and she's in a chauffeur-driven car. She wants chicken feed. He says, "I'm all out," and probably sits back chewing on a toothpick or a straw. So she wants hay. "I'm all out of hay too," he says, putting his boots up. She's getting irritated. "Why don't you just close this place up?" He pulls his hat down over his eyes. "I'm fixin' to if you'll just leave." I'm visiting and he tells the story at dinner and we all laugh because it is genuinely funny and it is a story of outsmarting the rich.

My father is a good storyteller and he will spend all of his time telling stories once he is given the opening. Any story. Army stories. Childhood ones. Historical. A lot of my poems come from family stories— "Stolen Trees," for example, from *Calling Myself Home.* My father and grandmother had talked about the black walnut trees they had that were stolen. People would come in and take the trees and use the hard wood for gunstocks. Once my family returned home to find all their trees gone, my father told me.

JB: Let me ask you about another of the themes in *Calling Myself Home.* There is a turtle which turns up a number of times. What is it about that turtle?

HOGAN: That turtle was the one I caught out in the tank close to my grandfather's house.

JB: What do you mean by "the tank"?

HOGAN: It's like a little pond. It was a giant turtle. Of course, I was not very big so it was probably not a giant, but it was bigger than my arms could reach about. I caught it on a fish line. It scared me to death. I knew this monstrous thing would eat me. I'd heard all those stories about these turtles. The mythologies of those things grow, you know, like those whip snakes that will beat on you. I'd heard how once those turtles got you they would never let go. For your entire life you'd have to carry a turtle around or lose a limb. I was terrified of this giant turtle that lived in the water. But we are turtle people. I don't know why that is, not from clan or anything I can put a finger on. It just turns out to be that way. My grandmother would have big land turtles that would come around the yard. One in particular she would talk to and, when she told it to watch out for the dogs, it would turn and come back just like it knew her language. The poems in that book were about that tank. It was a place where I spent much of my time as a child, out behind my grandmother's. It's my own center, heartbeat, a kernel of life I carry with me. There's also a well down there where I got a blue racer one time. I thought it was a giant worm because I had never seen a blue racer. I took it in. I was going to go fishing and catch the biggest fish with the blue racer. I carried this giant snake in the house and said, "Look at my worm." My mother screamed.

JB: That's a terrific story.

HOGAN: I was a very isolated person when I look back on it. Most of the things that I did as a child and even as an older growing person were outdoors and were alone. Outside was my church, my place of vision and dreaming.

JB: When you speak of being outside and being alone, the Oklahoma landscape comes to my mind.

HOGAN: It's like that here today. That kind of humidity. In Oklahoma the light makes the leaves extremely green and the soul is fire red. There is something very dense about it and at the same time very barren. It's a very old place.

JB: In one of her poems Joy Harjo says "Oklahoma will be the last song I'll ever sing." What does Oklahoma mean to you?

HOGAN: Well, it's the entire history of half of my life. It means a lot of violence, a lot of poverty, beauty, and good food—corn bread, beans. It means people who are related to me, the people I know in Oklahoma, my family and tribe. Oklahoma is a place of wet, heavy air, hawks on fenceposts, buckled linoleum, and oak and walnut forests that feel inhabited by ghosts that want to tell their history to mortals. Because I was born in Denver, when I was with my Oklahoma family that presence was obvious to me. It told me I would always be a part of the place and the people. I think my umbilical cord is buried there. Everything there, the land, is the oldest part of me and the wisest. The part that can survive. All of us Indian writers are historically a part of the whole body of our nations' histories and places, wherever we may do our writing, in New York City or at Rosebud.

JB: I have heard it said by traditionalists—if I may use that term—that we human beings have three parts. We have a physical part, a mental part, and a spiritual part and it is important to keep them in balance. I have heard them say that they feel there is great imbalance in American life. It seems always to go in one direction or the other, but never to integrate all three. Would you agree?

HOGAN: I really feel very fortunate. Fortunate that I have a place to live where I am grounded—surrounded, really—by the earth, the circle of the mountains. It's like being inside a bowl. I have children so my life doesn't get flighty. I have a whole life separate from the writing life, though they meet and join. That balance you mentioned between the spiritual and the physical and the mental—a lot of people who become interested in the spiritual tradition become very silly. They go off so far there is no balance or no footing, and our feet are very important in spiritual life touching earth. We're here on earth with our bodies. We're not meant for outer space physically or spiritually. People who go into the mental can go off too far into the mental. I don't know many people who can go off too far into the physical (I don't mean athletically or sexually, I mean awareness of body), but the physical draws down the other two, the spiritual and the mental. I suppose

LINDA HOGAN

physical labor is real good for that reason—chopping wood and doing whatever work you have to do in the world. It seems to me that is a very important aspect of tradition, to have that balance and keep and maintain it as much as you can. I think when people lose it is when they get caught up into the other things—when they lose that balance.

For me, the things that are very important, the spiritual and the political, are very united. You do not believe one way and act another. You see cruelty or injustice and you act. You do not sit and meditate and think you are making youself clean and pure by that. I know some tribal people l respect very much who do absolutely destructive things to themselves and would never consider sitting and meditating. They're too busy running around all the land speaking for tribes; yes, for the spiritual aspects of life: about federal policies or the destruction of energy development. American people need to revise their ideas about spirituality. Spirituality ends up being very much like capitalism. It ends up being a force to control other people or to make yourself look good—to give yourself a position of power and integrity.

JB: This may be a little bit to the side, but I think one thing people in majority culture sometimes find it hard to deal with in relation to spiritual things is humor. Yet humor goes with a sense of the spiritual as much as with anything else, doesn't it?

HOGAN: Sometimes lechery goes with it, too. Like I said, we have bodies, we have voices. We are here to rejoice with our full selves. We didn't come here to deprive ourselves. We aren't made for deprivation. We came here with work to do—balancing the forces—and with great capacities for love and joy to fulfill with/in our full selves.

JB: What is a traditional person?

HOGAN: It's not somebody who looks old and dresses a certain way and says certain things. I speak English. I did manage to survive a university education, I eat potato chips, and I have a T.V. I don't think that's very traditional. But what is? I guess one of the things I feel about tradition is that, in order to really understand what tradition is and to respect it and to fulfill what it means to be a traditional person, one first has to achieve a health and a kind of independence in a way that they can then return to that place within and do what needs to be done on the outside in any place and context, with any people. I don't see that happening with Indians. I see the "idea" of what's traditional, a concept only, and then people move into that idea of what's traditional without ever having a real sense of what it is. And being a traditionalist becomes like being a medicine person, like being a "priest" or the leader of people. It's simply not true. In tribal culture *every* person has their place and one who speaks more clearly with spirits than others is not a better person or is not in a higher position but simply performs one of many functions for the people. You and I have friends who do this daily and they make nothing of it. The woman who builds the fire is as important as the woman who guides the soul.

Also, we don't have to do anything special to have contact with the spirit world. It's just natural if you stop and listen. Just there, always. Like your own heartbeat. You don't have to run three miles to know it's there or use a stethoscope or get an X-ray. Really, being "traditional" means you have a great deal of responsibility. Rather than people cutting themselves off from white communities to be traditional, the more I think about it in my life the more I have thought that breaking down those barriers is much more important than building them up. Any kind of racism at this point is not good for any people. And to become anti-white is a mistake. It's self-destructive for those who do. Talk about a balance of things—talk about head and heart or head and soul—somehow I think that merging the two cultures in a really *healthy* way, not as done in the past, might be an integration in the way that we were talking about earlier. Indians have already begun that process. Years ago. Now I see white people integrating in that way. Mostly women at this point.

JB: Your second book of poetry, *Daughters, I Love You*, seems to me to be an even more spiritually oriented book than *Calling Myself Home*. It seems committed to issues which are spiritual and political at the same time. In the introduction to the book Elizabeth Jamieson says, "Women's relationships to the land itself, the struggle to preserve and nourish life in a poisoned and poisoning landscape form part of Hogan's poetic voice." The book appears to turn on that idea, preserving life. How did you happen to write this second book?

HOGAN: All of my life I really have been thinking about these issues, about any kind of destruction to the land. I have never really thought that hunting was a particularly appropriate thing because most people who hunt do not need to. It becomes a death sport, a very different thing than it once was. It's not for survival. All cruelty is needless. All fighting. Now do we need to build real estate in the Everglades or on migration lands or drill the earth? We have everything available to us for full, good lives, for peace. We must just simply step into it. Anyway, I just started thinking that being silent was in some way not being honest and that I did not want to be silent about the things that were very important and that our survival is very important. We've gone on—this progression is a very straight line progression into total destruction (Meridel LeSueur says this also), and we're just on the border now. Like the earth is square again and we stand on her edge. I guess I feel, if I'm going to be killed and if my family is going to be killed, at least I don't want to go quietly. I want to feel as if I have done something and not just passively accepted it.

The River Is the Past

An Interview with
KARONIAKTATIE

Karoniaktatie is an Akwesasne Mohawk writer and artist.
While he was still in his teens, his work began appearing in
Akwesasne Notes. At the age of 19, in 1972, he became the
poetry editor for *Akwesasne Notes*. His first book of poems,
Native Colours, was published shortly thereafter. Twelve years
passed before his second book, a chapbook entitled *Landscape*,
was published in 1984 by Blue Cloud Quarterly Press.

After years of travel, which saw him alternately attending
various colleges and following that now time-honored Mohawk
profession of working high steel, he returned to his home on
the reservation and began, once again, to work as an editor.

This interview took place at his mother's house, which
sits only a few yards back from the main road which passes

through the reservation. As we sat and talked on the front porch, the noise of passing trucks sometimes came close to drowning out our words. Corn picked from the garden was hung above us to dry and all around us on the porch were his paintings, landscapes of the river which has been so terribly polluted in recent years by the plants on both the American and Canadian sides of a border that divides the Mohawk people—a border which, if they are at all traditional or political in their beliefs, they do not recognize. His small son wandered in and out of the room as Karoniaktatie began.

Child of Mine

child of mine
has never seen   eagle

how long has it been   Akweks
since you were chased
from the Great Tree
the Standing White Pine

chased and slaughtered by
white devils in bluecoats
chased by Kanatakarias, the Town Destroyer
chased by his left hand, Sullivan
"not to merely over-run . . . but to
wipe from the face of the earth."

child of mine has not
           will not go to school
the square grey boxes & bars
           his school is the circle
           of people holding hands
           of animals of mother earth
the circle of grandmother moon
           of grandfather winds

child of mine eats corn, beans, squash
& sits in his own small garden
talking to plant people
       to bug people

child of mine talks in a beautiful language
speaks better than me   this tongue

child of mine   he is the bear
& is taught by his kinsmen
the roots & herbs & medicines

child of mine
           has never seen   eagle
but i wonder now
           does he not know the eagle
           better than i?

    —Karoniaktatie

JB: I'm struck by the way your writing reflects that combination of often-seeming opposites which seem characteristic of Mohawk life today. How do you put those things together in your poetry?

KARONIAKTATIE: Well, it's been part of Mohawk life for years—since colonization started, the last 300 years. It's just now really getting into the research in books on revolutionary and pre-revolutionary times. It's probably not that much different, what was going on 300 years ago and what's going on today. My poetry and my art are all about an individual caught in these cross-cultural goings-on. Sometimes that individual is talking from one side and trying to forget where he came from and looking ahead. Sometimes that individual is on the fence trying to look two ways at once. Sometimes that individual is on one side and wondering what he's doing there, wondering if it's the right way to go, wondering why he is alone and wondering if he can fit in with other people. Sometimes I'll go strong one way, trying to imagine myself a more traditional person, what it means to me and how I fit in. Other times I'll go on the other side. Being strong . . . it's ironic, I guess, knowing we have been colonized and raised that way, I can deal in the language of commercialism and consumers as well as anybody else. I've been educated that way. But when I speak from that way it's usually ironic. Like I was telling you, I think there's two sides to my stuff. When I was working at *Notes* I became known as serious, when I was editing poetry there, but humor, whether satire or humor, is necessary, from your own standpoint to keep from going crazy and to remind people that humor is a part of everything.

JB: Your first book, *Native Colours*, was published in 1974 by Akwesasne Notes. Where were you then as a writer and what led you to that title?

KARONIAKTATIE: I was out of high school at the time and dealing with other people who were going through the whole thing about identity crisis, Indian identity, Red Power, Black Power. It had been going on for some time, but I was new to it. I didn't like the feeling of being somebody's Indian. I ran into *Akwesasne Notes* and White Roots of Peace while I was in prep school and I was just amazed that this was coming from my home. So I decided not to go to school—which was Dartmouth, at the time—and joined up with *Notes*. When I went home I was really in a daze about what to do. You're sent away and supposed to be a bright student with As, sent away to school so you can become a lawyer or a doctor to help your people. So, naturally, I was wondering who I had let down. I was doing it on my own, but did I let my community down or what? Returning in this way? So I got my writings together and went to *Notes* and I fit right in there at the time with what needs they had, a regular poetry editor doing art work, working in the gardens, doing correspondence. *Native Colours?* Well, *Native Colours* is spelled with a "u," it's the Canadian, English type. I fool around with language a lot in the book. I couldn't explain it then, but I think now it's just that English is meant to be fooled around with. It has become my tongue—it's always been my tongue. When I was young all the Indians around could speak their native language but that didn't last long. English intruded right away, and once you get in school it's forgotten. Whether it was beaten out of you or not encouraged. I fooled around with the language because the language and the culture of English and America fooled around with me and my life. So, turn around is fair play. I just use the language, exploit the language, and turn it around on itself. *Native Colours*—I'm an artist as well as a writer. What you see and what you feel, colors are part of it. You can't explain it. Colors, everything, it's just part of the rainbow. Trying to explain relationships or anything, it's just colors, all mixed together.

JB: Is there any reason why it took you so long to publish another collection after that 1974 volume? Is it because your work went in the direction of performance or because of so many elements being involved in what you have been doing?

KARONIAKTATIE: Everywhere I go, every different situation, there are new toys, new tools, different things to exploit. I was an assistant printer at an Indian print shop in Quebec. When I got to IAIA in Santa Fe, oh that was just amazing! There were ceramics, printmaking, experimental painting, and the whole wealth of Indian art from the Southwest from all the other tribes there. Then I got into the degree thing. I was in creative writing at Santa Fe then, so I majored in sculpture and minored in creative writing. Sculpture was good because you could work any way you want, you could work in two-D with fabric or you could work three-D with metal or wood or mix it all up. I carried that through the Kansas City Arts Institute— sculpture major and creative writing minor. There I met head-on with art in America, a poetry teacher who was once a radical and seemed to be licking his wounds and showing us his favor-ite poets who were a bunch of neurotic American writers, obscure . . . and a mix of sculpture teachers including one who was very macho, a macho huge Viking from Minnesota who did huge, huge art pieces. He wasn't an apologist for the Ameri-can way, he was just gung-ho. He said there's no other place where the kilns are going all night and the gas is burning all night and the electricity is on all night, so you just go for it. He was no apologist, he just understood the way things were, but he was a teacher. He wanted you to go that way, not stay within your shell and withdraw, but use the tools available. The teacher we got along with naturally, me and my wife, he was a painter and a ceramics guy from Montana.

JB: The traditions of oratory and speaking out about events, political and human, seem to be of great importance in the heritage of most Iroquois writers. Would you agree with this and do you feel this is an element in your own work?

KARONIAKTATIE: Yes, I think oral literature is part of all folk cultures, no matter where you are at. All these things were used against us by the civilization in power at the time, yet there were documents and records kept through oral literature and through artifacts, different native and folk-recording de-vices. Just the tradition of the Great Law among the Iroquois was the message that had to be carried. It exploited a whole oral literature. The wampums with the oral literature, the message had to be continued. As it went from generation to generation, the message couldn't be forgotten and it was a forceful message and a message of brotherhood. You had to restate the message and the law for each generation, and you had to hone your skills to convince people, to convince people not to war, not to fight their brother. You had to be convinced and you had to talk. You had to talk from the ancients and you had to talk for the unborn. It just had to go that way. It was well developed among the Iroquois. Again, you get back to colonization, and what's happened to the Iroquois people for the last 300 years and the necessity was there to deal with the Dutch and the English and the French, to convince them of your authority. Your articulation was one way of convincing them. They could see the armies and the cornfields and the manner the people lived, yet you could convince them through articulation. It's still that way. If you have nothing to show and nothing to back you up, you can still use their language, you can still manipulate their ideals of articulation and education. I don't know whether that is positive or negative, but it is part of diplomacy, which is part of government, which is part of law. It's just there to be used. As time went on, dealing with the changing governments and the change from one society to another, the Dutch to the French to the English, and playing the part in the middle, trying to maintain your advantage, to maintain your people, to survive, all those skills of oratory and diplomacy were developed even further. Whether you look at it, as I am now, back through history in a revisionist way, whether some of these things were right or wrong, at the time it was the survival of the people. It's difficult looking back at it. What counted was the survival of the people. They had no way of knowing how things could have worked out, assuming the power of their nation would be unbroken and there would be a permanent place for their law and their territories. As you know, we still have our territories and our law, but it's been broken up in such a way that it's difficult to use that power. We still can convince people, but the proximity, the closeness is not there. What has broken us up is the distance between people. It is difficult to travel. We should start traveling to make over those bonds and relationships. I guess that is what art and poetry are about, long distance communication.

JB: What do you see in the river here at Akwesasne?

KARONIAKTATIE: Oh, the river is the past and it's an unchanging thing. In the present it seems unchanging, but the river is the past and it will be there in the future and that's the political end of it, what kind of life will be in the future, what kind of life will be left on the river. But the river is the past, whether the darkness of it or the light, trying to catch the light of the moment on it. The river, that's where the snapping turtle lives, those huge animals that live a long time. Some of those turtles are full of PCBs, but they are not dead. They may have cancerous growths on them, but it doesn't kill them. Those creatures are a symbol of history and ancient times. They're tough animals. The river is important to the people, to the culture here, there are changes on it. I don't do much fishing myself. There's other things I get out of the river. My wife's family, they're from the village. That's where I see it in other people, what it means to them, how it's very often a central part of their lives. And taken for granted, too. Because it is taken for granted and because pollution is not seen and not smelt most of the time, it is difficult for people to realize that their friend the river can harm them. That's very difficult to get across to people. You deal with that in your art, too.

JB: In addition to your own writing you are also an editor now.

KARONIAKTATIE: Yes, I edit for *Akwesasne Notes* now and a little bit for *Indian Time*. Then there's the literary journal *Akwekon*.

JB: Tell me a bit more about *Akwekon*.

KARONIAKTATIE: We're an independent group and we're starting with Mohawk artists and writers. *Akwekon* is largely a literary magazine, but you have to include the artists. We may call it a literary or a literary and arts magazine. It will go in circles a lot faster. It is a quarterly and will become international in a short time. We will have Indians from the south and we may have Polish writers. We will probably have African storytellers and Ainu stories and art work from folk people everywhere. Again, there will be some tough issues. Just as *Notes* has to deal with advocacy journalism and what is called "objective journalism," as our crtics would have us conform to their "objectivity" and give or abandon our advocacy. I guess you can be pro-Indian but they don't want you to be political. But we don't want to create a class of "objective" journalists and professional people whose professions are the ends to their lives, the rewards of professionalism. That's just a start. If you reach that level you can't stop, pat yourself on the back, try to gain the respect of corporate media who have no respect for anything. They can just chew you up and spit you out if they want. You're a hero one instant but you're not a hero very long. So I can't see going after that "respect" when that respect was never there. In *Akwekon* we also have to deal with the competition among Indian artists. People going for grants and the big book publishers. We have to deal with that. We have to honor those who have gone before us and not gotten recognition and we have to have the people who do sell well and are known. They have to be a part of it, but we have to recognize those who are still alive and are not well known but do need support. We're inviting all Native American writers and artists to participate in *Akwekon,* to discuss and honor people, to find out what is going on, what we're up to, how we should be going, to call together the minds and call together the people and push this forward.

Our Own Pasts

An Interview with
MAURICE KENNY

It was a cold January day when Maurice Kenny arrived on the
campus of Hamilton College to read his poetry. As we walked
across the campus we stopped to look at the cabin of the Rever-
end Samuel Kirkland, the missionary to the Oneida Indians
who influenced Indians toward the Christian way, an influence
which many Iroquois people today feel was disastrous to their
people. The land where the college stands holds a great deal of
history for Native American people. The stone marker only a
few hundred yards from the building where the class was held
was a mute testament to that history, for it marks the first of
what were to be a series of dividing lines between white and
Indian land as the treaties forced upon the Iroquois drove them
from their homes. Not many miles away were the Mohawk

River and the shrine to Father Isaac Jogues, the Jesuit missionary to the Mohawks whose controversial death and martyrdom are the subject of Kenny's epic poem *Blackrobe*.

We walked up the creaking wooden stairs of the old building and sat down in front of the class where fifteen students sat in front of us in a semicircle, and Maurice looked through his manuscripts. Maurice Kenny is not a tall man and, though his gray thinning hair held back in a ponytail is a sign of his Indian identity, it is not until he begins to speak, to "sing" his poems that one feels the powerful presence of his Iroquois consciousness and he grows in stature until he seems as tall as a pine tree.

KENNY: I was born and raised not too many miles from here. You can almost throw a stone on it. So, as I was coming up by the Greyhound bus this morning, which is my usual mode of conveyance across the country, I started almost growing hair again I was so excited to come here. It was a beautiful morning coming out of Brooklyn, where I currently live, and coming along the river was just so good. As you probably all know, I've written about this area a good deal, particularly in a new book, *Blackrobe*, so it was good seeing the river again . . . and being home.

This first poem I'm going to read I would have as a frontispiece if my autobiography is ever published.

First Rule

stones must form a circle first not a wall
open so that it may expand
to take in new grass and hills
tall pines and a river
expand as sun on weeds, an elm, robins;
the prime importance is to circle stones
where footsteps are erased by winds
assured old men and wolves sleep
where children play games
catch snow flakes if they wish
words cannot be spoken first

as summer turns spring
caterpillars into butterflies
new stones will be found for the circle;
it will ripple out a pool
grown from the touch
of a water-spider's wing;
words cannot be spoken first

that is the way to start
with stones forming a wide circle
marsh marigolds in bloom
hawks hunting mice
boys climbing hills
to sit under the sun to dream
of eagle wings and antelope;
words cannot be spoken first

—Maurice Kenny

KENNY: It was probably that poem which led me back into an oral tradition. And it was after that poem was written that I wrote most of what other people called "chants" or "incantations." I don't call them that because I decided that I didn't want to use words for the word's sake. I didn't want to build walls with these words. I wanted to use sound as much as possible, but I would have to use words rather than the sound . . . to a certain point. I wanted the sound to carry the *meaning* of the word and not the word. If we look around us today we see the misuse of words, in television ads, commercials, newspaper ads, or just in our daily conversations. We don't really know the meaning of the words we use and so we misuse them and misuse them constantly. They say it's the growing of the language. I'm not sure it's the growing of the language. I think it's the destruction of the language myself.

JB: What year was "First Rule" written, Maurice?

KENNY: Oh, let's see. It was published in '77 and I wrote that probably back in around '69 or '70. It was before I wrote "I Am The Sun."

JB: You mention home and family often in your work. What and where is home?

KENNY: Hmmm (chuckles). Every review and critic I've had asks that same question. "Where is his home? He's always talking about home, he's always talking about family. He's never locating home and he's never naming family." I do that on purpose. I want, if I use the word "home," I want everyone to identify with it, to think your home and your home and your home (looking at different people in the room). Not just *my* home. It's a way of bringing a reader into the poem. If I locate my home and you happen to be from Oakland, California, rather than, say, Clinton, New York, you're not going to see the home I'm talking about so easily if I name it because you're not going to see palm trees there if you're from Oakland. There are palm trees in Oakland. That sort of thing. So it's a way of drawing a reader's very rich imagination into my imagination. Naming the family? Well, for one, up until very recently I did not write personal poems. I saw no need to drag my mother's name through poetry, or my sister or my father or

anybody else, any member of my family. My family, my immediate family at least, they couldn't care less whether I write
poetry. They'd probably rather see me out there plowing the
backyard or something like that, planting in the garden rather
than writing poetry. So it's also kind of a way of keeping them
out of the poems. They don't want to share my work with me?
Okay, you stay out. However, recently this has changed. I have
a new book coming out in late 1983 called *The Mama Poems.*
It's a group of extremely personal poems. Most of them deal
with my mother and with my father. It's really the first time I've
gotten personal, where I've named names.

JB: When did you first have poems published?

KENNY: My first book was published when I was twenty-
eight years old. I wrote a great deal while I was in college, a
great deal. I published practically nothing. I was communicating with people such as John Crowe Ransom and William
Carlos Williams and Marianne Moore and I was studying with
Roy Mars, the Keats scholar Werner Byer, et cetera. Those were
all on the fringes if not directly in academia. Though I have
college degrees, I did not and do not come from academia. It's
not my culture. Something inside of me when I was back in
school studying was telling me not to go that way, not to get too
hung up on Richard Eberhart's poetry, on Robert Lowell's poetry. So I didn't. The one I got hung up on is Dylan Thomas.
He was perfect for me, just perfect. He was a singer, one of the
great lyrical voices of all time, not just the twentieth century.
Of all time. Then I heard some of his biography, the poverty he
knew even though he was well published and well received.
He and his family were very close to starvation. When I was in
college I was close to starvation, so I had empathy for his problems—and I couldn't handle it! He was a famous man and
almost starving to death. What was this world I was getting
myself into?

JB: What college were you attending?

KENNY: Butler University in Indiana. Then I returned
to the East and attended St. Lawrence for a year. I worked with
Douglas Angus at St. Lawrence, a novelist who said something
to me. We were doing a course on the Romantics and he asked

me to do an essay on Shelley, to write it in blank verse—which surprised me. It was pretty awful, but I did it. And he said to me, "I thought you were a poet. I knew you were hiding something. I'd like to see your poems." And I said, "I don't write poetry." He said, "Yes, you do." Well, actually I had written poetry, but I'd stopped. John Crowe Ransom had very little to offer me—though I can now sell his letters to me for a couple of hundred dollars apiece, I understand. I think I might just do that. He always made me a mechanic or something other than a writer. He always said I didn't have an ear for rhythm. I can show you the letters. Now I read him and I think *he* didn't have an ear for rhythm. Where I was going, where I wanted to go and where the poets of my generation were going was into natural speech—which John Crowe Ransom knew nothing about. We'd had enough exposure to William Carlos Williams and even Denise Levertov. She was not that much older than my generation. In age she *is* my generation, but she began writing very, very early and publishing major work in her teens. Those people were bringing in the natural speech. Then, what happens in 1957? Allen Ginsberg publishes *Howl* and the doors open for us. We can put our fingers to our noses to academia, to academic poetry. We have a vanguard, we have a platform, and we're there. Somebody asked me once why I wasn't a beat poet, because that's my generation. I said because Leroi Jones (now Amiri Baraka) wouldn't let me. And that's true, he wouldn't. He was publishing a magazine called *Yugen* and, when my first book, *Dead Letter Sent*, came out, it was published by the same press. They tried to get him to publish some of my poems in *Yugen* and he said no way, he wouldn't do it. So that saved me from being a beatnik, a beat poet.

JB: When did you make that first step in beginning to explore American Indian themes in your poetry?

KENNY: I think they're always there. Okay, there's that old bromide that if you're Indian you're going to write Indian. Not necessarily true. That's hogwash, quite frankly. The themes were there because that's what I grew up with. I didn't know there was anything different from that. It was already in my work when I was thirteen, when I was seventeen and heavily influenced by Whitman. He was one of the poets I read a great deal. It didn't come out of Whitman, but his being a singer naturally appealed to me. The poems I was writing at that time which were in natural speech, natural rhythm, reflected my Indian background.

JB: Many contemporary American Indian writers are of mixed ancestry but they've chosen—you among them—to make their central identification with the American Indian roots. Why is that so?

KENNY: Well, I'd have to be extremely personal there. My parents separated when I was nine and divorced when I was about thirteen, and I went to live in New York with my mother. When I got into this intense trouble in New York, I was very close to being sent to a reformatory. My Dad came down and saved me from that fate worse than death and brought me home. I began to identify at that point with my savior who was my father. My father is Mohawk. My mother is part Seneca, but my father is Mohawk. It was at that point that I said I must throw off what my mother has given me and take what my father has to offer. It was at that time I made the decision.

JB: What does being a Mohawk, being Iroquois, mean to you as a person and a poet?

KENNY: I'm not sure I know how to answer that. I don't think about it. I practice it. To answer that you'd have to follow me twenty-four hours a day. Then you will know.

JB: Let me make the question more specific. Do you think that your lyricism and some of the political nature of your writing—in such poems as "I Am The Sun" and "Blackrobe"—are in the tradition of Iroquois oratory? Of such orators as Red Jacket and Logan?

KENNY: I try to write in the oral tradition which is Indian, which is Iroquois. At the time I wrote "I Am The Sun," which was the time of the Wounded Knee confrontation in 1973, I personally was so angry and I physically couldn't do anything about it because I was suffering a heart attack. So I couldn't go to Wounded Knee. But there was all of this anger and frustration that many of us felt, not just Indian people, but non-Indians and Indians alike. Because of the heart attack I couldn't get out and do anything, so I had to sing it out of me. I sang it out in "I Am The Sun." I couldn't use an Iroquois traditional form because I was writing about Lakota people. So I chose a Ghost Dance song to pattern "I Am The Sun" after.

JB: You've patterned some of your other poems after Iroquois material such as the moccasin dance.

KENNY: Yes. In *Dancing Back Strong The Nation* there are several—I don't call them poems, I call them pieces—that are based on the social dances that are usually held on a Saturday night at this time of the year in the Longhouse. There's not a taboo, so I can attempt to equate the music to the poems. They're like dances at the local Y or whatever club people belong to. They're put together mainly to bring the young people, and I mean the little children, into the Longhouse so that they will hear the music, see the dances, and hear the language, to learn the language and to respect the language. In the Longhouse no foreign languages such as English, French, German, Spanish are allowed to be spoken. (laughs) Those foreign languages. There is something of a ceremony that does go on. Often an adolescent boy will sing. This boy has been practicing his song for a long time, several years perhaps, sometimes just a couple of weeks. But once he feels he has his song perfected he requests to sing and he sometimes is allowed to sing. It's a sort of puberty rite. Again, it's not a sacred ceremony so I can talk about it.

JB: What are the differences between a *piece*, a *chant*, and a *poem*?

KENNY: A *piece* is something like, in *Dancing Back Strong The Nation*, "Moccasin," and "Drums." I really don't mean them to be poems. I really don't mean for you to read them with the eye. I mean you to read them out loud, for the audience, the reader, to try to get the feel of the music of those particular pieces. They're not *chants* because there is nothing I am trying to cause to happen in any way with those. I'm not trying to turn heads. Now I avoided the word "heal." That I don't do. I'm not a shaman. I'm not a medicine person. I'm not a holy man and I'm not an elder. I am a *poet*, period. So I do not use the word "heal." But in the *chants*, I mean certain things to take place in your heads. I mean not just you students here in this room, but the general reader. I want certain things to happen there. I want changes to take place . . . the way Dylan Thomas changed my head when I heard him chant or even T. S. Eliot when I heard him read his poetry. Eliot was a magnificent reader, by the way, an elegant, elegant man. He was a *reader*. The *piece*, the *chant*, then the *poem*. The *poem* is something left over from my college days of the old form. I struggled to get the sonnet and the sestina out of my work. I don't like it. I feel encumbered by it. It does not come to me naturally. It's not of my liking, it's not of my roots, it's not of my culture. I'm not telling other people not to enjoy the sonnet and other forms, but I'm not comfortable with them. I still feel there is a—if Paula Gunn Allen will forgive me—a wildness in my spirit, my personal spirit, that is walled, zooed by those particular forms. They might work for you and I hope they do, but they don't work for me. And when I threw them out I began to write poetry that I was pleased with. Maybe, had John Crowe Ransom seen those poems he might have liked those a bit more than he did the sonnets I kept trying to write when he said I didn't have a sense of rhythm.

JB: I find a rather balanced picture of Isaac Jogues in *Blackrobe*. It's almost sympathetic to him.

KENNY: No, it's not really sympathetic at all. What I tried to do was to use some of the rules of the novelist or the playwright for the first time. *Blackrobe* is a departure. It's basically a narrative book and, as I said before, I'm not a narrative poet. It's a departure. I try to show him in the round as much as possible. So, here and there you'll see a speaker, one of the voices, talk favorably and positively about him. Then you'll hear someone talk negatively about him. It's their voices, not mine. They are all historical characters. They all knew him in one way or another, and so I'm allowing them to describe him. But what did happen with Isaac was that he had two visions when he came to this land, to this earth, to this part of the country totally believing the bilge that Indian people were just plain wild savages. Then he had his first vision in which was told, and he came to understand and accept, that the Indian people of that time were his brothers and sisters. That's very important. That's a lesson we can all still learn, not just about Indian people but about each other—particularly under the times of Ronald Reagan where now racism is rampant, it's licensed. We are licensed to hate again. And that bothers me tremendously because you here in this room may not remember it, but people died, heads were bashed in, people were mentally and physically and spiritually crippled for freedom, for civil rights in this country. And it's now being taken away from all of us. Not just blacks, not just Indians, not just Chicanos. All of us.

Anyway. Isaac Jogues came to realize through this vision that Indian people were his brothers and sisters. And his second vision told him that because he had finally accepted the people as his brothers and sisters that he must remain with them and die. Whether by natural causes or unnatural causes, he would never leave the village again. In other words he was throwing The Crown away. He would eventually, I am sure, have fought against The Crown had he lived longer. He died at 46. Had he lived another ten years it would have been a different story. But because of Isaac Jogues the state of New York, as we know it now, and the country of the United States of America is a different place. It's a different place. He was the first missionary to come to this area and survive for any length of time. Others had come in, but they didn't stay. They were killed or sent back to Montreal. So it is directly upon his head. So you see where I might favor him a little bit. What I'm trying to say is, had he lived longer, it might have been different. It might have taken a little longer then for the change to come.

JB: For some reason, whenever I think of missionaries I think of anthropologists. I've heard both good and bad things from Indian writers about ethnologists. As we both know, there are at least one or two American Indian poets who have made use of work done by various ethnologists to increase their awareness of their own people. We even know one American Indian poet who is an anthropologist herself—Wendy Rose. Yet I think there continues to be a lot of arrogance and misunderstanding on the part of some ethnologists and, I think, a related

MAURICE KENNY

trend on the part of certain non-Indian writers who treat American Indian culture (as described by ethnologists) as fair game, as material for their own poems and stories. What do you think about this rather complex issue?

KENNY: As an editor I'm confronted with this every time I go to the post office and pick up the mail. There is always something in there from someone who would like me to think they might be Indian or they might be black. They always say, "I'm very interested in Third World *culture* and here are my poems," or something like that. If the poetry looks halfway interesting, I will write back and say, "What's your background? Are you black, are you Indian, are you Asian, are you Irish, or what?" And usually that kind of note will get an answer of "No, I'm such and such and so and so, but I'm very interested. My great-grandfather lived next to a reservation." Or something like that. If they are not really using their own roots, I discourage them. Sometimes I've gotten letters back in four-letter words and sometimes I've gotten letters back saying, "Hey, thanks for helping me discover myself." That's what it's all about—discovering yourself, what's inside you. I'm interested in what's inside of you, but I don't want to write about what's inside of you. You should want to write about what's inside of you. And I don't want you to write about what's inside of me. We write out of our own experience, our own pasts.

Passing It On

An Interview with
HAROLD LITTLEBIRD

Of Laguna and Santo Domingo Pueblo ancestry, Harold Littlebird has done much to bring the unique vision of the Pueblo people into contemporary art, expressing very ancient traditions in new ways. In addition to being a poet, he enjoys an international reputation as an innovative potter, using Mimbres figures found on pots thousands of years old on his own pieces, sometimes also adding lines of poetry to go with the traditional designs.

Though frequently published and well known as a performer of his own work, it was not until 1982 that Harold Littlebird's first book of poetry *On Mountains' Breath*, was published by a New Mexico press called Tooth of Time.

The interview with Harold Littlebird took place in Taos, New Mexico, in a house he built with timbers cut in the nearby mountains. The house sits in a wide field of sagebrush, and Taos Mountain dominates the view from his front porch. I had driven up to Taos with Bo Scholer, a Danish scholar who is writing about contemporary Pueblo writers, and Bo sat in the workroom with us as we did the interview. Harold's wife and daughter were in the adjoining room and several times came in to bring us something to drink, to ask a question. The mood was very relaxed and Harold continued working on his pottery in his workroom as we spoke, his hands moving with delicate precision as he inscribed the designs into the clay.

Moon Light, Moon Bright

Way-ana, ay-ana, way-ana, ay-ana, way-ana, aya oh-hey na
Way-ana, ay-ana, way-ana, ay-ana, way-ana, aya oh hey hey hey ya
Way-ana, ay-ana, way-ana, ay-ana, way-ana, aya oh hey hey hey ya
                               oh hey hey hey
                                  hey hey hey ya

Moonlight, Moon bright
Glow upon the world tonight
Shine down for all to see
Spread your peace and harmony
Moonlight, Moon bright

Way-ana, ay-ana, way-ana, ay-ana, way-ana, aya oh hey hey hey ya
                               oh hey hey hey
                               hey hey hey ya. . .

—Harold Littlebird

JB: What relationship do you see between your poems and song?

LITTLEBIRD: It's very difficult for me to separate song and legend and myth. History, Pueblo history, has been passed on orally, and when you think of things, then you think of ceremonies and different rituals that go with things. . . and a lot of them have to do with song, chant, and *sound*. The way you express different cloud formations, for example; when you listen to that word being said, it has its own sort of song with it, just by the way you would say it and by the way you pronounce it . . . or the way something is stated in a person's voice. I think that has a lot to do with the way the person is himself. So many things that have to do with song come from those traditions. . . like different plant forms, animal forms, the sound of a name. Even your own personal name that someone gives to you, your Indian name, it has a certain sound. It sounds like a song. So it's hard to separate song and myth and language and all that.

"Moonlight, Moon Bright" was my contribution to a film that my brother and a bunch of filmmakers and I were working on out on Laguna. The song came to me after hearing my cousin Pete, who is now passed away, talk about how the Moon relates to everything around us and how we ask for strength from the Moon, not just from the Sun but also the Moon, because it's like the other side of the sun. I was also thinking about Paguate, where my mother is from. That's a location where one of the largest open-pit uranium mines used to be in operation. It's no longer in operation, but it was. And I was thinking about trying to talk to the people out there about what that uranium is about. A lot of them don't really understand, but they hold on. They hold on through the language. They hold on through the songs. And so this was my own sort of song of hope for the people. It has a traditional sound. The sound is very much like an Indian sound or a Pueblo sound, but then I try to incorporate the English language with it to help other people who are non-Indian to be more aware of Indian music.

Whenever I do readings and things like that, I always incorporate song, my own songs and some traditional things.

Even in pieces of poetry that I've written I've just found that all of a sudden there'll be a song that can go with the piece. Like "Coming Home in March." I never knew I would incorporate a song into that piece of poetry. It's about when I was in Pennsylvania and thinking about coming back and thinking about what I was missing here during the wintertime. Our side in the Pueblo was taking part and heading some of the ceremonies and things. I knew I was missing all that, and I'd call back here and my Mom would say, "Oh, they're having a dance over here and they're going to be doing this. . ." and, of God, so I was lonesome, really lonesome being that far away. But even though I was lonesome, I was having a good time with people that I met. And then they threw this big party for me before I was ready to leave, they had this big party. And I was thinking about that particular piece of poetry and I incorporated a song that I remembered from then. It sort of gives that feeling of how a person on the road away from home is thinking about home and feeling very lonesome and I've had that kind of lonely type feeling, too.

JB: This happened when I was interviewing Luci Tapahonso. I find that everything you're saying leads into every question I was going to ask you—such as this one. It's a very common experience for Anglo poets in the United States to feel isolated. Does that feeling of isolation, that feeling of a lack of community, seem to be true of American Indian writers?

LITTLEBIRD: No, I don't think it does. There's an incredible piece of poetry that Simon Ortiz wrote. I think it's something like "You meet Indians everywhere."

JB: That's from his poem, "I told You I Like Indians."

LITTLEBIRD: Yes, "You meet Indians everywhere. . ." It's really true. You're never alone because those Indian people seem to have that kind of reverence for one another that way. They know you by your location. They know you by your certain ceremonies. They know you by the kind of things you believe in. They don't know you by your names, they just know you by what your people are like. There was so much trading going on in these areas that people came in contact with one another all the time. They could tell by just the way you appeared to them where you were from. But *now* everybody asks you. And that's the first question they ask whenever you run into Indian people: where are you from? "Hey, where are you from?" You know? I mean, it's real good. It just seems like it always feels good when you see another person because that's what you want—to come up to them and ask them, too, "Hey, where are you from?" (laughter) It's really simple.

JB: Your book strikes me as being very carefully put together. The sections, the artwork, the little head notes, all have a relationship. Could you talk a little bit about *how* you put together *On Mountains' Breath* and what you see happening from section to section?

LITTLEBIRD: Well, just the title—*On Mountains' Breath*. The whole book itself is more like a written prayer. The whole thing. That's a part of being out here in this place, giving thanks for everything that's around you and what helps you and what strengthens you. And for me, coming up here to this area, Taos, you're surrounded. You just feel this enormous presence around you of mountains, especially when you look to the east—there's Taos Mountain. It's a very powerful place and a very magical place. I guess the first couple of weeks I was here that's all I'd watch—that mountain and the way clouds formed around there, early morning clouds, late evening clouds, and it was like. . . it's *like* breath. It's like that movement, when you watch the clouds come in and you feel that presence and that mystery that's there. It builds up there.

Then the drawings themselves. Being a potter and drawing on my pottery, it seemed very natural to illustrate my own book. Most of the things here are things that were not copied from something but things that I've experienced my own self. My daughter's poem in there and the drawing of the family entertaining this little baby. The *hunting* sequences. There's a deer there and the first thing I thought to use was a piece of poetry that I wrote for my brother when I was up in the state of Washington. How I felt about it when I got that deer up there. And, like I was telling you before, about the sequence of the Moon. The Moon plays a very important part in the cycle of hunting. People know different kinds of Moons are Hunter's

Moons and so forth. I tried to incorporate that into the book by using phases of the Moon for the hunting sequences. And the last one, the last drawing in there of the women with the burden baskets moving through the night, it's all reflected in that song, too. You know, "Moonlight, Moon bright, guide us safely through the night. . ." But also it is supposed to signify traveling, which is a very important part of any people. Wherever you move to, who you meet, what you do there, the kind of things that you see there, and the special way that you remember them.

So, as I said, it's all a real prayer. And it's all for anybody. It's not just Pueblo people that are involved in this book. It's for everybody. That's the way I feel about things. When people take part in certain things, especially ceremonies, when they're praying at the end, whoever has to pray, whoever has to say the last things to thank the dancers for coming, to thank the what-it-is you're giving praise to, at that time they say a number of things. But in all the things that I remember, I hear it said all the time that it's for *all* people. They say that all the time: All People. The way you would say it in Laguna, "Opa," that's what it means, *"All People."* It's not just here in North America that you're praying for, but it's all people. You don't make any distinctions of color, of race, of anything. We're all here doing the same thing, praising this Creation, this wonderful place that we are. So that's what the book is about.

JB: Um humh, um humh. It makes me think of the title of one of Simon Ortiz's books, *A Good Journey.* It contains that same theme of moving through the cycles of life, moving into different places, seeing different people, and always seeing a relationship between them.

LITTLEBIRD: Yes. . . I guess what I try to do is bring about a feeling of remembrance in everything. That's the incredible thing about being here on this earth—all the things that help you remember where you come from, what it is you are, *why* you're here. There are so many ways you can get caught up in all the political situations and things. I'm not a very political person myself. I'm not really outright politically active. My politics are just remembering, and they have a lot to do with repeating things but in different ways. That's why I try to incorporate songs. I think music-and-song is a very universal kind of thing that people can relate to very easily . . . with instruments and without instruments. That's the first time I've sung that song in a long time just without my drum. (laughter)

JB: But the sound carried it and the song had its own drum?

LITTLEBIRD: Yes. And everytime I sing it, I remember those things that were told me when I was thinking about writing that song—by my cousin Pete, by my brother Larry. You know, by other people, my uncles and even my aunts. When they were taking part in things, they were talking. They would say, "Thank you for bringing this dance to us and for bringing these things back to us to help us remember where we come from, who we are." It's repeated all the time. Repetition is a very important part of Pueblo history.

JB: Your poem, "After the Pow-wow," is a good example to me of a poem that in the hands of another writer might just be overtly "political." You start talking about the uranium mine and the pollution, about the people having birth defects and internal disorders in the elderly . . . yet in the end of the poem you turn it around. You are talking to this executive who works for one of those big companies related to the whole process of uranium mining and you say, "It's not his fault I know, so I sip my coke and/change the subject/ and we continue to talk about traveling/ but I will remember to sing for him also." Now that idea of singing. . .

LITTLEBIRD: For all people. I think if you were able to understand all the languages in the world, it would come around to that also. They're not just praying for themselves when they're taking part in certain things. All over the world people are doing the same thing, praising the Creation and the really powerful qualities of this Creation.

When I first started writing I never thought of myself as a poet, anything like that. I was just another person expressing myself in many, many different ways because I make pottery, I sing, I write poetry. But I do a lot of other things, you know. I chop wood—that's a part of it, too. I am beginning to be—work on my house—a builder, you know, and that's all part of whatever you're thankful for having. I don't consider myself a poet. I can't put myself into just one little bracket and say that's all I do or that. . . when I say "poet," this is what I mean by it. Because it's much more than that.

JB: We were talking earlier about hunting. Hunting is celebrated more lyrically in this than in almost any other book I've seen but it isn't hunting in the way of the white "sport" hunter, something violent, something which is against nature.

LITTLEBIRD: Well, I think the reason it became a very critical point in my life was because one of the first times I was introduced to Pueblo beliefs was in hunting. And my brother. . . I have that memory in the book, "For Larry." That really triggered the whole idea of being thankful for everything and not going out in a manner where you're just *saying* you're going to kill something. It's more like a "prayer of asking." And then when things happen, you really respect what happened and take care of it and wish it well and do all the proper things. That's the way it is in Pueblo life. You always hold those things real strongly in your own life, in your own personal life. You remember them daily and hopefully pass them on.

To me it just seems a very basic thing whenever you go anywhere. It's like respect and then remembering why you're being respectful. If you're not going to take something in a very reverent way, then it seems like a real waste. No, not a waste, but a real. . . *shame* that you're not being respectful to whatever it is you're going for. And it doesn't make any difference whether it's a rabbit or a deer or any kind of game. And even if you don't get something, you're thankful that you're out there. That's another important thing about Pueblo belief. It doesn't make any difference if you get anything or not. If you're with a party and they happen to get something, you're thankful that it's coming. It doesn't necessarily have to be a personal thing to you, but you're thankful that it's coming to the people and you know that the people will treat it right and you just add your thanksgiving to it.

JB: There's a kind of movement in your poetry which I call the movement of storytelling. You mention names and places in a very relaxed way, sort of like when you're sitting around a fire and telling stories. Is this storytelling structure something you try to create in your work or is it something that's come to you in a natural fashion?

LITTLEBIRD: I think it's just come to me in a natural fashion, but it does come from those basic roots of a narrative style of storytelling. You know, just listening and observing the way people speak to you when they talk to you, or when you're taking part in things—when people ask you to listen and you're there and are listening and you hear the sound, you hear the voice. I guess that's what I'm trying to convey when I read my poetry, when I perform. . . to make it like a story so that people will take time to listen. It does seem to be just a natural thing. I don't know how it comes. When I work with students or work with other people in different programs about poetry, I always talk about remembering because it seems to me that's what poetry is about—or for me it is to remember those things. Like you said, in dreams, in songs, in stories that are told to you . . . or just the way someone speaks to you, or just a memory. You know you have these memories in you and all of a sudden someone helps you remember it. I think that's the important thing about being able to share things with people. When you share an experience with them, you help them trigger something in their own memory and that's why it affects them that way. A lot of people come up to me and they'll say, "I really enjoyed that piece of poetry because I had a similar experience." Wonderful! I think that's all we can hope for when we try to perform or read—to help people remember things, in their own way.

JB: There have been problems, haven't there, for people who've written things about the particular Pueblo that they came from? How do you work with this?

LITTLEBIRD: All I can really do is express myself in any way I can. Writing happens to be the way I can do it sometimes. I know I have to be very careful, and I don't try to exploit anything when I'm writing. There's a lot of times when I figure I can say something, but then I go, "That's too touchy, you can't do that." Because you don't want to have to explain yourself to anybody or have to defend yourself to anybody. These are very personal kinds of things that are happening for you and for some reason they *are* happening for you. No one told you that they were going to happen—they just happen and in some way they affect your life. And it's all these changes that you go through throughout your lifetime that maybe one day will click for you and then maybe you will be able to understand, really, why you're here, what is the meaning of your life, what value was it to *anybody* and that's what I mean by communication. I don't speak my languages. That's another reason why I've chosen to write, because I *hear* it and I understand certain things when I'm spoken to at certain times. But if I were to go out and try to talk to anybody, I couldn't do it in either of my languages, either Santo Domingo or Laguna. But I listen. I listen for the sound of the way people talk to one another when they *want* you to hear. It's not like, "Sit down, I'm going to tell you something!" You know, it's more like "Just listen to me," it's like that. It's quiet in that sound, so that's what I try to do with my voice when I'm reading is to create that same kind of feeling for the sound, for the language as you would hear it. Of course it's all in English so maybe a broader audience can appreciate it. But I've read my stuff to Indian people and I think they understand what I'm trying to do, too, just because they've heard that song all their lives, except they've heard it in their own language.

JB: I was talking with Barney Bush about being an Indian poet. Barney said that when you're writing, what you write is like the shadow of the event. You don't write about those things which you're not supposed to talk about, but you do write things which people will understand if they're within that community.

LITTLEBIRD: Right.

JB: They'll know more, perhaps, than someone who doesn't live within that community. In one of your poems, "A Circle Begins," you make a reference to the sweat lodge. Yet the way you've written it you never said, "This is a sweat lodge.

This is the ceremony you go through in there." But when I read "A Circle Begins," I feel as if I'm back in the sweat lodge again.

LITTLEBIRD: I think that piece of poetry, in particular, was a very spontaneous piece of writing—which is the way I write anyway. But I mean *spontaneous*, I mean that it was just like it happened, just like that. We actually helped build a sweat lodge up in Utah. It was part of my brother's plan for his project while he was working at the Sun Dance Institute, and he used that sweat lodge as a place to help whoever was going to work with him center themselves so that the work would go well and also would be more of an asking kind of thing rather than something without any relationship to whatever was going on at the time in your own self. There were outside people who were helping us build that sweat lodge, and they wanted to participate in something ceremonial. They felt that you had to do something real far out and super to participate in something ceremonial. That's what I was trying to show them—that that *was* the whole thing. It didn't have to be something where someone said, "Look, look, they're doing a ceremony!" It was more like they participated in it. I wrote that poem for them, but other people could understand. I mainly wrote it for those people, though, so they could understand what we did while we were in that place, that ceremonial place.

JB: I've noticed what I call a "lack of anger" in your poems and the poems of quite a few other American Indian writers unlike, let's say, the black American writers whose experience has also been painful in dealing with majority society and who often responded in an "angry" fashion. Do you notice that "lack of anger" and, if you see it, why do you think it's so?

LITTLEBIRD: I've noticed it with a lot of the Pueblo writers, mainly, but also with Indian people. I know there are exceptions, but for the most part. . . I don't know. I really couldn't say why that is. I have ideas. My idea is that when you write something down it's a very physical thing. To write it down, to put it down on paper, it becomes a very physical thing. And what you achieve—or what I hope to achieve—is a very spiritual thing so that it transcends that paper and goes

into a person's heart. And for me to be very bitter about some-
thing would be to keep it on paper and make it very physical.
It's much more than that, but simply put I think that's about all
I could say about it.

JB: Do you read much work by other Native Americans?

LITTLEBIRD: Not that much. I used to. When I was in
school I used to read a lot of people's work. I don't even remember the names. And then I began to read people I know,
people I know personally. It seems to me that what I usually end
up reading is people's work I know personally because it's just
like following them. You see what they've written and what
they're doing at the time. But I don't like to pick up something
and read it just because an American Indian wrote it.

JB: Who are these people whose work you follow, whom
you feel close to?

LITTLEBIRD: Simon, Simon Ortiz. Leslie, Leslie being
from Laguna and I know her personally. I know Simon and her.
Luci Tapahonso. There's this Barney Mitchell. I used to read a
lot of his work. I really liked his work while I was in school. I
haven't read anything by him lately, I don't know what he's
publishing. There's a Navajo woman in Arizona. Her name is
Nia Francisco. Her stuff, when she *reads*—that's what I mean
by when you hear the sound, it's different. I've heard her read
different times and in different situations where I could tell she
was uptight, when she didn't want to be there, and then other
times when she was just in her prime and just going, going, and
just the incredible feeling you get from her work when you
hear it. I like a lot of Joseph's stuff, Joseph Concha. And there's
another guy, a fellow I just became acquainted with about three
or four years ago. He's from Iowa.

JB: Ray Young Bear?

LITTLEBIRD: Yeah, Ray. I met him. I think by being
involved with someone personally, just casually in a very social
kind of occasion. . . We were both invited to do readings at this
university up in Washington. I got to know him. We were sort
of across the hall from one another so we spent a lot of time
with one another. Then hearing him read. . . and he gave me
his book and I started to read a lot of his work. I think that, for

me, is a very important thing—to know the person personally before I really start reading their work. I like a lot of Scott Momaday's things, a lot of his things. There's probably people I'm forgetting.

JB: But again, it's the idea of a sense of community, isn't it?

LITTLEBIRD: Um-humm.

JB: Breath and life and the wind and prayer are all associated, aren't they?

LITTLEBIRD: Yes. Yes, they really are and not just . . . I mean it's a visual thing that you actually see happen, especially down here. But in many different ways it's a visual thing. You see it when someone offers a ceremonial pipe to you. Your breath adds to that breath, that life-giving breath. You always give back that breath and that's what it's like when you take part in certain things. Even when you're dancing—that breath, that breath that comes quicker from the exertion there, it's giving back, it's just revitalizing everything that you believe in and so you say your prayers. You can say them quietly or you can say them out loud, but your breath is always giving that back. That's another thing about *On Mountains' Breath*, that's what the mountain does. It gives that feeling that yes, you *can* continue, you *can* endure, you *can* be thankful that you are here because these things that are happening for you right now in your lifetime will be memories for you. And you hope you'll be able to pass those things that affected you on to your own children and keep it going, make it continue. Pass it on. Even if you don't know the language.

It was my Mom who told me that when I first started going hunting. She said, "You're getting ready to go out now, huh?" And I said, "Yeah." And she said, "Well, remember to stop and just say something." And I said, "Yeah, I'll remember." It was one of the first things that really made me think about prayer. When I started going, I used to ask her, "Well, how do I pray?" And she said, "You just say whatever you have to say and don't worry that you can't say it in Laguna. Just say it with an open heart. Something will hear you. Something is going to help you." It's true. I tell that to all people now. It doesn't make any difference if I can't speak the language. If what I say comes from where I hope it comes from, then it's helping. And I think that's all you can ask from anybody—that they help it, continue it through their words, through their voices, through their sound.

JB: That idea of seeing the breath and understanding what you see is very important. Again it's a contrast to what I call the "Anglo point of view," where people so often don't see and hear things that are so obvious and so simple.

LITTLEBIRD: Yes. It comes from just being observant, really *paying attention* to where you are and what it is you are doing. Whatever it is.

JB: So, whoever you are, if you're a human being you have that duty and that opportunity?

LITTLEBIRD: Yes, yes.

JB: You have done a videotape called *Songs From My Hunter's Heart?*

LITTLEBIRD: Yes. That was from the University of Arizona in Tucson. Larry Evers is the one who contacted me for that and they came out to Laguna to shoot it. It was really nice, I enjoyed it. I had a really nice time.

I think one of the neat things about that tape—I don't know if it comes across—was this one sequence they left in which I thought was really nice. I was talking with one of my cousins who is a younger boy. He, too, does not speak. I guess his father spoke to him but he just never picked it up and that's the same thing with me. My Mom and Dad spoke to me, but I just never picked it up. You have to be around it all the time to hear it and understand it and use it all the time. Consequently, he didn't pick up the Laguna language. I don't know if he feels the same way I do, he's really young. He's older now, but when this was shot he was still at that point where he was just a little boy changing into a young man. The sequence that I enjoyed doing with him was when we were just about finished with the tape. We got up and started walking and I said to him, "Hey, did you ever throw sticks in the water and have races with them?" And he said, "Oh *Yeah*, yeah, I did." He just opened up and this whole world opened up and he started telling me about it. So I said, "Well, let's do that." So we got our little sticks and said, "Ready, set, go!" and threw them into the water and just watched them go. The camera man panned on this whole thing with our voices and just watching the sticks going down through the water and disappearing. I thought that was important. For me it was like seeing—well, I just got through reading this piece of poetry for Larry—it was like seeing that happen again. This young boy goes along with an older person and has an experience to remember. It wasn't a hunting experience, but it was just a real simple thing of racing sticks in the water like you do when you're a kid. It really made me feel good to see that happen. . .

The Magic of Words

An Interview with
N. SCOTT MOMADAY

This interview with N. Scott Momaday, the first Native American writer ever to win a national literary prize—a 1969 Pulitzer for his novel, *House Made of Dawn*—took place on December 7, 1982. The setting was his office at the University of Arizona in Tucson where he is a professor in the English Department. After many years of self-imposed "exile" in California, Momaday has returned to the Southwest which is the backdrop for so much of his important writing. Few people have described that landscape and its people with such love and precision.

With Momaday's deep awareness of details in mind, I made a conscious effort to observe the particulars of this place he had chosen for our meeting. It was not that easy to do, for N. Scott Momaday is an imposing man of dominating, though agreeable, presence. More than six feet tall and large of body in the way a buffalo or some other great animal is large, he seemed to fill the room. The voice with which he greeted me was warm and deep, the words spoken in a way which gave weight to each syllable. It was the voice one might expect from a man who wrote and continues to write of the magical nature and power of language, whose essay "The Man Made of Words" is one of the most important contemporary statements about the American Indian writer. Clean-shaven (unlike the photographs on the backs of his books in which he wears a full beard and looks vaguely Japanese), his hair cut short, and his clothing of the sort one might describe as "informal academic," there was little to distinguish his appearance from that of a thousand other men sitting at ease in their college offices and awaiting the arrival, perhaps, of a student for a conference about a term paper. Yet there *was* something different, beyond his seeming self-assurance and the Kiowa cast of his features, something reflected most clearly, perhaps, in his beautiful voice. Perhaps it was only my own flawed perception, but it seemed to me that I was in the presence of one who was aware of and most careful with *strength*.

He carefully lettered a sign: DO NOT DISTURB, TAPING SESSION. As he taped it to the outside of his door I thought how much the contents of the room mirrored its principal occupant. A large desk was placed to face the door. A few papers were arranged on it neatly, but it was the two carvings placed there which drew my attention. One was a large, roughly shaped wooden bear. The other was a Plains Indian on horseback. Between the two of them was a big magnifying glass. There were only a few books in the case to the right of the desk, but there were two paintings on the wall, both signed by Momaday. One was a figure resembling a harlequin, the colors bright, the lines bold, almost idiosyncratic. The other was a man in late middle age with a dark face standing in the midst of a wide bare landscape which made one think of the plains of southwestern Oklahoma.

When Momaday was ready, the tape levels set, my questions in front of me, I asked him if he would begin by reading a poem. He reached out a hand to touch the carving of the bear and I thought I detected a faint smile.

The Bear

What ruse of vision,
escarping the wall of leaves,
    rending incision
into countless surfaces.

    would cull and color
his somnolence, whose old age
    has outworn valor,
all but the fact of courage?

    Seen, he does not come,
move, but seems forever there,
    dimensionless; dumb,
in the windless noon's hot glare.

More scarred than others
these years since the trap maimed him,
    pain slants his withers,
drawing up the crooked limb.

    Then he is gone, whole,
without urgency, from sight,
    as buzzards control,
imperceptibly, their flight.

—N. Scott Momaday

N. SCOTT MOMADAY

JB: In a recent book entitled *Four American Indian Literary Masters*, Alan R. Velie links your poetry strongly with those whom he calls "the post-symbolists" and your former teacher, Yvor Winters. Do you think that really was correct?

MOMADAY: Well, to an extent, yes. I don't remember what Velie had to say, exactly. "Post-symbolist," by the way is Yvor Winters's term, not Velie's. It is an important concept in Winters's critical canon, and I would not presume to say what it is or what it has to do with my work. Anyone interested in it ought to go directly to Winters's last work, *Forms of Discovery*. I didn't know much about the traditional aspects of poetry until I went to Stanford and studied under Winters. Winters was a very fine teacher, and no doubt he had a significant influence upon a good many of his students over the years. In 1959, when I went to Stanford, I was just ready to be educated in terms of prosody, and I owe a good deal of what I know about poetry to Yvor Winters. I think that my early poems, especially those that are structured according to traditional English forms, are in some respects the immediate result of his encouragement and of his teaching.

JB: Poems such as "Angle of Geese" or "The Bear" . . .

MOMADAY: "Angle of Geese" and "The Bear" are written in syllabics; that is, the number of syllables in each line is predetermined and invariable; it is therefore the number of syllables to the line, rather than the number of "feet," which constitutes the measure. I was just playing around a lot with syllabics at Stanford—I wasn't even aware of the term "syllabics" until I went to Winters's class in the writing of poetry. So, yes, those would be two examples. But I got tired of the traditional forms. When I left Stanford I had worked myself into such a confinement of form that I started writing fiction and didn't get back to poetry until much later—three years, perhaps—and when I did, I started writing a very different kind of poetry.

JB: I notice, before we talk about that different kind of poetry, that you chose the poem, "The Bear." What is it that made you choose that poem to read? What is important to you about that particular poem?

MOMADAY: It was pretty much a random choice, but I like the poem because it is early and it is one of my first really successful poems, as I think of it. It deals with nature, as much of my work does, and it is rhymed in syllabics, and so there are good, solid, controlling devices at work in the poem, and that, that aspect of control, is important to me. I wanted to see how closely I could control the statement, and it seems to me that I controlled it about as well as I could. "The Bear" won some sort of prize at Stanford—a prize awarded by the Academy of American Poets, I think. I was ecstatic.

JB: What forms do you think you're working in now in your poetry? I've heard them described as prose poems by Velie and other people. In some cases, I know some aren't.

MOMADAY: No. I continue working in syllabics. I have written what is called "free verse," though to my mind that is a contradiction in terms. I'm greatly interested in the so-called "prose poem," another contradiction in terms, but what I mean is, I like writing what is essentially a lyrical prose in which I'm not concerned with meter, but with rhythms and fluencies of sound, primarily. I wrote a piece, which no doubt you've seen in *The Gourd Dancer*, called "The Colors of Night," which is really a collection of quintessential novels, I suppose—very short, lyrical stories. I would like to continue working in that free form.

JB: As a matter of fact that particular poem is one of my favorites in *The Gourd Dancer.* I thought it interesting that in that book you combine both the earlier poems and the later poems, and they didn't seem to be combined in a chronological order but rather in terms of subject matter. When you put the book together, what was your structuring theory or device?

MOMADAY: I wanted, as you say, to group the several poems in certain ways. There is a chronological progression to it. The early poems, recognizably traditional forms, I think, are contained in the first section, then the second section is of a very different character, informed by a native voice, and the third section is, or was then, quite recent work. Much of it was written in the Soviet Union.

N. SCOTT MOMADAY

JB: Did it affect your writing when you worked in another country?

MOMADAY: I think it did. I'm not sure that I can say how, exactly. There was a great compulsion there to write, and that surprised me; I could not have anticipated that. But when I got there and had been there a while and had begun to understand a little bit about my isolation and my distance from my native land, this somehow became a creative impulse for me, and so I wrote much more than I thought I would. And I wrote about things I saw and felt in the Soviet Union. "Krasnopresnenskaya Station" is an example. The little poem called "Anywhere is a Street into the Night" is a comment upon my understanding of that distance that I mentioned a moment ago. But I also found myself writing about my homeland, the Southwest—perhaps as a kind of therapy. I wrote the poem that I dedicated to Georgia O'Keeffe ("Forms of the Earth at Abiquiu") there, for example, and it is very much an evocation of the Southwest, isn't it?

JB: This southwestern landscape which turns up in your poems throughout your writing . . . how do you define that landscape? What are the important qualities of it for you? The qualities of life in the Southwest which are important . . .

MOMADAY: Well, I think it's a much more spiritual landscape than any other that I know personally. And it is beautiful, simply in physical terms. The colors in that landscape are very vivid, as you know, and I've always been greatly moved by the quality of light upon the colored landscape of New Mexico and Arizona.

JB: Yes, that's evident in your work.

MOMADAY: And I think of it as being inhabited by a people who are truly involved in it. The Indians of the Southwest, and the Pueblo people, for example, and the Navajos with whom I grew up, they don't live on the land; they live *in* it, in a real sense. And that is very important to me, and I like to evoke as best I can that sense of belonging to the earth.

JB: I think that idea of belonging is also of central importance. In *The Names* or even in some of your poems, you present us with situations where there is a possibility for distance, or a possibility for alienation. But I don't see that alienation coming about. I see, rather, a motion in a different direction—toward a kind of resolution. Am I correct in seeing this?

MOMADAY: I think that's a fair statement.

JB: Why is that so? Why are you not an existentialist, for example, a "modern" man looking at the world as separate from the person?

MOMADAY: Well, I'm a product of my experience, surely, of what I have seen and known of the world. I've had, by the way, what I think of as a very fortunate growing up. On the basis of my experience, trusting my own perceptions, I don't see any validity in the separation of man and the landscape. Oh, I know that the notion of alienation is very widespread, in a sense very popular. But I think it's an unfortunate point of view and a false one, where the relationship between man and the earth is concerned. Certainly it is one of the great afflictions of our time, this conviction of alienation, separation, isolation. And it is certainly an affliction in the Indian world. But there it has the least chance of taking hold, I believe, for there it is opposed by very strong forces. The whole worldview of the Indian is predicated upon the principle of harmony in the universe. You can't tinker much with that; it has the look of an absolute.

JB: Do you differentiate between prose and poetry in a strict sense?

MOMADAY: When I talk about definitions, yes. Prose and poetry are opposed in a certain way. It's hard to define poetry. Poetry is a statement concerning the human condition, composed in verse. I did not invent this definition, skeletal as it is. I think I may be repeating something I heard in class years ago. In that refinement, in that reservation, "composed in verse," is really, finally, the matter that establishes the idea of poetry and sets it apart.

JB: I wonder, because I see in the work of a number of American Indian writers, for example, Leslie Silko, places where prose suddenly breaks into what appears to be verse in parts of *Ceremony*. There the stories that are told are in a form I would describe as verse. I see, also, in a number of other writers who are American Indians, if not a blurring of that distinction, a passing back and forth, rather freely, between verse and prose. I see it, also, in your work . . . your prose in such books as *House Made of Dawn*, and especially *The Way to Rainy Mountain*. There are sections which one could read as poems. Is this observation a good one? Why do you think it's like this, with yourself and other American Indian prose writers?

MOMADAY: That's a large question, and I've thought about it before. The prose pieces in *The Way to Rainy Mountain* are illustrations of the very thing that I was talking about before, the lyrical prose, the thing that is called the prose poem. The oral tradition of the American Indian is intrinsically poetic in certain, obvious ways. I believe that a good many Indian writers rely upon a kind of poetic expression out of necessity, a necessary homage to the native tradition, and they have every right and reason to do so. It is much harder, I suspect, for an Indian to write a novel than to write a poem. The novel, as a form, is more unfamiliar to him in his native context. That he does it at all is a kind of tour de force. I am thinking of Jim Welch's *Winter in the Blood*, for example, a fine novel, to my mind. Again, I have to quibble with the word "verse." Verse, after all, strictly speaking, is a very precise meter of measure. My "Plainview: 1," for example, is composed in verse. If you look at it closely you see that it is a sonnet, composed in heroic couplets, rhymed iambic pentameter. "The Colors of Night," on the other hand, is not verse. Meter, as such, is simply not a consideration in that piece. You can make the same distinction between, say, "Abstract: Old Woman in a Room" and "Forms of the Earth at Abiquiu." I will indeed quibble over terms here, for they are important. Verse greatly matters, though too few contemporary poets take it seriously, I'm afraid. Verse enables you to sharpen your expression considerably, to explore and realize more closely the possibilities of language. A given prose poem, so-called, may be superior to a given Shakespearean sonnet, but we are talking about an exception; the odds are against it. Sometimes, of course, it is worthwhile to go against the odds.

JB: Vine Deloria complained, in an interview in 1977 in

Sun Tracks that so many young American Indian writers turned to verse rather than writing in what he thought was a more useful form to communicate with the Anglo world, fiction or prose. Yet you're saying that really isn't so much of a choice, as a natural step.

MOMADAY: I think so. At least, that's how I think of it.

JB: I have noticed that certain themes appear to turn up again and again in your work. What are those themes? Do you think about them or are they there subconsciously?

MOMADAY: I would say that much of my writing has been concerned with the question of man's relationship to the earth, for one thing. Another theme that has interested me is man's relationship to himself, to his past, his heritage. When I was growing up on the reservations of the Southwest, I saw people who were deeply involved in their traditional life, in the memories of their blood. They had, as far as I could see, a certain strength and beauty that I find missing in the modern world at large. I like to celebrate that involvement in my writing.

JB: You don't think of yourself, though, as a person who is sort of conserving something that's disappearing, do you? I've heard that description of their work given by many non-Indian writers who have written about Indian ways. And I'm not just talking about anthropologists, but also some of the novelists of the early part of the century who thought of themselves as both celebrating and preserving—almost like an artifact—something which was vanishing. Yet I don't think that is characteristic of your approach.

MOMADAY: No, I wouldn't say so. There is an aspect of this matter that has to do with preservation, of course—with a realization that things are passing. I feel this very keenly. But I'm not concerned to preserve relics and artifacts. Only superficially have things changed in the world I knew as a child. I can enumerate them. When I was growing up at Jemez Pueblo—I lived there for several years from the time I was twelve—I saw things that are not to be seen now. I wrote about some of them in *The Names*. I remember one day looking out upon a dirt road and seeing a caravan of covered wagons that reached as far as the eye could see. These were the Navajos coming in from Torreon to the annual Jemez feast on November 12, 1946. It was simply an unforgettable sight. But the next year it had changed considerably; there were fewer wagons, and there were some pickups, and the year after that there were still fewer wagons and more pickups, and the year after that there were no wagons. And I had later the sense that I had been in the right place at the right time, that I had seen something that will not be seen again, and I thank God for that. But the loss is less important to me than the spirit which informs the remembrance, the spirit that informs that pageantry across all ages and which persists in the imagination of every man everywhere.

JB: Yes, that's a great example. Are words magical?

MOMADAY: Oh, yes.

JB: How so?

MOMADAY: Well, words are powerful beyond our knowledge, certainly. And they are beautiful. Words are intrinsically powerful, I believe. And there is magic in that. Words come from nothing into being. They are created in the imagination and given life on the human voice. You know, we used to believe—and I'm talking now about all of us, regardless of our ethnic backgrounds—in the magic of words. The Anglo-Saxon who uttered spells over his fields so that the seeds would come out of the ground on the sheer strength of his voice, knew a good deal about language, and he believed absolutely in the efficacy of language. That man's faith—and may I say, wisdom—has been lost upon modern man, by and large. It survives in the poets of the world, I suppose, the singers. We do not now know what we can do with words. But as long as there are those among us who try to find out, literature will be secure; literature will remain a thing worthy of our highest level of human being.

JB: You mention poets and singers. Are they related or are they different?

MOMADAY: I think they are the same thing. You might

make this sort of superficial distinction. The poet is concerned to construct his expression according to traditional and prescribed forms. The singer, too, composes his expression according to strict rules, but he is a more religious being, on the whole, less concerned with form than with the most fundamental and creative possibilities of language. The American Indian would be in the second of these categories. This distinction, of course, requires elucidation, but, for the time being, I shall spare you that.

JB: And do you think there are some Indian poets who are still singers or vice versa?

MOMADAY: Yes.

JB: Could I ask you to read this one? I think it goes well with what we were just talking about.

MOMADAY: Yes.

The Delight Song of Tsoai-Talee

I am a feather on the bright sky
I am the blue horse that runs in the plain
I am the fish that rolls, shining, in the water
I am the shadow that follows a child
I am the evening light, the lustre of meadows
I am an eagle playing with the wind
I am a cluster of bright beads
I am the farthest star
I am the cold of the dawn
I am the roaring of the rain
I am the glitter on the crust of the snow
I am the long track of the moon in a lake
I am a flame of four colors
I am a deer standing away in the dusk
I am a field of sumac and the pomme blanche
I am an angle of geese in the winter sky
I am the hunger of a young wolf
I am the whole dream of these things

You see, I am alive, I am alive
I stand in good relation to the earth
I stand in good relation to the gods
I stand in good relation to all that is beautiful
I stand in good relation to the daughter of Tsen-tainte
You see, I am alive, I am alive

JB: I've always liked this poem of yours very much. As you may know I chose it for translation into some European languages. This is your own song, isn't it?

MOMADAY: Yes.

JB: This is the name which you were given by an older relative?

MOMADAY: The name was given to me by an old man, a paternal relative, actually. His name was Pohd-lohk, and he gave me the name when I was very young, less than a year old. Tsoai-talee means "rock-tree boy." It commemorates my having been taken, at the age of six months or so, to Devils Tower, Wyoming, which is a sacred place in Kiowa tradition. And the Kiowas call it "rock-tree." Therefore, Pohd-lohk gave me the name. All of this is set down in detail in *The Names*.

JB: This poem or song makes me think of some very traditional poems or songs. I feel as though I can see, for example, that southwestern influence, the traditional songs of the Navajos and Pueblo people. Especially the Navajo people. I also feel I see something which comes out of Plains Indians' structures, a statement of who you are. Not so much a boasting song as a definition of being alive. Do you see all those things coming together in this? Is this part of what you did consciously or did the form of the poem come in and of itself?

MOMADAY: I see those things in it, but I'm not sure that I set out to reflect them consciously in the poem. As I recall, the writing of it came quickly, without effort . . . it's not a poem that I crafted over a long period of time. It is more spontaneous than most of my poems.

JB: Yes, you mention the word "dream" in here. Again it seems to me like the poem that comes out of a dream . . . the poem that traditionally would come as an inspiration from an-other voice.

MOMADAY: Dreams, I suppose, are also a constant theme in my work. I'm very much aware of the visionary aspect of the Plains culture, especially the vision quest, so-called. I have more to say about that, I think, in another context. I'm writing a piece now, based upon a vision quest. It will be a novel, I think.

JB: The idea of dreams, then . . . what are dreams?

MOMADAY: Yeah, what are dreams? Has there ever been an answer to that? There is so much we have yet to know about dreams and dreaming. Dreams are prophetic, mean-ingful, revealing of inmost life. But no one knows how they work, as far as I know. I have powerful dreams, and I believe they determine who I am and what I do. But how, I'm not sure. Maybe that is how it ought to be. Mystery is, perhaps, the necessary condition of dreams.

JB: The term, "the great mystery," is often used by some of the Plains people to describe the Creator or that life force which is beyond and above all human, in other life. That's not a mystery that, I sense, native people wish to pierce. It's a mystery which they live in the knowledge of, without wanting to know "what" it is. It seems rather counter to the Western ap-proach to things. The Anglo approach is to *always* know.

MOMADAY: Yes, yes. I don't know.

JB: I was talking about the contrast between the Western, Anglo, view and the American Indian view. I'd like to take that back directly to literature and ask what you think the difference is between, let's say, an Indian view of what literature is, and I don't mean just a traditional Indian person, but, let's say some-one who has been raised in the twentieth century and who is writing still as an Indian, as opposed to that writer who is non-Indian.

MOMADAY: I think there is only one real difference be-tween the two, and that is that the Indian has the advantage of a very rich spiritual experience. As much can be said, certainly, of some non-Indian writers. But the non-Indian writers of today are culturally deprived, I think, in the sense that they don't have the same sense of heritage that the Indian has. I'm told this time and time again by my students, who say, "Oh, I wish I knew more about my grandparents; I wish I knew more about my ancestors and where they came from and what they did." I've come to believe them. It seems to me that the Indian writer ought to make use of that advantage. One of his subjects ought certainly to be his cultural investment in the world. It is a unique and complete experience, and it is a great subject in itself.

JB: One thing which I'm concerned with is a sense of the continuance and the survival of various things which seem to be central to a number of American Indian writers. Do you see your work as continuing some tradition?

MOMADAY: Yes. I think that my work proceeds from the American Indian oral tradition, and I think it sustains that tradition and carries it along. And vice versa. And my writing is also of a piece. I've written several books, but to me they are all parts of the same story. And I like to repeat myself, if you will, from book to book, in the way that Faulkner did—in an even more obvious way, perhaps. My purpose is to carry on what was begun a long time ago; there's no end to it that I can see.

JB: That's a question that I was going to ask. I'm glad you led into it. In *House Made of Dawn* there is a sermon which is given by a Kiowa character. He's not terribly likable in some ways. Yet those words turn up again in *The Way to Rainy Mountain* out of, I assume, your own lips. The things that happen in *The Gourd Dancer* also seem to be a continuance of that same voice and, of course, in *The Names* you have that repetition. I've heard some people say, "Momaday's repeating himself. Doesn't he have any new material?" But I've suspected this repetition was a conscious thing.

MOMADAY: Oh, yes. In a sense I'm not concerned to change my subject from book to book. Rather, I'm concerned to keep the story going. I mean to keep the same subject, to carry it farther with each telling.

JB: Some traditional songs and stories begin each new movement by repeating. They repeat and then go a bit further. That's the structure in your work?

MOMADAY: Yes, indeed, and I believe that is a good

way in which to proceed. It establishes a continuity that is important to me.

JB: What are the links in your everyday life to American Indian traditions?

MOMADAY: Well, I have the conviction that I am an Indian. I have an idea of myself as an Indian, and that idea is quite secure. My father was Huan-toa; my grandfather was Mammedaty; my great-grandfather was Guipagho. How can I not be an Indian? I'm a member of the Gourd Dance society in the Kiowa tribe, and when I can, I go to the annual meeting of that society, and it is a great thing for me, full of excitement and restoration, the deepest meaning. Since I've returned to the Southwest I feel new and stronger links with the Indian world than I felt in California, where I was for twenty years in exile. Then, too, I have children. And my children are, much to my delight, greatly interested in their stake in the Indian world. So that's another link for me as well as for them. Of course I have Indian relatives. I lost my father, who was my closest tie with the Kiowa world; he died last year. But there are others who sustain me. I keep in touch.

JB: You could say then, perhaps, of "The Gourd Dancer," of your poem, although it's dedicated to your grandfather, that Gourd Dancer is also you.

MOMADAY: Oh, yes, yes. Again the continuity. That part of the poem which refers to the giving away of a horse: I wasn't there, of course. But it really did happen; my father was only eight years old, but it remained in his memory as long as he lived. And I absorbed it when I was the same age, so that it became my memory as well. This is a profound continuity, something at the very center of the Indian perception of the world. We are talking about immortality, or something very close to it, though the American Indian would not have that name for it. He would say, perhaps, if he were Kiowa, *Akeahde*, "they were camping." In that word is the seed of the same idea.

JB: The American writer some people might link you most closely to who is non-Indian is Walt Whitman. Whitman's life was a single work, *Leaves of Grass*, which went through different stages of development. Vine Deloria and Geary Hobson have both pointed out (Geary in an article in *New America Magazine* and Vine in that *Sun Tracks* interview), that there have been cycles of interest in American Indians and in the publication of American Indian literary work. As you know D'arcy McNickle more or less stopped being published after a certain point in the late thirties and only was published just before his death in the current resurgence in the late seventies. In the thirties, it was Luther Standing Bear, twenty years before that Charles Eastman. Do you think that this kind of cycle will happen again with American Indian literature or is there something different about the current surge of writing by American Indians and interest in their writing?

MOMADAY: I really don't know the answer to that. Oh, I suppose there will be cycles; the popularity of books by and about American Indians will pass, and then there will be regenerations of interest, *ad infinitum*. That's the nature of the publishing world, isn't it? I'm not worried about it. The American Indian is indispensable to the soil and the dream and the destiny of America. That's the important thing. He always was and always will be a central figure in the American imagination, a central figure in American literature. We can't very well do without him.

JB: I also wonder if it might not be different this time because we now have more Indian people who are literate, who do read. We now have also our own audience as opposed to an audience of people who are non-Indian.

MOMADAY: I'm sure that's true.

JB: What is it that contemporary American Indian poetry has to offer to the world of literature or to the world as a whole?

MOMADAY: Well, I think it's a legitimate and artistic expression in itself, first of all. Here is my voice, and my voice proceeds out of an intelligence that touches upon the inexorable motions of the world. There is design and symmetry in the pattern of my speech, my words. That in itself is a noteworthy thing. Another such thing is the perception that we were talking about a moment ago. I believe that the Indian has an understanding of the physical world and of the earth as a spiritual entity that is his, very much his own. The non-Indian can benefit a good deal by having that perception revealed to him.

JB: I've been interested in the place that women seem to be taking in American Indian literature. There seems to be a good deal of strong writing coming from American Indian women, perhaps more so than any other ethnic minority, if you want to call it that, in America. Why is that so? Do you have any ideas on that subject?

MOMADAY: No. It's not something that I have thought much about. But it doesn't surprise me, what you say. Women in the Indian world have always had strong, sometimes supernatural, voices. In Plains culture those voices were often understated for obvious reasons—it was a warrior society, after all—but even in that culture women have always had a prominent position. And it is appropriate that we see Indian women writing now. You're right, there are many, and more to come. And some are doing remarkably fine work. I spoke at the Institute of American Indian Arts in Santa Fe a few months ago. I was speaking particularly to the creative writing students there, and I met several young women, in particular, whose work was very impressive. I met very good young men who were writing well, too, but the women won the day.

JB: In a recent interview, as a part of a National Public Radio program that focused on American Indian women poets called "The Key is in Remembering," Paula Gunn Allen said that reading *House Made of Dawn* was one of the major turning points in her life. It made things possible for her that were never possible before. And it is certainly true that you've been a very important inspiration for many American Indian writers. Just the fact that the two best anthologies of American Indian writing, *Carriers of the Dream Wheel* and *The Remembered Earth*, both draw their titles from your work, is a very clear indication of how important people think you are to them. What do you feel about your place as a sort of, to use an academic term, dean of American Indian writers?

MOMADAY: It's something that I don't often think about. I don't know what that's worth, really. I do very much appreciate people who say the sorts of things that Paula Gunn Allen said on that occasion. But I'm not conscious of my place in that whole scheme of things as yet. And I'm rather reluctant to think in those terms, really, because I want to get on with my work. I'm afraid that if I started thinking of myself as the dean of American Indian writers I might not work so well. I might be tempted to slow down and accept the deanship when I really want to be out there among the subordinates doing my thing.

JB: Deans tend to be administrators, right?

MOMADAY: Exactly.

Closing the Circle

An Interview with
DUANE NIATUM

Klallam poet Duane Niatum published his first work, including his book *After the Death of an Elder Klallam* (The Baleen
Press, 1970), under the name of Duane McGinness. Born in
Seattle in 1938 and raised by the family of his maternal grandfather, he later changed his name to Niatum, a family name
given him by one of his elder relatives. It reflected his growing
commitment to express the reality of being a contemporary
Native American in both his writing and his life.

Since that first volume, his work has continued to grow in
that direction. His books include two collections of his own
poetry published by Harper & Row, *Digging out the Roots* and
Ascending Red Cedar Moon, and a 1981 collection from the

University of Washington Press, *Songs For the Harvester of Dreams*, as well as several chapbooks. While working in New York City in the mid-'70s as an editor for Harper & Row's Native American Writing Series, he edited a landmark volume of contemporary Native American poets, *Carriers of the Dream Wheel* (1975), and was working in 1985 on a followup to that volume for Harper & Row.

In 1983 Duane Niatum was invited to Holland to address an international conference on world literature. On his way to Europe he stopped to visit in Greenfield Center, where this interview took place. Slender and intense, there are times when Niatum's face takes on the exact cast of one of the old men whose faces appear in the Curtis photographs of Northwest Indians of the turn of the century, though just as quickly the quick laugh of Trickster may spark in his eyes. A careful technician to whom revision is of vital importance in the process of writing, he decided to begin by reading an early poem which he had revised.

The Novelty Shop

More grotesque than a laundromat,
Novel shopkeepers pun the city like skid row,
Outside the entrance
A cigar-store Indian,
With the entombed stare of a museum sculpture,
Draws the tourists into the damp shop
Of seashore ornaments for manufactured bores.
With the forest serenity of a shaman,
And the black eyes of a renegade priest,
The cedar Indian abandons the city of red rain,
And dives into the sea at the end of the pier.

—Duane Niatum

JB: What led you to read this particular poem?

NIATUM: I'm not quite sure. At first, because I was looking for a poem that was brief, but another reason is that I think I'm returning to the protest movement again. That's one of the few protest poems I've written and I think it has a lot to do with that.

JB: The image of the Indian in that poem, both in the sense of the cigar store Indian and the picture of a person in an environment, has a lot of irony connected to it.

NIATUM: Yes. I think the Native American is constantly faced with the ironies of life and the paradoxes. He shares those with everybody, but I think he's in a much more poignant position because of the fact that complete survival is at stake, survival of the traditions and survival of what he represents as a people . . . although I think there is a new movement to hold together what is left. It's a real struggle and it demands a great deal of energy and concentration by everybody that's still living.

JB: You're touching on some points which I feel are very important in relation to your work and to things going on now in contemporary literature, but first let me back up a bit by asking you some questions about your early years. What are your memories about growing up in the Northwest?

NIATUM: I've been thinking about this recently, as I've been putting together my *New and Selected Poems* and going back over the work which goes back twenty-five years. It's made me think about my childhood and it's pretty exciting, actually. When you get close to those old poems which involve experiences from childhood it brings all the memories back to the surface, and it's amazing what comes out of it. As I get older, now that I'm forty-five, I realize how much more important my grandfather was to me in terms of my psychic stability, my social and aesthetic values, and his people and what they represented in terms of Northwest culture. It's more meaningful now than it was when I first began to use it in my work, and it wasn't an extrapolation from the outside; it's a spiritual thing, it's an integral part of myself. . . and ourselves, because we have many. It comes from within and when it becomes art it's an unconscious impulse. It's not anything I try to fabricate consciously. I don't believe in that. I believe that genuine art has to come from the unconscious but it requires work once it surfaces. I'm against the surrealists' feeling that everything that emerges from the unconscious is art, which is delusion.

JB: Was there anything different about your childhood because of your Native American background?

NIATUM: Well, yes. There were a lot of things. One of the main things was the teaching of my grandfather and his parents about the Klallam traditions. . . fishing, hunting, which gave me a strong sense of my relationship to the sea, to the land, to the animals, which I retain. This was training when I was a child from a very small age, say, four or five, till I was a teenager. So it was an important part of my background but I didn't realize how important until years later. Of course, I think this is the case with anything that you lose later on in life. You don't realize how important it is until after you've lost it. Another example is I didn't realize how important my grandfather was to me until years after he died. I knew he was important to me because he was my surrogate father. He took the place of my father because my father left—my mother got divorced when I was about five. It was after the divorce that I spent a lot of time with my grandfather. I was the black sheep of my family, and he took my side, always, and gave me support all through my life until he died. He died when I was seventeen and in my first year in the Navy. Yet, he had laid the groundwork for my art without my knowing it. It was only when I became self-conscious about being an artist that I realized the significance of his role in my life, showing me the way, the right way—because there's so much hype in pop culture, so many wrong paths that a young artist can take if he gets trapped in the various fads and fashions of "pop culture." Artists have to resist the pressures of consumer culture if they're really going to do anything significant in the form or try to make any breakthroughs. They have to constantly resist the temptations to trivialize their art.

JB: What were some of the particular things you were taught as a young child about the sea, the animals?

NIATUM: Well, one simple thing was digging clams. One of the ways I used to make my spending money as a child was digging clams. My grandfather taught me each type of clam has its own hole. They're also at different levels, different depths. You can recognize the clams from the holes they make. Also there were oysters and crabs. The Dungeness crab is one of the greatest edible crabs in the world and it's only found in Klallam country. It's a wonderful food. So there was crabbing, there was fishing—salmon, trout, all kinds of fishing. There was hunting—deer, duck hunting—and so those things I learned from my grandfather. How to build a bow and an arrow, some wood carving. Those are some of the things. He taught me how to walk in the forest at night, how to notice certain birds, recognize certain animals—the kind of things that we were doing this morning. Part of the training was for you to recognize all of the animals around you, all of the birds, all of the fish, the different kinds of crabs because there are different kinds of crabs and many of them are edible and some not. Everything in the environment, you were shown. The berries which you could eat, the different kinds of trees. All of these things I learned about as a child. Another thing is that I was half the time in the city and the other time in the country, so there was exposure to both and what helped me survive in the city was the fact that I was trained by my grandfather to be fairly independent as a very young child. Consequently, I could live on my own in the city and get around easier because I had that training.

JB: You learned then that kind of self-reliance—or being able to rely upon the world around you without the intercession of other people? And it helped you even when you moved out of the natural world and into the world of the city?

NIATUM: Right. It helped me survive. It reinforces your reliance on your own instincts, intuition. You need that in the city as much as you do in the country. In fact, you need it more. Those things that you learn, how to use the senses, how to make these judgments, are really important to know in the city because of the complexity. In a way, it's more of a forest to deal with than the forest itself, because it's an alien forest, not a natural forest. If you learn how to survive in a natural forest, it's then much easier to survive in the city.

DUANE NIATUM

JB: In your book *Digging Out The Roots*, the poem "Street Kid" opens on that world. You stand before the window which looks out on a field of sagebrush. It is interesting to me that in that poem your perspective is not looking toward the city, as everyone else does, but toward the natural world which is beyond the city. That is a result of your early training?

NIATUM: I think so. Yes, you're right. I didn't think about it, but that was instinctual. I would survive in that environment which was totally alien and hostile by holding onto that tie.

JB: Where does "Street Kid" take place?

NIATUM: California. Martinez, a reform school.

JB: You were in reform school twice?

NIATUM: Three times, actually. I spent two months in Martinez and twice in the Youth Service Center in Seattle. The first time just for a couple of weeks or so and the second time for about two months.

JB: Did that experience shape you at all or have much effect on your childhood?

NIATUM: No, I think the street itself had more effect. It wasn't long enough. But it did show me what it was like to be locked up, what prison life must be like. In that way it showed another kind of a reality that at the beginning is really horrible. What I've grown to admire about humanity is its incredible ability to survive. You adjust to these extreme situations. A more extreme situation that I experienced was the time that I spent thirty days in the Marine brig. There the men are brutal, and it's even more dramatic and more terrifying and more demanding that you hold on to your senses.

JB: Were there also things you were taught by your grandfather about the *way* you should relate to the natural world?

NIATUM: Oh yes! I think one of the things is that you have to respect the fact that in the natural world the animals and the plants have a position equal to your own. I think that was a very important training. You have to respect that world and know that you share the same world and that means that there is a mutual dependency. When you take from nature you have to give back something. You're only allowed to take your fair share. You can't be a pig about it. This way was the original, traditional training. I realize that has changed, even among Native American people—which is a tragedy because it's an integral part of their training from the very beginning, from the first tribe. There are some Native Americans that are abusing that now, but I imagine you can also find that abuse in Africa among Africans hunting elephants for their tusks. It's not just a problem with Native Americans. I'm not saying it is a large problem, but I'm not saying that it doesn't exist. I feel that you should always face reality and that's one of the realities and it needs to be turned around. There are Native Americans who have been killing eagles, which I don't think is a good thing— for making money. You make big bucks. The eagle is an endangered species and you should respect it. When Native Americans do such things they have to be held responsible the same as anybody. . . *it's against the traditions of their people.*

JB: Stories appear to be a very important element in your work, not just in your prose, but your poetry as well, though the stories seem more suggested than said in your poems. The cutting edge of the story is visible, but the rest is left to the imagination of the reader. Is that intentional?

NIATUM: Yes. I think that is part of the oral tradition. I've tried to create these stories in such a way that the reader has a lot of space to work, him or herself, using their imagination on an equal basis. I think creating art is reciprocal. It requires almost as much energy from the reader—especially if the artist really does his job. He just merely—or she just merely—sets the groundwork. The art piece is finished by the reader. The circle is closed with the imagination of the reader. It has to be both of them working on the art object for it to become a whole. It's not a finished piece, it is always unfinished to a certain degree and this is just part of the tradition. It's not only part of the oral tradition, it's part of the contemporary aesthetic. I think it is paradoxical, too, because the contemporary aesthetic has gone too far. It's left black holes. Whereas, the oral tradition—you could fill in the spots that were missing with your imagination. I think contemporary art leaves so much

DUANE NIATUM

fragmented, so many holes that they can't be filled in by the imagination of the observer, and so in that sense, it is not the same as the oral tradition. The oral tradition believed in the closing of the circle, the wholeness, *that value*, that social and aesthetic value was an absolute necessity for anything to be exchanged.

JB: So the oral tradition always gives you the outline and you fill in the individual features in that outline?

NIATUM: You can close the circle.

JB: Whereas, in some contemporary literature—too much, you say—you don't have an outline at all? You have lines going off in random directions?

NIATUM: Right. No point of convergence, no sense of trying to tie anything together; thus, it is totally fragmentary. No sense of unity, no sense of continuity, and they don't value it because the attitude doesn't exist. It's where I separate myself from the modern movement. I feel myself to be a contemporary, a twentieth-century artist, a modernist—but fortunately, I'm a modernist with Native American roots which have saved me from getting trapped in that attitude that is so prevalent in the modern arts that there is no necessity for wholeness—everything can be left fragmented without the continuity of a circle. It's not just an aesthetic opinion. Modern science has reinforced it. It's been abused. It's just like the philosophy of Nietzche, which is good philosophy but if misread can be very destructive—just like the Nazis. But they misunderstood it and it's not Nietzche. He would be appalled by the Nazis, I'm sure. It's the same way with what modern science has done. People who have looked at it naively and superficially have drawn certain conclusions and missed the real meaning.

JB: There are a few characters which turn up frequently in your poems. Who is Trickster?

NIATUM: Okay! Trickster is universal. It's found in the oral traditions in Africa and the Occident and Native American cultures. The most prevalent Trickster figures in the Northwest are Raven, Blue Jay, Crow, Fox, Wolf—to name just a few. Raven and Crow, especially, come back to mind. My grandfather used to call me "Little Crow" when I was a child. The

Trickster can be both benevolent and malevolent, and he's a teacher. I like to think of him—if you want to think of him in terms of contemporary psychology—you could say he was the Irrational Self. It's an attempt to balance the psyche. Trickster teaches us to live with the dark side of our natures, for the most part, to come to terms with the dark side. The figures in Western culture that are equivalent teachers are Fox, for example, Bre'r Rabbit. Those are figures that teach about a certain part of our nature. That's one of the reasons why the Trickster keeps coming back in my work so often. He also represents dealing with reality, never giving up the value, the sense of the real world. I think our culture's become so extreme, so mad, that there's this tremendous impulse in us to escape to any place other than the present moment because it's so bizarre. Reality is so much more surrealistic than art can ever be. Art will never duplicate the irrational face of reality. So, I think, Trickster is important because it forces us to keep our feet on the ground.

JB: Do you think that explains why Trickster turns up in the writing of practically every Native American poet and fiction writer?

NIATUM: I would think so. They're at a more extreme position because it's the survival of the people, and the breaking down of the whole social structure is even more extreme there. I think, though, that throughout the globe people are facing the same dilemma, but because there's a chance of the Native American losing his tribal roots entirely, everything that represents the Self as a Native American, I think it's a much more extreme position.

JB: Who is Cedar Man?

NIATUM: It is meant to represent the Native American tradition in Coast Salish culture. Also, it's a reference to my grandfather and what he represents traditionally. So it's a symbolic reference to my own family traditions and to the Native American from the Northwest Coast. There was a lot of overlapping of the traditions in the Northwest. We were, for the most part, salmon fishermen, as were most of the Northwest tribes, because there are five different species of salmon that go up the rivers along British Columbia, Washington, Oregon to spawn. So we were salmon fishermen for the most part. Cedar was *the* tree of the culture and it was made into canoes, totems, and even clothes. Bowls were made out of cedar. Other trees, too, but especially cedar. Spoons, forks, houses, almost everything in our lives was associated with the cedar, and it was a sacred tree.

JB: You also mention Cedar Berry Woman. Yet another character?

NIATUM: Yes. All of these characters come from the tradition, from the Northwest Coast, and, particularly, Klallam. I might refer to characters from another tribe nearby, but for the most part they're almost entirely from the Puget Sound area. If I talk about Native American culture in any part of the country other than my own, the references are there and can be recognized. If I speak of Sitting Bull, then almost anyone will know in the context of the poem that he's not a Northwest figure.

JB: I notice that you make frequent references to the moon, also.

NIATUM: Yes, I think that has to do with a contemporary Jungian principle, but it's also traditional in Native American culture. I think it also represents the imagination. There's a story that we see best in the dark. The clearest light is in the dark. I think that has to do with the fact that we are blinded by day from really seeing. You can see this idea in Oriental culture, too. They say the best way to see is to close your eyes. You see most clearly with your eyes closed. Too bright light gets in the way of real perception. It takes away the power of the imagination. Imagination blossoms the greatest in the dark. So I think that's what that alludes to and also a few other things. I think that alludes to the cycles—that is very important. And the moon is the sun's opposite. It represents the relationship between the sky and the earth, man and woman. You can go on and on. It symbolizes so many things that are important in terms of connection. The older I get—and I don't want it to be a fabrication—the more I feel a responsibility to retain some of the values of my Native American ancestors in art. I think one of the best ways they can survive is in art. They might even survive longer in art than in any other form. So I feel it is very important. These are things that can make survival easier if you maintain these kinds of ties.

JB: What does it mean to be an ethnic writer in the United States?

NIATUM: One thing it means for sure, as far as I'm concerned, is you're an outsider. You walk a tightrope between the two cultures and you never really are a part of either. As an intellectual, as an artist living in a city for the last twenty-five years of my life, it's really separated me from my Native American people to a certain degree. Art puts you in a different place, especially if you try to be innovative. If you're a traditional carver using the traditions of the Northwest Coast, you're not faced with those kinds of problems. But, if you're trying to be innovative and break ground, you come up against trouble in both societies. You're looked at with suspicion by your own people and you're also looked at with suspicion by the Anglos. So, you're right in the middle of things, and I think it's a lifetime position.

JB: You also said, when we were talking last night, that at one time you just tried to be seen as a writer, not as a Native American writer.

NIATUM: Right, I've always resisted the stereotype of being a Native American poet or an American Indian poet. I mentioned this in an essay. In fact, it haunted me so much I once wrote an essay on stereotypes. I tried to deal with this conflict. I feel that it puts shackles on the reader and sets up preconceived notions of what to expect in the poem or the story, and I didn't want that. I want the reader to approach the poem or the story free of preconceived notions. But, my resistance has failed on that, and I can't seem to get away from it. So I have to live with it and hope for the best. It works out. I don't think it is as big a problem as I thought at the beginning of my career.

JB: Then there are positive aspects? If you approach the traditional inheritance that you have as a writer with respect?

NIATUM: That should save you. That should make it. So I shouldn't worry about anything else. But the stereotype, I think, is with you all your lifetime.

JB: You've been concerned with larger issues both in your private life and in your writing, haven't you?

NIATUM: I've always been involved in the human rights struggles, I've always been for the people. All of my life I'll be a fighter for the people. I haven't tried to do too much of that in terms of my writing. I'm not a didactic writer for the most part. It goes against my aesthetic, because I don't think you should force anything. It should be natural, as Keats's saying goes, "as a leaf falling from a tree." If it isn't, it shouldn't exist. I feel that would be going counter to my nature, so I'm an activist in other ways. I protest, I march, and I write letters. I'm concerned about the struggles and the persecution of the individual in societies, not only our own but others, persecution for being an artist, for being an individual, for going against the established government order. The possibility of the nuclear holocaust involves me in politics. Social concerns, ecology, what we're doing to nature, too, is another concern. There are endless problems, but all of them are related and go back to the central problem of our arrogance. The key problem of all mankind is arrogance.

JB: Don't you think there is a kind of political poem which is not polemic? It may not even be obviously political, but it contains a very real politics. Certain of your poems which contain a certain aesthetic, no, an ethic, ethic is a better word, which you were taught by your family, by your experiences. That, too, seems political.

NIATUM: Oh yes, yes. I think so, too. But I use it in such a way that it's not tied to the moment and it goes beyond time. Also, it's tied to a physical reality, not just the abstract world. Yes, in that sense I do deal with a lot of political issues in a very indirect way, but that is about the only way I can do it. I think some things that you have inevitably will become political by their very nature because there are so many problems in contemporary society that all things seem political. Important values that I have are in danger and so they will be political.

JB: Last night you said you felt one of the big problems with contemporary writers was that they lacked a connection to the people.

NIATUM: There's an arrogance against the community.

JB: And the ethnic writer, by definition, is connected to a people and a community, for better or for worse?

NIATUM: Yes, whether he or she likes it or not. That is a significant difference. They care about having an audience. I think that problem is relatively recent with Western culture and stems from the Romantic tradition. It evolved out of a Byronic arrogance, but it has moved all the way to the extreme today of the Punks. It's found in the Romantic tradition, the Surrealists and the Dadaists and the Pop artists. Hostility. I think one of the reasons we have a small, and growing smaller, number of readers is the fact that the artist has alienated his audience. He has as much responsibility for this decline in readership as other people! He's been so hostile that he has helped this decline.

JB: At what point in your life did you find yourself directly in contact with other poets?

NIATUM: I was lucky that it was when I was relatively young and first starting out. I started college when I was twenty-one. I became exposed then to poets and writers of our generation and developed friendships. I had a lot of exposure to the arts at that time, at the beginning of my career as an artist. It happened at a good time. That's the most exciting time because everything is new and so you're discovering all these new things. I think that kind of intensity, that kind of discovery is never found again. It's not that you can't discover things all your life, but it doesn't have the same power. It has to do with youth and not knowing a lot. You know almost nothing—well, I'm not sure when you get older that you do know that much more, but you do know a little more and something in our chemistry changes where it's not exactly the same thing when you discover something new. It can still be intense, you can still get excited about it, but it's not the same as when you're young.

JB: This is when you were at the University of Washington?

NIATUM: Yes.

JB: Who were your teachers there?

NIATUM: I was with Roethke for a while, and Nelson Bentley had an enormous influence on me. Roethke, too, though I wasn't an official student of Roethke's. I sat in his class back in 1961. It was about the same time I studied with

Nelson Bentley. I was also a student of Elizabeth Bishop's and Leonie Adams and, later on, Susan Sontag. Those were the central writers in my life in terms of molding my philosophy and setting me straight as to what was real poetry and fiction and what wasn't. They got me on the right road.

JB: Do you have any specific recollections about any of your teachers, Sontag, for example, or Roethke? Things they did which made a difference for you?

NIATUM: I think with Roethke it was to pay attention to the ear, to hear the song aloud. The poem aloud, the poem leaving the page becoming a spirit outside, a song in the air. I think that was one of the most important things. That and to pay attention to both traditional and free verse. Sontag encouraged me to explore art and society, beyond the limits of my own American tradition, particularly the writers and artists of Europe.

JB: One of the things you learned from Roethke was the importance of working in both free verse and traditional forms?

NIATUM: That is one of the most important things he gave me as a teacher—besides his wonderful gift as a poet himself. Some teachers of poetry aren't really great poets themselves. He was, fortunately, and he was able to express this in the classroom. He was one of the greatest readers of poetry we've had in America. He had hundreds of poems memorized and he showed the power of the ear. . . and in conjunction with the rest of the senses, in terms of molding a real solid sense of what the poetry form means. He emphasized the fact that you really need to work not only in free verse, which has become the dominant form in contemporary poetry, but you need to try to discover what the ancient forms meant and to use them and to make them new. I think that was a very important thing. It established an interest in me for the traditional forms which I have carried right to the present day.

JB: You've been working on a sonnet sequence, haven't you?

NIATUM: I've finished a sonnet sequence in honor of Roethke. It's a nice paying back of what he suggested years and years ago, working in a form that I've always loved but never worked in, using the Shakespearean rhyme scheme or any other rhyme scheme of the sonnet form. I had written a couple of Shakespearean sonnets in the '60s but I didn't like them. I've written several unrhymed sonnets like those of Robert Lowell's in his *Notebook* and *History*, but nothing using any particular rhyme scheme. These four poems for Roethke are a Shakespearean sonnet sequence. I've also done two or three others using the same tradition. I'm very happy for that. He also emphasized the importance that poets know as much about the historical aspect of their form as the present, and also that poetry should pay attention to the other art forms. All of this somehow has to be integrated into your poem, your experience not only with the poem, but your experience with the play, with the novel, with the quartet, with the dance, and your relationships with the people—again, the importance of the community. I think I've discovered another reason I became so fond of Roethke as a poet. It is the fact that many of his poems reflect the Native American tradition—that is, Native American tribal culture emphasizes the importance of the nature of the universe and your relationship to this Nature. It's an important part of the Native American tradition.

JB: Were any of your other teachers as influential as Roethke?

NIATUM: Yes, I think Nelson Bentley was, surprisingly so, even more than Elizabeth Bishop. I am a great admirer of Elizabeth Bishop. I think she is one of the greatest poets that we've ever had, but I didn't care for her much as a person or a teacher. Nelson Bentley had a tremendous influence because I think he modeled his teaching after Roethke's. He followed Roethke out from Michigan. He was from Elm, Michigan, a little town that I guess no longer exists. He also believed in working in and out of traditional forms. Too many teachers tell the young that the ancient forms are dead and free verse is the only form for the contemporary poet. Bentley resisted the fashion mongers. He also had a tremendous range in his reading and his knowledge of literature—like Roethke—which he could bring to bear on his teaching. I think Roethke and Bentley were the two most important teachers, in terms of laying a foundation for growth, when I left the classroom.

JB: What have you done since leaving the classrooms?

NIATUM: Sometimes I've taught, sometimes I've done editing work. I've done other things. I've worked for social programs and school programs. For the most part it's been teacher-related, but the jobs have been few and far between. I haven't been able to get an academic position like a lot of my contemporaries. But I think an advantage of being poor and out of work—for a certain amount of time—is that you have an enormous amount of time to work. It's paid off in the long run and I'm not sorry. There were times when I really regretted it, the poverty and the paranoia that's involved with that—where are you going to get the money to pay the rent or buy the next meal—but when you're young you can handle that.

JB: You've now put together your new and selected poems?

NIATUM: Yes, and it's exciting because I never thought of myself as reaching this position. I always thought of myself, when I was young, as dying young. I think it was part of the Romantic tradition. You were supposed to burn out in youth. But as I grow older I become a little bit more Classical. I think that might have to do with a natural biological and psychological and spiritual change in us, too. We evolve out of our Romantic state like a snake out of its skin. There are self-destructive elements in the Romantic tradition and, as we get older, we have to preserve our resources, and among them are our biological and psychic resources. If we're going to survive we have to pay attention to that, whereas, when you're young, you can do a lot of terrible things to yourself physiologically and psychically and still survive. Some of the things I've done when I was young terrify me to think I would ever do them now—a dictionary of self-destruction. I think it's just because of ignorance and fear, ignorance and fear working together. I'm not so sure your wisdom with time helps you improve matters much, other than letting you relax more. I think that much of it is so personal that you're not able to pass it on—unless it is transformed into art. If it's transformed into art, it is different. But the little things that you learn about life that are important, the little bits of wisdom you get from your experience and making syntheses, are pretty much your own, unless you do transform it into art.

JB: In a recent letter to me, you quoted what Kline said about Brodsky: "Brodsky sees literature in general and poetry in particular as a mode of endurance, a way of facing and perhaps surviving the ghastliness of both public and private life." What attracted you to that statement?

NIATUM: I think that is one of the central problems of modern man, and particularly the artist, because he is the visionary, he's close to the mystic—these are dangerous terms, "visionary" and all that, because they are so abused, but I do think the artist is a visionary. There's the spiritual element and it's a very important one. But I think art gives the individual a chance to deal with the complexity and the chaos, a chance the average human being doesn't have. I think the gift is a survival instrument, tool, artifact, if you will, that he should revere because he is the only one with it. It can be a filter for the struggle and he has an advantage and that's why he should respect it. It's a gift. I believe it's a gift from the gods. It's something that everybody who goes into the arts has an opportunity to use or abuse. Since it is a gift that belongs to the universe, then you should respect it. I think one of the major problems with contemporary society is that we don't respect that gift. That's why I was so impressed with that quote, because it is true! It's a way you can strengthen yourself in resisting the chaos of the modern world, which is a problem, I feel, not of our generation only. However, in terms of the possibility of nuclear holocaust, we have a struggle to deal with that earlier man never had. Our responsibility, if we recognize it as such, is the salvation of the universe.

The Story Never Ends

An Interview with
SIMON ORTIZ

The interview with Simon Ortiz took place in his home in Albuquerque, New Mexico. The author of half a dozen collections of poetry, including *Going for the Rain*, *A Good Journey*, and *From Sand Creek*, as well as a collection of short stories entitled *Fightin'*, his work is characterized by a storytelling voice which has earned him wide recognition. It would be hard to find a poet better known by other American Indian people, who respond to Simon's words as those who gathered around the winter fires at night once did to the old time storyteller. It is no coincidence, then, that Simon's father was famous as a story-teller among his people or that when Simon speaks it is with that quiet strength one associates with the old tales.

I see two children
on the northeast shore
as I walk.
They are almost hidden
by a tall gray bush.
Leaning into a bit of wind,
I hear them murmuring.

I think of a storyteller
who listens for the wind
to bring things.

When I get to the children
I say, Hello.
And nothing else.
I sit on the ground
listening to their silence,
listening to the wind.

They have nylon lines
wrapped around beer cans.
They are catching nothing.
The afternoon has been hot.
The shadow from the bush
is beginning to lean
into the lake.
Maybe soon.
I say nothing more
and they say nothing more.

I want to tell them things,
And I think they would understand
I am the father of two children.
I smoke a cigarette
and carefully put it out
in the sand, and then I get up
and say, Goodbye.
And they say, Goodbye.
And I leave.

SIMON ORTIZ

When I leave and angle away
from the lake,
the shadows of sage and juniper
are long.
I think of a story, listening.

—Simon Ortiz

JB: That word "listen" is very important to you, isn't it?

ORTIZ: It is. You have to listen all the time. If I know anything it's because of listening. Ever since, I think, I was a child I would listen to everything. I guess I have trained myself to listen to three or four conversations at a time. I'm a great eavesdropper. My parents used to have to shoo me away because I would be listening. And my father used to tease me with a name when I was a boy. He would call me "Reporter." Listening to people, to wind, whatever is murmuring, has been an important part of how I perceive and how I learn.

JB: I also see a lot of interest in children in your work.

ORTIZ: I guess children appear in my poems as an expression of my own childhood . . . and also because they are the future, the generations down the road. It's also that I have three children and that I was a child once and probably am a child somewhere inside of me still. The image of the children is both the very real image and the possibility of the future.

JB: What was your childhood like?

ORTIZ: I grew up at Acoma Pueblo homeland in the small village of McCartys. And I grew up pretty normally as an Indian child. There were conditions, social and economic conditions, that resulted in our community being pretty poor. People, years and years ago, generations back, made their living by farming, but by the turn of the century agricultural occupations were no longer extensive or possible to make a living by. So people began to go for wage work. My father was a railroad worker. He was away from home quite a lot, working at jobs he could get like other men of the tribe.

My childhood was normal, but sometimes it was stressful. In Indian communities or other communities where people are poor, the conditions are sometimes not good. I mean people are poor, so they suffer. But, through it all, the sense of community, the sense of who I was as an Acoma person and what was meant for me to do as a person in that community, in my family, it was always there. Sometimes spelled out very deliberately. Other times, maybe most times, it was just the way you did things and the way you were. That was my childhood.

I lived there most of the time except a couple of times our family went to where my father worked, to Arizona and California. Then, when I was in the seventh grade, I went to boarding school—St. Catherine's Boarding School and Albuquerque Indian Boarding School—because the school at McCartys only went up to the sixth grade. After I was about nineteen, I basically left home to go to college, Army, work, et cetera. But you never really leave. You're always a part of there. Acoma is sixty-five miles west of here, Albuquerque, and all of this is really Acoma.

JB: There's a sense in your work of being firmly grounded in who you are and in the tradition from which you come. I find this is a contrast to many non-Indian writers who are always searching for who they really are.

ORTIZ: I think for Indian writers to be able to use their talent and their beings to write they have to know some *place*. And to know some place you have to *let yourself*. It's a choice, then, that you really have to make. Non-Indian writers, perhaps, don't have a choice partly because of their cultural upbringing. The kind of history this nation has and the philosophies developed in the Western tradition don't allow that. But for Indian people, who have grown up within an Indian community, something is there that insists you allow yourself that choice. That you make that choice. That you are affirmed for making that choice. Belonging somewhere is a real affirmation. Perhaps non-Indian writers are just not affirmed when they find a place or desire a place. I hope, though, this is coming for them. I can't really see any value in not knowing a place. You have to have it. Otherwise you are drifting. You remain at loose ends and you're always searching without ever knowing where you are or what you're coming to. I guess the background, the heritage of Native American people at least offers this opportunity to have a *place*. We have something that we can choose.

JB: Can you compare the education you received in a traditional sense with the education you received in Western-style schools?

ORTIZ: I was thinking of this as I was going across town to meet you. I thought about the experience one has within his family, his home, his community—which is the whole tribal group and its way of life. It's *experiential*. You live it, breathe it, talk it. You touch it. You are involved with the motion of it. When you're born you are of your family, you're of your clan, you're recognized, and you are given a very particular mission or duty to acknowledge this. You're then a living part of it, and you're always going to have to be aware of this. Otherwise your life has no value, no meaning, no real part of anything.

Then you go to school. I first went to school when I was about seven years old to learn to read and write English. You learn *about* it. You learn about life. You read about it, you study it, you solve problems. But it's not an experienced learning; rather, you acquire it. You learn it mentally. You learn mentally certain processes, procedures, and results, and it's something that's outside of you, almost. What this, of course, means is that you learn because you are alone. You learn not within a communal experience. You learn because you, as an individual, have solved this problem or looked in the dictionary and sought out the meaning of this particular word. That's one of the differences and it's an important difference. Now, of course, this other way of education is a part of us. I think some of it is good and some is totally useless. In fact, some of it is contradictory to what that other *experienced* life is—the gathering of knowledge into us and how we are a part of that knowledge.

JB: How does writing—which is basically a Western form—fit into the work of an American Indian poet?

ORTIZ: I look at it as just language itself. That's why listening is so important, because that's the way you learn language—listening as an experience. Listening not really to find any secrets or sudden enlightenment, but to be involved with that whole process and experience, that whole process and experience of language. That's the way we understand how we are, who we are, what we know, what we'll come to know. So, when I look at language in terms of writing, it's the language itself I'm concerned with, not that those symbols on a printed page have any meaning. What I try to be aware of is its core nature, the basic elements of language itself. So that writing is a furtherance or continuation of what is spoken, of what is emotion in terms of sound, meaning, magic, perception, reality. . . Native American people write of many, many things in various ways, in various forms.

There's something else you probably might want to ask with that question. What about the topics that have been chosen by Indian writers? I think we should write about anything and everything and that we should write a lot. In fact, we must! Indian people love knowledge and have always sought knowledge. I know that U.S. history, especially from the 1890s onward, has characterized Indians as not wanting to learn. But I know that knowledge and the seeking of knowledge is a main requirement for living a life that is fulfilling. Writing, using language—whether it's in speaking or singing or dancing or writing—is a way of using that knowledge. So we should write about everything. I don't think there's any real limit we should impose upon ourselves—as long as it's good. When I told my mother I was going to be a writer—I was about nineteen or twenty years old, around 1961—one of the first things she said to me was, "All right. As long as it's good!" I think she meant it on a very practical level—like don't write pornography or useless things. That was very good advice. My collection of short stories, *Fightin'*, is dedicated "For my mother—who told me years ago to write only for good things." l hope I have. But I think it's important to write in all areas of knowledge. We're talking mainly about poetry and fiction, but we need writers in history, economics, sociology, philosophy, any other areas of human experience.

JB: When did you begin to write?

ORTIZ: My first published poem was when I was in fifth grade. It was a Mother's Day poem. But I don't think I thought of it in terms of being a writer. But I loved to read. Once I learned how to read it was like a world just opened up in front of me, all around me. Again, I think this interest came about purely because of language. I would listen to stories when I was small. My life was always stories. I call them stories even though they may have just been talking about somebody—gossip, anecdotes, jokes. My father or my mother telling me what they did that day. My aunt coming over and crying over some problem. Or an old man talking about how it was a long, long time ago and how it wasn't anymore. I call these stories, whatever they may have been, because that's the way they were experienced. But when I learned to read, that was the thing that was happening, I guess. I began to read almost anything, whatever we had. We didn't get much reading material. My father would bring the newspapers home sometimes and I would get books from the school at McCartys. Comic books, whatever. I read whatever was available. It was, I think, at about twelve or thirteen that I was inspired to write something. The thing I wrote was song lyrics, song lyrics in the folk music tradition. My father was a railroad worker and would sing songs, working kinds of songs he had learned in his travels. He was a good singer in Acoma, in English, in Spanish, and in other languages like Zuni and some Navajo. He had a beautiful voice. He was an inspiration to me. So writing song lyrics was really my beginning, but don't think I knew anything about what a writer was. I think it was in high school when I first began to be encouraged. As a skill, I knew it was something that I was good at, to express myself. I started out writing stories when I remember first consciously thinking of myself as a writer. That was partly because of the romanticization that came about when I read stories by F. Scott Fitzgerald, Ernest Hemingway, Thomas Wolfe. My background in writing had a lot to do with that. I also kept a diary when I went to St. Catherine's Indian School, a journal—a secret one. Being away from home, family, clan, community, life is very tenuous, especially being a preteen. You're scared and you're lonely and you're homesick, and so writing is a way to reassure yourself. That was part of it, how I came to be a writer.

By the time I was nineteen I was very aware that there was such a thing as a writer, that he was a certain kind of person. Probably I had that ideal of the American writer in the Western tradition, that he was a special person, an artist, a creator, an individual fighting the world, sitting in a garret composing his great novel. I got rid of that idea later. That period in the '50s was also the beatnik era. I read Jack Kerouac and Ginsberg and others—mostly the San Francisco poets. Snyder, Phillip Whalen, Rexroth. Those poets were very important to me. I'm not sure why. By the time I was twenty-one, I think I was committed. I would tell people that I was a writer, though I was still slated for a real job as a mechanic or something that seemed more real than a writer. By the time I was twenty-two, probably about 1963, I knew that's what I wanted to do as a profession and a career, though I didn't publish anything until '65 or so.

JB: Someone told me you were a great runner while you were in school.

ORTIZ: That was my brother.

JB: Your brother was the runner? Are you sure?

ORTIZ: Well, I ran. Yes, I still run. I can do a pretty good five or six miles up the hill and back. I almost would say I'm a better runner than I was in school. For Acoma and most of the Pueblo people running is just something that you do. I remember my grandfather saying, "Get up in the morning before the sunrise and run." It's a way in which you stay healthy and when you're running you experience life. You know what your capabilities are. You're not just running by yourself— you're running *with* everything. I wasn't a great runner, though, compared with some Pueblo runners. There are some great ones. There have always been.

JB: I see the act of running tied in, then, to the things we've been talking about—the relationship of language, poetry, song to life.

ORTIZ: Yes. In fact, I have several notebooks that almost have only to do with running. When I lived in California, I would get up in the morning and go down to the beach. I loved that, to just run with the ocean life, being at the edges of the land and the great body of the mother water. You're right in there, running in between them. When I run, I try to think of songs or prayers or to think of where you've been, where you're going, what each step means, what the breath of air you're breathing means throughout your body, what part you have in all life. Running is like that, and I think that writing and language certainly relate to what the act and experience of running is.

JB: Running makes me think of those journeys which occur so often in your writing, especially in your book A *Good Journey*. Why is there all this traveling in your work? Is a poem like a journey?

ORTIZ: Yes, think it is. I use an image which is very prominent in my consciousness: *Heeyanih*, which is road. A road of life. A road of experience. A road of learning. A road on which one travels from the time he is born until he goes back into the earth. And there is a certain process. Another book of mine, *Going For the Rain*, has a preface which describes some of that process—the preparation, setting out on the journey, and returning. So, it's a motif that I am aware of throughout my work, particularly in the poems. I look at journeys as a way in which I can further experience knowledge. In my poems I note places that I've been, note people that I've met, conversations that I've had, experiences that I've had—some good, some bad, some absurd, some that shouldn't have been. But all this is part of that journey of setting out and returning.

You're always on a journey. Especially in this age. Indian people are much more mobile. I think Indian people were always mobile. Not that they weren't settled, not that they didn't live in one place and call it home, but that they didn't always just stay there all the time. The Pueblo people, Acoma people and others, have a mixture of various cultural traditions. Some are from Mexico, some from the seacoast. This means that people either came from the seacoast or we went to the seacoast. We went south to get the parrot feathers. There was a great movement of people who were on journeys, and it's still happening today. Some peoples, in the past, followed migrations of animals—buffalo hunters—and those were journeys. That didn't mean they were a homeless people. They belonged somewhere. But the journey was important. Those are some of the reasons I use the motif or symbol or theme of the journey in my work. I've been pretty much all over this United States and I've learned and I'm still learning a lot.

In 1970, I went looking for Indians. This relates to your

question about education. You know there are Indians because you grew up with Indians, you were born with Indian parents, but formal, institutionalized, United States education tells you in very clear, though sometimes subtle, ways that there are no Indians. When I was a kid we weren't Indians. The picture books showed you Indians were in teepees and rode ponies and there were buffalo. At Acoma there are no buffalo and there are no teepees. There are ponies, but they are usually ridden by Indian cowboys, ranchers, people who had cattle. Some, something tells you that you're not a real Indian. Then, further, the books tell you there are no Indians in California. They all just disappeared. They tell you the same thing about the southeastern United States. They went to Indian Territory or they just disappeared. Where did they go? There was this feeling that there were no Indians, that the Indians you were growing up with were not really Indians. So, by 1970, I really wanted to find Indians again. I wanted to debunk the myth of the "Vanished American" finally, for all time, for myself. It was important for me. I wanted to see for myself. I had Indian friends in the South I had met a couple of years before, Adolf Dial from South Carolina, a guy from the Seminole people in Florida, some people in Mississippi. I knew these people individually, but I wanted to see for myself. So I went through the South, starting out from Arizona, through Texas and Oklahoma, throughout the South: Louisiana, Georgia, Florida, South Carolina, North Carolina, Tennessee. Indians all over the place—all over the place! People who were mixed with black people, with white people, and some who were in communities who call themselves Indian. So, once and for all, the myth was cast aside. There are Indians everywhere! In one of my poems, I say, "You're damn right, there are Indians everywhere!"

JB: Do you think of traditional ways as being threatened or disappearing as anthropologists often say?

ORTIZ: I think the anthropologists are wrong. I think what they think is disappearing is their own version of Indians. Their own images of Indians, their own stereotype of Indians. One time up in Alaska, about six years ago, with the Before

Columbus Foundation, we were conducting a workshop with a lot of emphasis on the oral tradition. There was a man from England who has written about Alaskan native literature who happened to be in Anchorage at the same time. On the panel he said something that was absolutely horrible and clear evidence of how anthropologists look at native people. He said, "There are no more storytellers. The last one spoke to me and he died." I just blew up! There were several young Alaskan native writers, Eskimo, Aleut, and Tlingit, sitting across the table from him and he says that there are no more native Alaskan storytellers! What he was referring to, of course, is that version in their own minds, the stereotyped Indians on the ponies, setting upon a wagon train. That's what they bemoan the loss of. Their version is unreal, it always was. It's best lost. Indian culture is dynamic culture; it's not a static culture. If Indian cultures were static, they would be gone. But cultures evolve and they evolve creatively. The fact that there are Native American writers, singers, dramatists, screenwriters is clear evidence that this tradition continues.

During the 1950s, especially after the period of termination and relocation, there seemed to be a period of real depression. I think we were forced to relocate mentally as well as emotionally, breaking away from the spiritual nature of our lives. People left to go to school because we were told there were no longer ways in which you could make the right standard of living at your home, your foods were no good for you, you had to go to San Francisco and eat commodity foods or starve because you were becoming an American. You were really learning how to be a "full and equal" citizen in this United States. It was a period of real depression in the '50s. But I've seen the '60s and the '70s and now the '80s. It has been a real growth period, a real affirmation back to what our values were, back to what those values meant to us. More people, young people especially, began to participate in dances. More people wanted to learn, to protest, to stand up for their Indian rights, their Indian identity, their Indian lands, and human rights in general. It's been a healthy period.

JB: How do you define poetry?

ORTIZ: Yesterday when I was up at the Four Seasons Elderly Care Center in Santa Fe I defined it pretty well. I forget now exactly how I said it. It had to do with that idea I talked about before—experience itself. I was talking about song as poetry, song as motion and emotion. Song as the way in which I can feel those rhythms and melodies and how those things give me energy or make me aware of an energy that is really the life force, a part of all things that we are part of. Then I said that song is poetry and poetry is the way in which those images become possible for me to obtain, that become realized in me. I think I also said that poetry is the way in which we make the connections between words, the connection between all things. Poetry is a way of reaching out to what is reaching for you. Poetry is that space in between what one may express and where it is received. Where there is another energy coming toward you—it's that space in between. Poetry is stories, certainly, for me. When I began to write poems I wrote them mainly because they were stories. Prose fiction was really my first love. I think, basically, it still is.

JB: How can history be used in poems?

ORTIZ: You have to use history. History is the experience we live. I suppose "history" in the Western definition means something that is really a kind of contrived information to support the present case, the present United States existence and aims. That it is a super power because in the past the groundwork was laid and we were destined to be great. Well, we have to look at that. But when I use history I mean for this to happen: that history be studied, that history be acknowledged. We are a part of that, even though scholars, academicians, policy makers, corporations may not acknowledge it. Indian people built this country. Indian land, Indian labor, Indian resources built this land, and we have to say it, we have to study it, we have to look at what the motives were and are. We have to acknowledge that certain terrible things happened. If *they* don't want to say it, then we have to say it for them. If their writers, their historians, their sociologists, their artists, their minds don't want to accept it and say it, we have to say it for them.

To some extent, I think Indian people have not acknowledged this history, recorded history. For example, I know that it's
usually difficult for Indian people, Pueblo people particularly,
to acknowledge how we have been colonized, what those events
in colonization were. It's really *hard* to talk about. Some people even go so far as to say those things didn't really happen.
We were never slaves. Acoma was never burnt and razed. Yet
history records it. When Onate's men in 1598 burned and
destroyed Acoma, they killed people. They cut off their arms
and legs and they took people to Mexico as slaves. This is the
experience of all the Pueblos—and other Indian people. And
then they don't really acknowledge certain things later on. We
talked about education. That education was a device, a strategy,
a policy by which we would become separated from each
other, that we would be broken. And then we don't acknowledge that there was religious persecution. The reason why most
of the religion is underground, why foreigners are forbidden, is
just because of that, because you had to hide and people are still
hiding. For all public purposes, at Acoma and most of the
other pueblos there are no native religions because it's still dangerous. People don't see and they don't admit to this danger
readily. And why don't they do it readily? Because suppression
and colonialism are still in effect here. There are still those
pressures upon Indian people to hide and not to allow ourselves
to see. I think that the only way in which we will become not
scared anymore, not hide anymore, is to know the truth. And to
know the truth of history and to acknowledge it, use it to foster
knowledge, not only foster our own knowledge, but of non-
Indians and those policymakers who have used ignorance
against us and themselves. I know that when you tell the truth
it's a political act. When you acknowledge history and point out
such things as Sand Creek—maybe nobody wants to hear
about Sand Creek—it is a political statement and the truth. It is
necessary to talk about it because it's a part of how we are
going to live, how we are going to fulfill ourselves on that
journey. It has to happen for the national consciousness. If we
don't, there will always be a black blot, a dark spot in our

SIMON ORTIZ

minds. There will be a continued sickness if you don't talk about it.

JB: You think of your audience as not just Indian people, but American society?

ORTIZ: Someone in Farmington, New Mexico, asked me that question once. I told them my audience was really everybody. Of course, I direct it, based on certain information to certain issues. Those two books, *Fight Back* and *From Sand Creek*, certainly have to do with United States history. They point out conditions and circumstances and areas where people may be sensitive, and I address them to those people who *are* sensitive about those things. In *Sand Creek*, I address Indian people and non-Indian people. It's necessary to address Indian people. I don't say that I do it first of all for them or that it's my priority, but I think Indian people are the ones my words are intended for. That is partly because I am an Indian person and it's like I'm speaking to myself. I'm speaking *with* myself. Language is an important act which has to do with a reaffirmation of self, and so the poetry has that, is intended for that—to reaffirm one's self.

JB: It's been said, though, that poetry doesn't reach many people in the United States.

ORTIZ: Poetry is suspect all the time, I think. Poetry is suspect because this goes back to how art is seen, in general. Art is something extracurricular. Art is something you hang up on the wall. You can enjoy it only if you can afford it. That's a separation from reality. The idea becomes: I don't have time to appreciate art, I don't have time to appreciate poetry, much less write it. So, poetry doesn't reach an audience. It's suspect because it has nothing, supposedly, to do with your real life. Knowledge and intellect and aesthetic tastes are over here, removed, somewhere else, far removed. Poetry is not a part of our complete lives as compared to cultures where art is something that you do all the time, where language is important to you and you do it, you live it, you experience it, you communicate with it. I think the fact that Indian people are very artistic people—whether it's in certain crafts like pottery making or weaving or in music and drama—is evidence of art being a part of life and not separated. The act of living is art. But poetry isn't seen like that in United States society. Poetry is suspect and is only for weird and strange people like Bohemians, Hippies, lost souls, and Indians.

JB: So what do you do? Do you stop writing poetry and try to write things people will read?

ORTIZ: I think you should become more determined. One of the things I've done lately is sing more and explain that this is poetry. For some reason, with singing you can make a real connection in spite of people's hesitancy about poetry, in spite of people's curtains and walls. Those are not really their own walls, but learned behavior. The song breaks down or goes through those walls. You can even sing about those walls and people will understand.

I think, also, to reach a wider audience poetry has to be somehow more conscious of the tradition of its oral source. That's one of the ways. Luci Tapahonso's poetry works in that manner. I tried to pattern my book *A Good Journey* almost wholly on the oral tradition, intentionally. I wanted the word *as act*, you know, poem *as act*. As close to it in its written form as possible. If poetry is to reach more people, this is one of the things that has to happen. It has to be aware consciously and insistently of its source in the oral tradition. And singing probably achieves this in a very definite way.

JB: Your name is immediately recognized by Indian people wherever I go. in the United States. Perhaps that is because within American traditions there's still that sense of art, that relationship to art?

ORTIZ: And also to art as political statement. I think a lot of people know me because of that. I'm involved with events that are purely political in nature, which are statements about Indian people, lands, and what we must struggle for with all human people. The spirit of humanity is thriving and fighting back. I think a lot of people recognize that. The human spirit doesn't really stay in one place. In order to ensure a good future we must resist and have certain goals in mind. I think I suggest in *From Sand Creek* that we have to be revolutionary poets.

Decolonization requires it, decolonization as African peoples, as the people in Central and Latin America, are determining for themselves. For the past ten years I've looked to African writers—Chinua Achebe, James Ngugi—and Ernesto Cardenal and Pablo Neruda of Latin America. What I think poetry means in a social, economic, political, cultural context in other countries is applicable here. I think people recognize me as a poet, but also as a person who is speaking for himself and maybe, in a sense, for them.

JB: Yet even in your poems which depict those situations in which Indian people are brutalized, jailed, exposed to radiation, disenfranchised, I find a lack of obvious anger and bitterness. Why is this so?

ORTIZ: It probably has to do with seeing the value that language has itself. You have to say certain things and what you say should be worth what you're saying. Perhaps how we can best say it is to affirm ourselves. We're not lost. We're not just fighting for survival. We're going beyond survival. There is meaning beyond mere breathing and walking.

It may be just a different style of saying it. I have a poem called "Time to Kill in Gallup." First of all that means just time to spend there. Other times, I have been angry enough to kill Gallup! There are certain things that point out, that say implicitly, that there is such an anger. But again, as you say, it doesn't come out and say "I'm going to go down the street and I'm going to get Whitey and put his children to death or hit them over the head with a piece of cement." I think the bitterness and anger *is* said, but I think it's said in a different style. Also, with what I said about language being a means of affirmation, that's a quality we can't waste, we can't misuse. It's something we have to hold onto in whatever way we can. But there are angry poems I've written. The *From Sand Creek* poems are very understated. One of the poems says that they don't know that Indians are counting their bullets. Of course, that book ends with "that dream shall have a name after all."

JB: You and Peter Blue Cloud are known for using Coyote in your poems. Who is Coyote and why does he visit your writing so frequently?

ORTIZ: I think Peter writes more about Coyote than I do. I don't write much about Coyote anymore. Partly, I have a reputation for using Coyote because of A *Good Journey*, in which I used it a lot. Some of my early work used it. I have used Coyote mainly to demonstrate the oral tradition and its transformation into the present in writing—and the continuation of the oral tradition itself. Coyote *is* there all the time. I don't mean to say that I don't use Coyote anymore, absolutely. In fact, some of my recent poems have coyotes. Just the circumstances change. The events are different, but the figure is there. He may have a different name or she may have a different name, but the Coyote figure is there because they're stories. Coyote has, for me, been the creative act. The act of creation and beyond. It is something that never dies. It is a symbol, for me, of continuation. No matter what the circumstances are— like in the traditional stories when, through some mishap, maybe his fault, maybe another person's trickery, Coyote sort of dies. But something happens and he or she comes back. Maybe a skeleton fixer comes along and says, "Hey, I wonder whose bones those are. I think I'll put him back together." So he or she is brought back to life and the story goes on. The story never ends.

You *must* tell a story. That's the way I think it's possible for life to have meaning and for it to continue. That's how we have to maintain ourselves. And Coyote, for me, is a symbol of that continuation. Indian people have various totems—at least I've read so in anthropological journals. But there are figures— animals—who are relatives, who are our brothers and sisters in life through whom human qualities or lack of qualities speak. It's human aspiration and human desperation, but the human experience is spoken through some relative being; he may be Coyote or Raven or Bear or others that speak for us and with us. Peter Blue Cloud sent me some stories. I really like them because they are transformations of Coyote in present-day circumstances. This is evidence again that the story may be old, but you have to make it new in order for it to be useful now, in order for it to be healthy and useful in today's terms.

SIMON ORTIZ

JB: Talking of Peter reminds me that your name turns up in the poems of some other Indian poets. Mentioning each other's names seems about as common among Indian writers as it has been among the Beats or the New York School.

ORTIZ: It's a big family, it's a big family. Naming each other and sharing each other in stories and poems has to do with a tradition. And, it being a mobile society, we're really all over the place. That Indian I met in Flagler Beach knew somebody, an Archembault from South Dakota whom I'd been with in the Army. You talk to somebody in California and you talk about New York and you mention names. You go to Alaska, you go to Phoenix, and you see somebody who knows somebody else. "Yeah, he's my kinfolk," or "He's my brother-in-law." It's amazing. It's more than just the fact that you're in a group like the beatnik generation. It has to do with that relationship between Indian peoples, a sense of community. Every place I go I know somebody who knows somebody and usually in a very close way. It really helps us to maintain that community—not necessarily as writers, but as people who share a common origin and will have a destiny that is communal and important because it is interconnected. That's why my name pops up every now and then—not just because of some crazy episodes, which sometimes have been the case. It's healthy to recognize each other. You're not alone, you're not separated from what's happening.

Something That Stays Alive

An Interview with
CARTER REVARD

The interview with Carter Revard took place in his office at
Washington University in St. Louis. Just before we talked, he
walked me around the campus, pointing out that it was part of
the site of the great St. Louis Exposition, showing me the place
where Geronimo was exhibited in chains for tourists. We had
started walking from his house, not far from campus, where
he'd played a tape of his grandmother speaking in Osage. He
nodded as he listened, translating the words.

Carter Revard is a tall, even-featured man with a precise
way of speaking which reflects both his years at Oxford and Yale
and, somewhere in the background, the resonance of voice
which one hears in Oklahoma—his birthplace. Because of an

auditory disorder, he wears hearing aids in both ears which, as he adjusted them, would sometimes cause a high-pitched noise to fill the air. Despite, or perhaps because of, that hearing disability, he is one who listens closely and well to others, and he pointed out and named the birds as we walked under the trees of the campus.

His office was piled high with books and papers, a sort of ordered disorder with Chaucer texts mixed in with American Indian anthologies. It was a warm spring day and as we talked, through the open window behind me, came the sounds of birds singing.

Dancing With Dinosaurs

1.

Before we came to earth,
        before the birds had come,
they were dinosaurs,
        their feathers were a bright idea
that came this way:
            see, two tiny creatures weighing
two ounces each keep quiet and among
        the ferns observe bright-eyed
the monsters tear each other
and disappear; these two watch from the edge
of what, some fifty billion spins
        of the cooling earth ahead, will be
called Nova Scotia; now with reptilian
whistles they look southward as
        Pan-Gaea breaks apart and lets
a young Atlantic send its thunder crashing
up to the pines where they cling
        with minuscule bodies in a tossing wind,
            September night in the chilly rain and
they sing and spread
        small wings to flutter out above
surf-spray and rise to
                twenty thousand feet on swirling
                    winds of a passing cold front
        that lift them over
the grin of sharks southeastward into sun
and all day winging under him pass high above
        the pink and snowy beaches of Bermuda flying
through zero cold and brilliance into darkness
        then into moonlight over steel
    Leviathans with their mimic pines that call them down
        to rest and die,
            they bear southeast steadily but the Trade

Winds come and float them curving
　　　back southward over the Windward Islands and
　　southwestward into marine and scarlet of
　　　　their third day coming down
　　　　to four thousand feet still winging over
　　　　　Tobago, descending till
　　　　　　wave-wrinkles widen into the surf of
　　Venezuela and they drop
　　　　　　　　through moonlight down to perch
on South America's shoulder, having become
　　the Male and Female Singers, having
　　　put on their feathers and survived.

　　2.

When I was named
　　　　　a Thunder person, I was told:
　　here is a being
　　　of whom you may make your body
that you may live to see old age;
　　　now as we face the drum
and dance shaking the gourds, this gourd
　　is like a rainbow of feathers lightly
　　　　fastened with buckskin
fluttering as the gourd is shaken.
　　The eagle feathers I
　　　have still not earned,
　　　　　　it is the small birds only
whose life continues on the gourd,
　　　whose life continues in our dance,
　　that flutter as the gourd is rattled and
　　　we dance to honor on a sunbright day
　　　　and in the moonbright night
　　　the little girl being brought in
　　　　becoming one of us
　　　　　as once was done for me,
for each of us who dance.

The small birds only, who have given
their bodies that a small girl
        may live to see old age.
I have called them here
    to set them into song
who made their rainbow bodies long before
    we came to earth,
    who learning song and flight became
  beings for whom the infinite sky
and trackless ocean are a path to spring;
    now they will sing and we
  are dancing with them, here.

—Carter Revard

REVARD: "Dancing With Dinosaurs" appears in the volume *Ponca War Dancers*. It came out first in *Denver Quarterly* magazine in 1980. Several stories came together for this poem. In 1979 the St. Louis Gourd Dancers that I belong to danced, at the invitation of Bob and Evalyne Voelker, at the bringing into the Indian community of their granddaughter. Evalyne is Comanche and she and the others had taught me as a gourd dancer, so I was happy to honor her and her granddaughter in the dancing. At the time I was reading, in *Scientific American* and *National Geographic*, about the tracking of bird migrations between Nova Scotia and South America, how small birds— particularly black-and-white warblers—fly nonstop for three days and nights over the Atlantic at heights up to 20,000 feet and more. Those are two of the stories in the poem—our dancing and birds migrating. The third is that of the dinosaurs turning into birds, and how they learned to put on feathers and fly and sing. A fourth is that of the continents drifting apart to let the new Atlantic Ocean between, and I imagined the birds as having migrated before the ocean came between their spring and autumn homes.

When I wrote the poem I was up in South Dakota where Norma Wilson had invited me to talk about Indian Literature and the sense of place. I had been meditating on Osage naming ceremony and songs in relation to our places on earth. It hit me that we as Indians survive as the dinosaurs learned to do, transforming ourselves by learning the songs and putting on the feathers, traveling between red and white ways (the "powwow circuit" is one version of this, summer dances up on the Rosebud, winter dances in school auditoriums). I had to be thinking, too, when I looked at our old Osage naming ceremony, of our Creation stories, how we came to be a people, came from the stars and made our bodies of the Cardinal Redbird or the Golden Eagle, powerful and friendly beings whose ways we follow as we follow suns and stars, to live into a peaceful and serene old age.

JB: Themes of transformation are important not only in that poem, but in a lot of your work, aren't they?

REVARD: Yes, in order to survive the Indians did like the dinosaurs. They put on their feathers and became something else. You can talk about paths, Indian paths. How is it the birds learn the path around winter into spring? They never see the winter, those little birds up there. They start in Nova Scotia and fly over the Atlantic for the three days and nights and come down in South America. They go from the end of one summer to the beginning of another. That's why I say they make *the infinite sky*—which has no limits—*and the ocean* with no track at all—a path to unending spring. So what I'm talking about there is the way in which you transform yourself out of something which is an obsolete and extinct species, according to a lot of notions of Indians that non-Indians have, into something that stays alive.

JB: And that mention of "leviathan with mimic pines" . . . ?

REVARD: Yes, the ships that the birds want to come down on. Once they come down they seem not to want to make it again. They can't lose that height. They have to make that passage without eating, without drinking. It reminds me a lot of the vision quest. If you read *Black Elk Speaks* and *The Sacred Pipe*, crying for a vision, you see going out and seeking for a vision. My uncle Gus went through that. So, in the title poem "Ponca War Dancers," I talk about him as having gone and found his vision. That's what I'm referring to.

JB: Why was it that you had your own naming ceremony?

REVARD: That was given me in September of 1952. My grandmother, my Osage grandmother Josephine Jump, was from the traditional Osage people. This is my stepfather's mother. My own father was part Indian, but my mother and he split up when I was young. My stepfather, Addison Jump, is almost fullblood. They say about fifteen-sixteenths. His mother, my Grandma Josephine, arranged for me to have the naming ceremony. They did it in part because I had been given the Rhodes scholarship to go from Oklahoma to Oxford. So this name was kind of an honoring thing, and I felt it was important to me, it made a huge difference. I came up from Tulsa to Pawhuska. In the Legion Hall there was a lunch at the beginning of the whole afternoon, and I was introduced so the people saw me as *this being, here*. All the people participated. It wasn't just a lunch where my grandmother gave me the name. It was the whole day, and in the evening there was a dance and a hand game. The hand game is optional, not always part of the old ceremony. I have a book, John Joseph Mathews's *Talking to the Moon*, which my folks gave me that night and which a lot of people signed for me. It has the signatures of all the people there that day. A lot of them, Mr. and Mrs. Wakon Iron, for example, are names the oldtime Osage people would know. Paul Pitts was the chief then when that was done.

JB: For you this represents a strong connection to what some might say is only a small part of your blood ancestry?

REVARD: Yes, I grew up in a family with four brothers and sisters who were half-Osage. My older brother, Antoine, from another father is quarter-Osage. So I grew up in a mixed family. My twin sister and myself were the least Indian of the whole group. When we would go and visit Grandma Jump, my great-grandmother Grandma St. John was still alive. She lived into her nineties and could remember back into the time before they came down from Kansas into Oklahoma in the 1870s. She didn't speak much English at all. She died about 1941. I was nine or ten when she died. She came and sort of made a little feast in 1938 when my sister was born at our place out at Buck Creek. I remember the meat pies and stew. I didn't know at the time this was traditional food. Indian grandmothers are special. All grandmothers are special, but the Indian ones always seem to be so delighted with the kids. Neither she nor grandma was a demonstrative pick-up-and-hug type, but the expressions that would come over their faces when they would watch the kids running around. The kids might be doing something naughty or mean, but that wouldn't bother them. There were times when they might say, "No, no. Don't do that."

My grandmother, Josephine, did not speak English till she was about ten, when she was then taken and put into a convent school for about three or four years and learned to speak

CARTER REVARD

English there. So she spoke with an accent, but she spoke it pretty well. She was taken and married then. Her family arranged the marriage with Jacob Jump—whose picture is in *Ponca War Dancers*, right there. He looks almost exactly like my Uncle Kenneth. That was taken around 1915. They were married around 1908 or '9. Jacob died after the war down in Texas. That flu epidemic got him.

JB: I notice in your writing certain rhythms and even line breaks, which might seem random, but to me indicate a possible influence of the rhythms of Osage language or speech patterns.

REVARD: I hadn't thought about that, to tell the truth. But what I was doing in the dinosaur poem—"when I was named/a thunder person I was told . . ."—that is almost straight out of the ceremony there. I hadn't thought why I break it there in the middle but I wanted it, as I recall, to say "when I was named," as a separate unit. I didn't intend it to be an Osage-sounding thing, but when I wrote poems for, with, and about the Indian things, a person does have in his mind the way the Indian people talk. If you remember hearing the recording of my grandmother that I played this morning, she didn't speak English till she was ten and has that Osage accent. There is an Indian way of talking. It is as much pitch and cadence as it is particular words and pronunciations. So, when I am talking or have people talking in the poems which are Indian, I have a feeling that comes through without my thinking about it. If I were to think about it, I probably would mess it up.

JB: How early did you begin to write?

REVARD: The school people make you do certain sorts of things. I wrote stories and poems for the teachers and in the eighth grade they were pleased with the stuff. Mr. Loyd, the teacher in my one-room school at Buck Creek, praised that sort of thing. In high school I had some very good teachers, Miss Corbin, Miss Paxton, and Miss Wentz, who liked what I wrote. When I went to college I thought I would be an engineer because I didn't know what else would make a living for me. They kept insisting you had to pick a career, and I had no family background in education at all. None of my folks had gone to college and only my mother and one uncle had gone to high school. My uncle Kenneth, on the Osage side, had gone a little while to Notre Dame. So I had no advice or knowledge on how to do this. So I wanted to be an engineer, when I got out of high school. Over the summer I decided I wanted to do some writing, and so when I got down there I tried to sign up for creative writing. I discovered, though, that the creative writing program wouldn't do anything for me, and I wanted to learn about the literature. If I learned about the literature I could write on my own. And that took care of that. I never took a creative writing course, but I was always starting to write.

Once I got in college, I got stuck with the idea that I would write in traditional form. I picked a sonnet of Keats's and decided I would write a sonnet. Now I know what a sonnet is supposed to be now, ta-da, ta-da, ta-da with an iambic rhythm, but that sonnet of Keats, "Bright star, would I were steadfast as thou art,/Not in lone splendor hung aloft the night . . ." and so on. You try to scan that stupid thing and you're in very serious trouble. I tried to write a sonnet that had its stresses placed where his were and it drove me nuts! I got one written, though I hope to God it's not around anywhere. I was crazy about this girl or that girl, and this was a sonnet about one of them. It was a sonnet imitating Keatsian rhythm, and it really persuaded me I had better find out something about metrics before I did this again. There were things like that. But I was trying for the most part to do some kind of rhyme. Before I got over to England I had written and gotten into a literary magazine that was started up by a friend of mine, who was a much better writer and much brighter, knew more about literature than I did at that point, Ken Rucinski, who went later and taught at Smith College. I got into the literary magazine, thanks to Ken. When I got over to England I was still trying to write but I didn't tell people because I didn't want anyone messing with it. So I got stuck. I was trying to read everything and know everything. And I was trying to get as much as possible into the poems—which really got them—well, the volcano was just plugged. There was no way to get all of that out without a big explosion. So I wrote quite a bit in terms of lines but nothing that was any good. It was all the wrong kind of stuff. I was trying to get Hindu stuff in, medieval stuff, Latin and Greek and Italian and French. I was using metaphysical conceits. I think my ideal poem at that time was ten lines which would take two weeks to explain and, generally speaking, six weeks to write. (laughs) So I did a lousy job. The only time I got to a point where I could write well was when I was teaching at Amherst after I got through the Yale graduate school. I discovered one morning, up in the Emily Dickinson house, that I could talk about something. This was the coyote poem. I've talked to various people about this. It's the first poem in my book. It's a sonnet, eight and six. That year, '57–8—I was twenty-six—I was renting the top half of the old house where Mabel Loomis Todd, a friend of Emily's who edited some of her things and, I guess, her brother's mistress, had lived. That's the house that had the old camphor chest of Emily Dickinson's poems in it for a long time. I was in the top half of that house and it was raining, and I woke up in the morning about 6:00; it was starting to get dawn. I heard that dripping sound, but my ears were going out on me: I've got what is called osteosclerosis. It made me think, "Gee, I can hear that now and that's a sound I really like. I wonder how long I'll be able to hear that." Here was the rain coming down and I was thinking of the second rain off the roof and all the different sounds. Then I remembered when I was about fourteen, hiking up Buck Creek Valley, up toward Doe Creek there. There were some huge boulders up there with cave-like places under them, and we used to like to climb on those. We were up there and a thunderstorm came up, so we got under the rocks. Under there were things we took to be coyote sign. I was thinking about this because I was remembering the sound of that rain coming when I was a kid, and I remembered all the different sounds there. Then I said to myself, what would it have been like for that coyote, the pups especially? They're born, they've been around a little while, then all of a sudden the first thunderstorm comes. And, I said to myself, how much better they hear than we do. And then I said, but coyotes *sing*. They don't just get the sound in, they get it *out*. They bring it in as that sound and they put it out as coyote music. So I said that was how I would do this. I would have the coyote talking. Now once I took the coyote's voice that freed things, and I could talk Oklahoma and I wasn't trying to talk Oxford and I wasn't trying to talk Yale. So, a lot of times when I read I start with that poem because I think that is what got my voice out.

JB: It was the thunder gens or clan which you are initiated into and thunder is a transforming force in that particular poem, isn't it?

REVARD: That's right. And I hadn't thought of that when I was writing it, at all. I hadn't thought of the coyote as a special being. The beings that I thought about as my particular ones were the raccoons. As a kid I thought they were the cleverest, and I would see the tracks. I even hunted them some. But I never thought of the coyote other than as something that was trying to get our calves or our chickens. Then, when I needed the Oklahoma voice, the coyote gave it to me. So it isn't the beings you pick, but those that come to you, who give you earth-time.

JB: What is the Oklahoma voice?

REVARD: Well, it's for me the rhythms and sounds of Osage County people, Indian and others. I had a sense of it as going with stories and families and people living around each other—and not thinking in terms of literary language. It was talk about things that mattered, that were part of their own lives; just the way people actually sounded when they were talking about things that mattered to them there. I can still imitate, but my voice has lost that except when I go back there. I don't sound Oklahoma now unless I'm directly reading one of the things from back there. I lost that in the second year in Oxford. The first year I didn't get messed up but the second year I did, and from then on I've been different voices. The sound in *The Coyote*, though: I had been trying to write iambic or dactylic, but here, I said, I'm going to have six beats, a variable number of syllables, and it's not going to rhyme. So this is going to sound like what I remember people sounding like. So I heard it, as talk. What I'm doing is probably what Keats was doing, moving the stuff around as he wanted it. Probably there's a basic beat in here, but I don't know that I could now get six actual

CARTER REVARD

beats per line out of it. "The thunder waked us" I did mean to wake us in more than just an "I've been asleep" sense. I think I had in mind from the beginning something more. But "The storm made music when it changed my world . . ." is a line I didn't get until the end of the day. I had thirteen lines, and I realized if I had another it would be a sonnet. And that last line turned out to be the theme of the whole thing, it summed it up. I just thought that what the coyote did was to hear all these terrific sounds of the thunder and the rain drops coming, and then, as he listened, he would hear the stream start singing. Now there wasn't any actual stream near those rocks—I had to imagine that—but when you're a kid you build dams on little streams. Of course, inevitably, the water will build up and over-run your dam. If you've built a good-sized mud dam, when the water starts to spill over, at first the sound is kind of high-pitched, but, as the dam gives way, the whole pitch shifts in-credibly to a lower gurrrggg sound. So I was thinking of what the coyote heard first as the stream swelled, then when a rock dropped and the whole pitch changed. That means, all of a sudden, the coyote realized there was music and not just sound there. The transformation from sound to music or from just hearing to organizing the hearing is what I talk about. I needed the speech, I needed the sound. Getting from the mass of talk to this fourteen-line poem was like the coyote getting the music there.

JB: There are a number of American Indian writers of your generation—Scott Momaday, Ralph Salisbury, and your-self, for example—who were schooled in very strict Western literary traditions and who began writing work not terribly "Indian" in form. Yet, as you've matured as writers, you've moved away from "Western forms" and gone back toward those Indian roots.

REVARD: I think for me that was it. I always had in mind that what I was going to do was work with where I was, where I was from, the whole business of *place*. As I went from Oklahoma, through my college days, over to England, I found people were incredibly unknowing. I had been, even up in Kansas, among people who didn't know there were Indian reservations and didn't know what Indian people there were. I went to the wheat harvest in '49 and I was shocked to hear from people up there they'd never heard of Osages. So, as I kept running into this all around, I kept being more and more determined that some way or another it was time for people to see that there were people *here*. That's kind of stayed the same, but finding the voice, finding the rhythms, finding the sounds that would be that place's voice and my voice, that is what I think I was doing without knowing what I was doing when I finally got into this coyote thing. Some of the poems that aren't in here, in *Ponca War Dancers*, were also in that form. Then I tried to do a lot of narrative in the blank verse form, but even there I was determined it was going to sound like someone from Oklahoma telling the story. Scott Momaday—although I didn't read Momaday until later as he wasn't published till I was well into my own medieval studies—in what he says in "The Remembered Earth" and in *The Way To Rainy Mountain*, I see very much the resemblances there in these things he's had to do to kind of come back to where he is. He's got a double thing— he's got New Mexico *and* Oklahoma. There's no place else that I write about, though I've been to the Isle of Skye and have written a little bit about Greece.

JB: How do you characterize the landscape of Oklahoma?

REVARD: Where I come from, in fact, is the cross-timbers and Flint Hills country. I grew up in a valley with hills and trees all around, but the valley itself is mostly bluestem meadow. Out to the west is the great prairie, and over to the east past Bartlesville is prairie and plains again. I was in hilly, rolly country something like the Ozarks with shallower hills. It's also a country of slow streams and muddy streams, not the spring-fed streams of eastern Oklahoma. Winding, slow bottom land. A land of sandstone hills and limestone prairie, and blackjack oak and hickory, redbud, dogwood.

JB: I see the land strongly in your writing, both your poetry and that essay you've written on the prairie. It reminds me a bit of a book by the Osage writer, John Joseph Matthews.

REVARD: *Talking to the Moon*. Matthews is a wonderful writer. I have his book *Wah Kon Tah: The Osage and The White Man's Road* on the shelf here. *Talking to the Moon* was published by Chicago Press about 1945, and it's just been put out again in paperback by Oklahoma. I read him after I had done my own beginning writing. I was twenty-one. I didn't use his book in the way I wish I had until later. He's certainly got a sense of it and he helped create Oklahoma for me. I always thought of it as being an extremely beautiful area, but since there was nothing written about it directly, you always felt, "Well, I know it, but they will never understand it or recognize it." Then, when I saw he'd written about it, it made a considerable difference.

JB: Matthews, like several others of his generation, has been almost completely neglected.

REVARD: I think so. I think in Oklahoma he's well known, but he is treated as an Indian writer and not taken out and treated as a novelist and a thinker in the general community. I think "neglected" is a good word. His book on the Osage has a double reputation. On the one hand, it is regarded as very poetic; on the other hand, there are anthropologists who are dubious of it. Myself, having looked at LaFlesche and other people he uses, and having written stuff of my own about the naming ceremony and so on, I think he's accurate. If anything, what I would fault him for is not giving enough credit to the Osage creativity and philosophic capacity. But I think the anthropologists faulted him for giving too much credit. Garrick Bailey at the University of Tulsa, who did his dissertation on Osage culture and who knew Matthews quite well, gives him credit for the achievements there—though Bailey has a different patterning and clan organization than either Matthews or LaFlesche. I haven't taught *Talking to the Moon* and I haven't taught *Wah Kon Tah* in my current American Indian Literature class. It is a problem of having enough time. What we're doing with American Indian Literature is comparable to teaching a course in all of English literature in one semester.

JB: You raise an interesting issue when you say Matthews is only known as an "Indian writer," not as a fine novelist or essayist in the tradition of Thoreau.

REVARD: I think that is what he wanted very much.

JB: How do you deal with this particular double standard?

REVARD: I don't deal with it very well, I'm afraid. I got over to Oxford in 1983 and I took *Earth Power Coming* to Blackwells and said, "This is a very pretty book, you should put this in." And they said, "We don't take books like that. Our anthropology things don't do very well." There is that whole assumption about where you put Indian literature. Wendy Rose and other people have talked a lot about this and rightly so. It's a double bind, too. Indian writers want to be known as Indian writers but also as writers and not just as Indians. We're pleased and proud about being Indian, but we don't want to be kept "on the reservation." There's always that question, "Are we good enough outside the reservation?" That is the implicit thing which makes Indian writers so angry about bookstores and the rest. That is the attitude. Other writers are fiction writers. These are "Indians." It gets you published and keeps you from being read. Almost as bad as being labeled a "poet" on Wall Street, I guess.

JB: There is, in much Indian writing, a different sense of time, isn't there?

REVARD: I think with so many of the tribal things, there's just a sense that these things operate according to events that are important. For example, in the Osage dances, there are certain things in the year, in Pawhuska, that matter to the Osage, which matter very differently to the non-Osage and those outside. Things are set in relation to those. Obviously they involve anticipating getting ready for the dance—your clothes and those things—so it isn't as though it's just a matter of things occurring outside themselves. That's one way. There are seasonal ritual times which have nothing to do with the outside world. The other thing is that a lot of the cultures have notions of previous worlds. With the Osage, we come from the stars. When I got into that naming ceremony and studied it, there was just a different sense of the formation of a human being. I think for a lot of Indian people that sense of a ceremonial time—which is their arrangement of the year that differs from the others—that sense in those ceremonial things connects not merely to what we did last year and what we're going to do next year but to what people have done time out of mind and to the beings who were here and from whom we come into the world. I'm talking of the Hopi and the others, but, when you look at the other myths and legends, you see it's true of all the different people. I'm sure it's true of the Abenaki.

JB: Yes, the sense of emergence, of connection, of cycling and circles. I'm sorry, by the way, that the transcription won't show the hand motions you've been making. The circling, the raising up, the pointing inward.

JB: You're both a writer and a teacher of American Indian literature. What directions do you see for the future?

REVARD: I couldn't possibly say about American Indian poetry. I couldn't have predicted Louise Erdrich's coming along. Her writing is different from Jim Welch's, though it resembles it more than Momaday's. There are other good Indian writers, but she seems to fit right with those two as very strong. Looking at *Jacklight*, the poems in there, I couldn't have predicted that book, either. She's combined a kind of mythical dimension with a naturalistic "this is the way Indian people live" sort of thing. She's combining things in ways I like to see done. I think, if we're lucky, we'll have writers come along who know the mythical dimensions and are very, very honest, fiercely, unflinchingly, almost meanly vivid about the tough parts of Indian life and will not neglect either dimension. Which really means I'd like to see American Indian writing be a standard for this country. I'd really like to see this country judged by its Indian people as a civilization and brought into the dock and given its good and bad marks. Until you do that you don't have an epic, and I'd like to see the Indian people do the epic for this part of the earth. It may not be just one person, it may be a bunch of people. That's what I'm looking for.

What I have really been concerned about is why the poems are dead in terms of influence and power and why the prose is not. Reagan may say he doesn't read much fiction lately, but novelists still have a kind of power that poets lack in terms of the impact. What I want is to see reestablished, for the uses of language and imagination that we call poetry, some of that which has gone off into what we think of as novel and fiction. They need not be separated. But poetry has lost *story.* I don't think it has lost it so much among American Indians, and I think there is more hope there. Among American Indians, blacks, Chicanos, and others, they write because it matters like hell. You can say God is Dead, but not if your people have just been wiped out. If you are Job, you're in a different place. You can afford to worry if culture has finished itself only until you are the victim of it. I think the victims, those who need a deity, *have* the Deity. To those who absolutely *need* the powers above and below and past and future, the powers offer themselves, not forever but through certain windows in time and place. Coyote came over to me in 1957 and made the world musical instead of noisy, the black-and-white worlders brought me a vision for the dances here in 1978. When I look at writing that has only a personal vision, only stories of the writer in an eternal present, I feel what's missing, why poetry lost its audience. Virgil needed Homer and Venus, Dante needed Virgil and Beatrice, we need Uncle Coyote and Grandmother Spider, Grandfather, Stone Boy . . . The stories have gone out of a lot of poems, along with the rhymes and the song, the tears and laughter, but this is less true in every case with those we call minority writers. There's a live force and strength there. You can hear in the poetry of American Indian writers a genuine felt concern for what is going on. It's different from just wanting a literary career. I know the same ego stuff gets hold of all of us, but I feel there's a more genuine concern for the human condition and people who I know are suffering things among these groups. The stories have got to come back, the sound stuff, the rhyme, all of that, more of it and better.

The Bones Are Alive

An Interview with
WENDY ROSE

My first meeting with Wendy Rose took place more than a
decade ago in California while she was still writing under the
name "Chiron Khanshendel." It was a name she had given
herself as she sought for some truth other than what she'd been
shown by the white urban culture which, as a person of mixed
race, was only partly her own. Some of the poems in her first
collection, which Greenfield Review Press published, hinted at
the power inherent in her voice. The illustrations she did for
those poems made it clear why she would develop into one of
the most sought-after illustrators of American Indian books of
poetry. In addition, she would become one of the few Native
American anthropologists and, with her as yet unpublished bibliography of writings by Native Americans—stretching from

the 1700s through the present century—an important chronicler of American Indian creativity. Included in every major anthology of Native American verse and the author of eight published collections of her poetry, she was teaching at the University of California in Berkeley (her alma mater) at the time of our interview.

The interview took place at Paula Gunn Allen's apartment in Berkeley. Wendy is an intensely serious person—though not slow to laughter—and her well-informed anger showed in both the poem she chose to read and in the directness of her responses.

Truganinny

"Truganinny, the last of the Tasmanians, had seen the stuffed and mounted body of her husband and it was her dying wish that she be buried in the outback or at sea for she did not wish her body to be subjected to the same indignities. Upon her death, she was, nevertheless stuffed and mounted and put on display for over eighty years."

—Paul Coe, Australian Aborigine Activist, 1972

You will need
to come closer
for little is left
of this tongue
and what I am saying
is important.

I am
the last one.

I whose nipples
wept white mist
and saw so many
dead daughters
their mouths empty and round
their breathing stopped
their eyes gone gray.

Take my hand
black into black
as yellow clay
is a slow meld
to grass gold
of earth

and I am melting
back to the Dream.

—Wendy Rose

Do not leave
for I would speak,
I would sing
another song.

Your song.

They will take me.
Already they come;
even as I breathe
they are waiting for me
to finish my dying.

We old ones
take such
a long time.

Please
take my body
to the source of night,
to the great black desert
where Dreaming was born.
Put me under
the bulk of a mountain
or in the distant sea,
put me where
they will not
find me.

The Bones Are Alive   251

JB: In his preface to your collected poems—*Lost Copper*—N. Scott Momaday said that it was a book, "not made up of poems, I think, but of songs." Would you agree with that distinction of Momaday's?

ROSE: In a subjective sense, yes. I don't think that the poems are literally songs the way that we usually understand the term. But I use them the way that many Indian people traditionally use songs. They, in a sense, mark the boundaries of my life.

JB: So that would be one of the differences between your poetry and traditional English verse.

ROSE: Yeah, I think so. My perception of them. The way that they function in my life.

JB: Is there any other way in which they're song?

ROSE: I think oftentimes that audiences feel them that way. People sometimes call them songs when they talk about them but, I don't know, I couldn't speak for what it is they are perceiving. I couldn't really put words in their mouths to try to clarify what they mean, but people call them songs and maybe they're feeling the internal parts of it the way that they have meaning for me.

JB: In that same introduction Momaday also spoke of your language, saying, "it has made a clear reflection of American Indian oral tradition." Do you perceive a relationship between your writing and that oral tradition?

ROSE: I would like to but I would have to say probably not too much. I think that there are some important differences, and I think that my particular work probably leans more toward European-derived ideas of what poetry is and of who poets are than Native American in spite of the subjective feeling that I have of the way that the poems are used in my life. There are some important differences, one of which is the sense of self-expression. The need to express the self, the need to make one's own emotions special and to explain it to other people, I don't think really exists in most Native American cultures. And I think that is an important component in my work.

JB: Are there any other distinctions that you'd see or any other things that you would use as definitions of the American

Indian interpretation as opposed to the Western interpretation of the use of song or poetry?

ROSE: One way that I think perhaps they do function, and I hope it doesn't sound like I'm contradicting myself too much, is that gradually the various Native American communities are re-establishing links with people using oral tradition. And sometimes this extends even to those of us who use the printed word and who publish. So in recent years I'm finding that the poet is right there with the orators and is speaking in council. I'm finding more and more that, when there are gatherings of Indian people, there will be poets who will contribute to what's happening. This was lost for awhile because of the effect of the white man's education in that for a while Indian people were discounting the contribution that poets were making in the same way that the white man discounts the contributions of his own poets. But increasingly I think that contemporary poets in Native American communities are coming to be valued in a traditional sense even though the work itself might be different.

JB: What are the roots of your poetry? How did you personally become a writer—and then a writer who identifies so strongly with your Native American roots?

ROSE: That's a complex question. Influences as far as poetry are concerned—they're just so multiple. Perhaps the earliest one that I remember is Robinson Jeffers, who of course was not an Indian poet. But some of the first published poetry I was ever exposed to was his and that was important to me, and I think it was my first sense of being able to think in terms of putting a poet in a landscape that's familiar, because the area that he was writing about was where I grew up—the northern California and central California coast. That was an early influence. Other influences that were fairly early—I figured out that it was okay to be an Indian and a writer at the same time probably, as many of us did, through the influence of Scott Momaday. His getting a Pulitzer prize in fiction made a real difference to us because I think so many of us had assumed that no matter what our individual goals might be, we had to somehow choose between fulfilling the goal and having any degree of integrity as Indian people. Whatever influences there are from Native American culture—I'm being fairly careful not to cite tribe here because I was born and grew up at a distance from my tribe, so I'm trying to deliberately separate myself from saying Hopi literature or Miwok literature—my community is urban Indian and is *pan* tribal. But whatever Native American traditional influences that might be in my work, I don't know if I can pick them out individually. I missed out on a great deal by not being exposed to tribal traditions as a child. In the city I was exposed on the one hand to a great many traditions and on the other hand to nothing that was really complete. I don't know. Perhaps that's an unanswerable question. I know that there was also this: in terms of identifying as an Indian writer, that was partly and perhaps mostly a function of how literature is published and distributed in this country—which is that in this particular instance if you are of a minority group and you are a writer, you are simply not allowed to do anything other than be a minority writer.

JB: I think this would be a good place to ask you this question. In your poem "Builder Kachina," you have these lines—"a half breed goes from one-half home to the other." And of course *The Halfbreed Chronicles* is the name of the collection you just read that first poem from. That word "half-breed" seems to be very important to you. What is it? What does that mean?

ROSE: Well, again, I have to answer on at least two different levels. One is the obvious thing of being biologically halfbreed, being of mixed race. I was in a situation where I was physically separated from one-half of my family and rejected by the half that brought me up. And in this case it was because of what there is in me that belonged to the other half. The way that a lot of us put it is you're too dark to be white and you're too white to be Indian. James Welch expressed it well in *The Death of Jim Loney* where Jim Loney answers someone who says to him (to paraphrase), "oh, you're so lucky that you can have the best of both worlds and choose whether or not at a given moment you will be Indian or you will be white." And he says, "it's not that we have the best of both worlds, it's that we don't really have anything of either one." I think that's really a very true statement. You don't get to pick and choose but rather you're in a position where you have no choice whatsoever. I was in that situation where the white part of my family had absolutely no use for any other races that came into the family. The white part of the family had no use for it. The Indian half is in a situation where, among the Hopi, the clan and your identity comes through the mother, and without the Hopi mother it doesn't matter if your father was fullblooded or not, you can't be Hopi. So that left me in that situation. The first years of writing, perhaps, the motivation from the very beginning was to try to come to terms with being in that impossible situation. But then maturing as a person, halfbreed takes on a different connotation and that's where *The Halfbreed Chronicles* are coming from. Now *The Halfbreed Chronicles* depict a number of people, and genetics doesn't have a great deal to do with it. For instance, the poem "Georgeline" is relating to people who are a fullblood Lakota family. There are other people who are depicted in *Halfbreed Chronicles* who would not be identified as halfbreed. People who are Japanese-American. People who are Mexican-Indian but spent their lives as sideshow freaks. People like Robert Oppenheimer. You don't think of these people in the same sense as you usually think of half-breeds. But my point is that, in an important way, the way that I grew up is symptomatic of something much larger than Indian-white relations. History and circumstances have made half-breeds of all of us.

JB: Then maybe you wouldn't be offended by my bringing in something I just thought of . . . a quotation from Matthew Arnold. He described himself back in the Victorian era—"one half dead, the other powerless to be born." There seems to be, as you see it, a world dilemma not just of people of mixed Indian and white ancestry but of the modern culture that we find ourselves faced with.

ROSE: Yeah, and I think that the point does come out in *The Halfbreed Chronicles* because one of the responses that I get is from people who are genetically all Caucasian, or all black, or all Indian; people who are genetically not of mixed race come up to me afterwards and say I know just what you mean by those poems. I feel like a halfbreed, too. So I know the message is getting through. We are now halfbreeds. We're Reagan's halfbreeds and Dukmejian's halfbreeds.

JB: I find it interesting, too, that that poem, which I cited a quotation from, is called "Builder Kachina" and there is no Builder Kachina as I understand it.

ROSE: No there isn't.

JB: But you have imagined a Builder Kachina?

ROSE: In a sense, yes, but based on things that my father really said to me. The poem is based on an actual conversation that I had with my biological father, which is the Hopi side of the family. And the conversation was basically my going down to the reservation and sitting down and talking to him and presenting the situation to him at a point where I was in crisis over it and saying what can I do because I can't be a member of a clan, because I can't have your clan? You're my father not my mother, I'm not entitled to any land or any rights or any privileges on the reservation. Yet, at the same time, my mother's family doesn't accept me, never has, probably never will, because of the fact that you are my father. So what do I do? His answer to me was, "Well, sometimes it's difficult, sometimes people don't point out to you what your roots are but your roots are on this land, and you just have to stand here yourself on this Hopi land and build them," and from that came the imagined person of Builder Kachina. I've invented lots of Kachinas. I hope that it's not thought of as being too sacrilegious. But I've invented Kachinas that go into outer space. I've invented Kachinas that are in the ocean and a lot that have appeared in the visual arts. This particular one appeared in poetry.

JB: Yes, the Kachinas are something I find occurring again and again in your writing. What are the Kachinas to you? How would you define them. I know there's a definition on strictly a tribal level . . .

ROSE: Well, there's no real agreement even on that definition because they aren't any one thing. They're not strictly nature spirits and they're not strictly gods. They're not strictly ancestral spirits and yet they're all of that. They are spirit beings who grow and evolve and have families and live and possibly die. Humans have to communicate with them and have to relate to them. One way that they can be thought of is if you think of the entire earth as being one being and we as small beings living on that large being like fleas on a cat. The Kachinas in a sense are aspects of that cat that are communicating with us. This is one way to look at it.

JB: I see then in your "Builder Kachina" a sort of balance emerging out of that duality and chaos caused by the conflict between two forces which seem to be mutually exclusive. The two worlds of the European Indian. The two worlds of the two parents that you describe in your own life.

ROSE: Well, of course, one thing also is that the Hopis say that the Europeans being on this continent is something that isn't all that important in the long run, that eventually the continent will be purified. The evil parts of that influence will be gone, and things will eventually return as they were and the cycle will continue. This is really only a small thing that we inflate with our own self-importance into meaning more than it does. For those of us who are in my position, I don't know whether I'm supposed to be saved with the Hopi or wiped away with the whites.

JB: Thinking of evils, I've seen several particular evils singled out numerous times in your writings. Let me give you some examples—the California missions, the attitude of anthropology toward Indian people in general, cities and the concept of modern cities. Why do you choose those particular targets?

ROSE: I don't see cities as evil first off. I don't think there should ever be more than, at most, a couple of thousand people living in one unit. I think beyond that it's impossible to be governed with any sense of integrity when you don't recognize each other and have no obligation to each other. But in any case I don't see cities as evil per se. They're evil for me. I'm not able to adapt to living in cities even though I've tried. I become intensely uncomfortable in cities and I see cities destroy people that I love. As for the other things, the California missions, of course, were not a spiritual endeavor; they were an economic endeavor. They had more to do with the conquest of a new bunch of natural resources by the Spanish crown than they did with the saving of souls. The point behind incarcerating Indian people there was to have a cheap labor force, a slave force if you will, to make blankets and to make pots and pans and various kinds of things for the Spanish settlers, for the colonist. Also to have everybody in one place so there wouldn't be any Indian people to stop settlement and there wouldn't be any Indian people out there able to act on their own. So they were incarcerated. Reduced is the actual Spanish term, the *reducciones*. It killed off some incredible number, something like during just ten years alone, in the early nineteenth century, the California Indian population was reduced by some incredibly high number like 80 percent. It was because of a combination of disease, of unnatural living conditions, and the punishment for running away. What a lot of people don't realize is there were a number of revolts against the Spanish mission by the Indians. But they don't tell you this in the museums. In fact, the museum right here in Oakland paints a ridiculous picture of the missions with the happy little natives making baskets in the shade of the adobe with the benevolent padres walking around rattling their rosaries. That just is not the way that the missions were.

JB: And then there is the attitude of anthropology toward the Indian people. It seems linked to what we were just talking about with the missions.

ROSE: In fact there's a saying that—I've heard versions of this saying from people from Africa, from Australia, from New Zealand, various American Indian people—first comes the explorer, then comes the military, then comes the missionary, then comes the anthropologist, then comes the tourist. Actually, though, as you know, in one sense it's ironic that I should be so highly critical of the field since at the moment I am teaching lower division anthropology at a junior college. However, I'm teaching it in an unorthodox way, and I hope I don't get in too much trouble for it. But, yeah, anthropologists have certainly been one of the main targets of some of my anger, probably stemming from my intimate association with them as a Ph.D. student in anthropology at Berkeley which contains both the best and the worst. I've run into some incredible racism in that department and, as faculty now, I see my Indian students running into situations that are even more bizarre than things I had experienced because it's becoming increasingly okay among the general population to become racist again or to express the racism that was always there. It's no longer cool to try to be tolerant or understanding or liberal or even to recognize that America is a plural country. There are a number of anthropologists, however, who are very, very good people and are sensitive to these issues. Unfortunately, I think they are still in a minority probably because anthropology is part of a European-derived institution run by the white male power structure. So Indian people along with many other kinds of people—women, gay people, people from fourth world nations and from third world nations—all of these people are coming into anthropology now and changing the face of it. But it's very slow because that old guard of course is still there. A lot of Indian people are going into anthropology just to become super informants and don't realize it.

JB: In part two of *Lost Copper* there are some poems that were originally published as a chapbook under the title *Academic Squaw: Reports to the World From the Ivory Tower*. I'm always interested in titles. What did you intend by it?

ROSE: Well, obviously, it was intended as ironic. The publisher inadvertently left off a postscript that was supposed to be on the title page. I think in *Lost Copper* they did put the postscript in. In the chapbook it originally appeared in, it was inadvertently left off. It explained how the term "squaw" is used in a purely ironic sense. That was really an important thing for two reasons. One is because "squaw" is an offensive term, regardless of its origin. It is now and has been for many, many years an offensive term much like "nigger" or "spic" and has been degrading not only in a racist way but in sexual ways as well. Because the image of the so-called "squaw" is a racist and a sexist image. So, on the one hand, people who are aware of that might otherwise think that I was using it without any kind of clarification, that it was just as if it were part of my vocabulary. As if I really saw myself that way. And people who don't know any better might assume the same thing not realizing there's anything special about the word. I have run into people who simply think that that is a word for Indian women. Just like they think that "papoose" is a word for Indian children and so forth.

JB: Or "pickaninny" is a word for a black child.

ROSE: Yeah. I know a man who thought that Jewish men really were called Jewboys and would call people that to their faces in total innocence because that's the only way he had ever heard Jewish men referred to. Things like this. So there is an innocence there in one sense but there's also a maliciousness.

I meant the title, of course, in a completely ironic sense and the poems were written in that context because I had just spent two years as an undergraduate at the University of California at Berkeley in anthropology and had just, in fact, by the time the book came out entered graduate school as a Ph.D. student. So the book encompasses experiences at both the graduate and undergraduate level as an anthropology major. And, as I was saying, there were some racist things that happened. There were a lot of things that happened that I had to come to terms with. There were many times when I almost dropped out. I spent the entire first year at Berkeley, in my junior year as a transfer student from a junior college, huddling in a corner in Native American Studies drinking tea and trembling. This is all coming from somebody who was raised in a relatively urban area right next to the university all her life, so I can't imagine what it must be like coming from a reservation, from someplace that's very different from Berkeley. The poems were written as a survival kit, really. And in fact one of the most pleasant things I have ever done was the day that the book came out from Brother Benet's press, I went and stuck copies of it in all my professors' mailboxes.

JB: Why have you chosen to enter that Ivory Tower world? That world of the academic?

WENDY ROSE

ROSE: I'm not in the Ivory Tower. I'm a spy.

JB: Okay, good. You say also in the poem "Handprints," "in this university I am a red ghost."

ROSE: I'm a spy.

JB: A spy. Great.

ROSE: Don't blow my cover.

JB: Oh, no. No, we'll never tell. (laughter) Let me move on to another area, Wendy. How has your art affected your writing? You now have a reputation both as an illustrator and as a writer. In fact, in some of your poems you speak directly of that world of art in rather magical terms. Sometimes you even speak as a mother speaks of her children. I'm thinking of the poem "Chasing the Paper Shaman," or the poem "Watercolors." How has your art affected your writing and how do they work together?

ROSE: I can't imagine them really working apart. Nobody bothered to tell me until I was an adult that there was anything wrong with being both a visual and a verbal artist. I think that's the only reason why that isn't the case with more people, and I think that's the reason why it is the case for so many Native American people. Look at the number of Native American authors who illustrate their own work and who illustrate other people's work. There is a tremendous number. There is nothing unusual about it among Native American people at all. There's a tremendous percentage of writers who do so in contrast to the non-Indian writers, where it's very seldom the same person who does both. But the way I think of it—now I don't really know where the poems or where the art comes from, I don't know where the images come from—but however they come or wherever they come from is like communicating with a person. It's a whole person. That person shows you things and has a certain appearance but also tells you things. So as you receive images, they are either received through the ear or through the eye or through the tongue and that's just the way it feels.

JB: Another thing that I find different about your work and also that of a number of American Indian writers (as compared to the typical writer of the traditional English mold) is your attitude toward death. Death seems to be very important in your work. Why is that so?

ROSE: I don't know. I never really thought of it as being important to the work. I guess if I really think about it, yeah, I've got a lot of bones rattling around in there. I guess there's a sense of feeling—sometimes I feel like I'm dead. Like I'm a ghost. Similarly, sometimes I feel that I'm alive but there are ghosts all around me, so that's part of it. But as far as the symbols go, of things like the bones for instance, I think maybe it's argument against death. Maybe what I'm saying is that the bones are alive. They're not dead remnants but rather they're alive.

JB: You have these images of returning to the earth and images of bones. These don't strike me as morbid images, as they would be in, say, a poem written in the eighteenth century in England.

ROSE: Well, you know, the rocks are alive and all the components of a tree, for instance, live. A pine cone falls down from the tree and it's alive. It carries the life of the tree in the seeds that are in the pine cone. And I think the parts of the body must be the same way. The brain isn't all there is to human life. The consciousness that's inside the skull is not all there is.

JB: There is a poem of yours in *What Happened When the Hopi Hit New York*—"Cemetery, Stratford, Connecticut"— with these lines: "I know that what ages earth has little to do with things we build to wrinkle her skin and fade her eyes." You also say "I have balanced my bones between the petroglyph and the mobile home." These different things, balanced in some way, seem bound to lead in a different direction than just finality.

ROSE: Well, that's really what we are, isn't it? We're bones that are just covered with flesh and muscle. The part of us that is spirit is just a component that is part of that entirety. We are parts of the earth that walk around and have individual consciousness for awhile and then go back.

JB: I could see someone looking at your poems and saying these are evidences of bitterness, of hopelessness, of a very dark perception of life.

ROSE: That's what a lot of white people see in them. Indian people almost never do.

JB: As a matter of fact, I'm playing the devil's advocate because I think there is a question we may have to address. What do you think American Indian poems have to offer to non-Indians? Are there problems of perception like this which may make them inaccessible to the non-Indian reader?

ROSE: I don't know. I want to say no, they're not inaccessible because it's a great frustration when people won't review our work, for example, in the usual professional way, saying that they don't have "the ethnographic knowledge" to do it or something. That's a frustration to me because some of us—people like Joy Harjo or any number of other people that actually have M.F.A.s from prestigious writing schools—come out and then find that they're being told that they're culturally too obscure to be reviewed as a real writer. That isn't true. I think that a person does need to stretch the imagination a little bit, perhaps, or to learn something about Native American cultures or Native American thought systems or religion, or philosophy. Just a little bit. But I don't think any more so than you need to become a Kabbalistic scholar in order to understand Jerry Rothenberg. This is a plural society and all of us have to work at it a little bit to get the full flavor of the society. I have to. Boy, do I have to work at trying to understand the Shakespearean stuff! I have students in my creative writing classes who are into Shakespeare and write tight verse and rhyme and do it very, very well. They're not doing it unsuccessfully, but I have to really work to understand where they're coming from. Just simply that what they're expressing is a dominant cultural mode in this particular country is not sufficient reason to say that that is the only way it should be. If I have to work at understanding that stuff, then I don't see why they shouldn't work a little bit to understand mine.

JB: Hasn't it often been the other way? Literary critics have celebrated the greatness of someone like James Joyce because *Finnegan's Wake* and his other books are so complicated.

ROSE: If they think the complication is individual rather than cultural, then they really love it, sure.

JB: Good point.

ROSE: But if they think it's cultural then they think that we're insulting them somehow by expecting them to understand it. That we're asking them to go out of their way. And of course, really, we're not asking any more of them than they ask of us when we pick up books in this society and read them.

JB: What images, aside from those I've already mentioned, seem to be recurrent in your poetry?

ROSE: I think I have a lot of female images. A lot of times I think that just talking about rocks or trees or spirits, where there's no real reason to put a gender on them, I automatically tend to make them female. I think that's something I've noticed more recently. Themes? I've been writing a little bit of science fiction poetry lately about colonizing other planets. But of course it's not from the colonizing viewpoint, it's from the viewpoint of the people on the planet. But that's sort of off the wall. I don't know, it's pretty hard to see the themes in your own work. I'm always amazed at what other people see in them. At first I don't believe them, and then I go back and I read it again and I realize they were right. Sometimes.

JB: Which of your already published poems express most clearly for you what you want to say as a writer?

ROSE: As a writer? Oh, boy! Of the published poems? I don't know. I guess the things that are most current in my mind or the things that I most want to say are what I've said most recently, which usually isn't published at that time. I guess what I want to say is bound up in *The Halfbreed Chronicles*, and as of now few of them have been published. One of the major focal points in *The Halfbreed Chronicles* section was published in *Ms. Magazine* in the June 1984 issue. That's kind of exciting to me to finally get a "pop" readership.

JB: Is this the one about the woman who was . . .

WENDY ROSE

ROSE: The woman in the circus, about Julia Pastrana, yeah. They're publishing that one.

JB: That's a particularly powerful poem, to me, for any number of reasons. I heard you read it about a year ago and was very moved by it.

ROSE: Well, it's about a Mexican Indian woman who was born physically deformed. Her face was physically deformed to where her bone structure resembled the caricature of Neanderthal man that you sometimes see in museums. She had hair growing from all over her body including her face. So she was Neanderthal looking and hairy in visual appearance, but she was also a graceful dancer and a singer in the mid-nineteenth century. She was a very young woman. She was billed as the World's Ugliest Woman and put on exhibit, where she would sing for the sideshow. The poem is not just about the exploitation of her being in the circus but is like a step beyond that. It's an ultimate exploitation. Her manager married her and it was, presumably, in order to control her life in the circus. She believed that he loved her, though, and really, what choice did she have emotionally? When she finally had a baby, the baby looked just like her. The baby had all the same deformities, but also had a lethal deformity of some kind and died just shortly after birth. Then she died a day or two after that. And her husband—and here's where the real *Halfbreed Chronicles* come in—her husband had her and the baby stuffed and mounted in a wood and glass case and continued to exhibit them in the circus even though she couldn't sing anymore. There was just something about the horror of that which in *The Halfbreed Chronicles* is coupled with the poem called "Truganinny" about an Aborigine woman who happened to be the last living Tasmanian native.

Truganinny went through a similar situation. She had seen her husband stuffed and mounted by the British museum people as the last Tasmanian man. She asked her aboriginal friends to please make sure that when she died that didn't happen to her. She wanted to be buried way out someplace where they couldn't find her body or just be thrown into the sea or something. And they tried but they were caught, and so she was actually stuffed and put in a museum too. Just like her husband, as the last specimen of a Tasmanian human being. The two of them together, Julia and Truganinny, represent the ultimate colonization. They're not side by side in *The Halfbreed Chronicles*. They're separated slightly by a couple of other poems. But they're intended as a pair in a sense because of the similar fate and because the circus treatment of the so-called freaks is another kind of colonization. Then too, what is it that happens to the colonized if not being made into a sideshow? So that's basically the point behind the Julia Pastrana poem and also the Truganinny poem. We are all in that situation. We are all on display that way.

JB: There seems to be a growing consciousness on the part of American Indian women, both as writers and as people speaking up. In the postscript poem in *Lost Copper* you say "Silko and Allen and Harjo and me—our teeth are hard from the rocks we eat." What do you have in common and why choose those particular women?

ROSE: This will sound sort of funny, I guess, but I could have gone on and named many, many more Indian women writers. I chose those particular ones because I felt that they were fairly well known, that a reader who has been reading very much contemporary Indian literature will immediately recognize the names. I feel that they have all made strong statements about being Indian writers, both in their creative work and peripheral statements in interviews or in articles that they have written. The actual fact of the matter is that I stopped after naming just those ones because that was the meter of the poem. (laughter) What I intend there is to go on with the list—and Hogan and northSun and Burns and Tapahonso and so on and so on. They're in there.

JB: What is exciting about their work for you?

ROSE: I know that when I read their work it makes chills go up and down my spine in a way that really most other people's work doesn't. It's not just Indian women's work, but work by minority American writers, by writers of color in general. It very often has that effect on me. When I read work that does have that effect on me, it is usually by such a writer. I tend to be terribly bored by the writing of white academic poets. Hopelessly bored. I really don't care how many sex fantasies they had watching a bird on a fence. If you'll pardon the phrase, I think in academia, in English departments, that the writers are just masturbating.

JB: Of course there are also the writers who are putting on headdresses.

ROSE: Yes. Yeah. There are those, but even they are not generally in the academic situation. Even they are a little too peripheral for academe.

JB: Um. Those white poets who would be Indian as you title that one poem of yours.

ROSE: Yeah. And of course that needs some clarification too because it's widely misunderstood—the whole thing about the "white shaman" controversy that Geary Hobson and Leslie Silko have addressed themselves to, that I have addressed myself to. It's widely misunderstood. It's assumed that what we're saying is that we don't want non-Indian people to write about Indians. That's not it. Many non-Indian people have written beautifully and sensitively about Indian people. Even in persona. The difference is that there are those who come out and say that they are Indian when they are not, in the case of some. There are those who come out and do not claim to be genetically Indian, but who do claim that what they write is somehow more Indian, or more legitimately Indian, than what real Indian people are writing. There are these people who claim to be what they're not. They claim to be shamans and it's impossible to be a self-declared shaman. Your community has to recognize you. And we know that the word is Siberian but we also know what is meant by it in popular usage. Yeah, it's directed toward these people and it's a matter not of subject matter but of integrity in the way in which the subject matter is approached.

JB: You've been editor of *The American Indian Quarterly*, taught Native American Literature, worked on a major bibliography of Native American writing. What do you see happening with American Indian writing today?

ROSE: Well, I think that there is a small nucleus of people who are primarily associated with the Modern Language Association who are acknowledging that it is a legitimate field of study. People like Karl Kroeber and LaVonne Ruoff and Andrew Wiget, Larry Evers. There's a whole crew there. These are people who have been interested in it all along. But through their influence and the influence of Indian writers who have become involved in that end of the writing business, the scholarship end of it, it's becoming better accepted in academe. But it's very slow as in the fact, for example, in the University where I taught (Berkeley), we were just recently told by the English Department that they would not hire people to teach anything about American Indian literature "because it's not part of American Literature." So, it's very slow. But it's gradually happening because of people like the scholars that I named . . . although it took a long time even to get to where Indian people could go speak for themselves, where Indian writers could go deal with their own work even in the Modern Language Association because the tradition for so many years was that the white scholars would sit around and talk about the work without having the writers there to deal with it themselves. That's changing.

JB: You feel then that the current small popularity of American Indian contemporary writing is more than just a fad? That its message is large enough to go beyond this moment?

ROSE: The message is large enough to go beyond the moment—whether anyone is listening or not, I'm not sure. I think that the way that a lot of us started, particularly those that are around my age in their thirties and forties, was on the basis of a fad. We were brought into it, many of us, before we were mature enough as writers, really, to do it. We were brought into anthologies and so forth, and our work was exposed to critical masses, so to speak. But I think that maybe if we work hard enough at it that we will somehow be able to make sure that it is incorporated into general American literature. And here I'm not just talking about Native American, I'm talking about Afro-American, I'm talking about Asian-American, I'm talking about Chicano and Puerto Rican, Indochinese. All of the various cultural elements have their literature that becomes modified and yet retains its cultural integrity as they come into America. Or as they leave the reservations and go into the cities that are in America. I think this is going to happen, whether anyone is out there listening or not, it's going to happen. And I know that the Indian communities respect their writers more now and that's the part that's really important to me. I would much rather be respected by the Indian community through my writing than to have my books reviewed in the *New York Times*. I really would.

JB: Last question. What would you say to young American Indian writers now in the way of advice?

ROSE: Like that old civil rights song says, don't let nobody turn you 'round. Although they probably never heard the song. (laughter)

For What It Is

An Interview with
LUCI TAPAHONSO

The middle one of eleven children, Luci Tapahonso was born in Shiprock, New Mexico, where her family still lives on a farm three miles from the town up on the north mesa. Speaking of her early years in the biographical statement in her first book of poems, *One More Shiprock Night*, published in 1981 by Tejas Art Press, she says, "I know that I cannot divide myself or separate myself from that place—my home, my land, and my people. And that realization is my security and my mainstay in my life away from there."

After attending school at the Navajo Methodist Mission in Farmington, thirty miles from Shiprock, she graduated from Shiprock High School in 1971, served in 1974 on the Board of

Directors of the Phoenix Indian Center, and took part in a training program for investigative reporting at the National Indian Youth Council. In 1976 she began studying journalism at the University of New Mexico but switched her major to English after studying with Leslie Silko, graduating in 1980. Currently a graduate student at the University of New Mexico, she is pursuing a doctorate in Modern Literature. Married to Earl Ortiz, an artist whose drawings illustrate her first volume, she is the mother of two daughters, Lori and Misty Dawn.

This interview took place at the home of Geary Hobson in Albuquerque, New Mexico.

Hills Brothers Coffee

My uncle is a small man
in Navajo, we call him little uncle
      my mother's brother.

He doesn't know English but
      his name in the white way is Tom Jim
      He lives about a mile or so
      down the road from our house.

One morning he sat in the kitchen
drinking coffee
      I just came over, he said
      the store is where I'm going to.
He tells me about how my mother seems to be gone
everytime he comes over.
      Maybe she sees me coming
      then runs and jumps into her car
      and speeds away!
      He says smiling.
We both laugh to think of my mother
      jumping in her car and speeding.

I pour him more coffee and
      he spoons in sugar and cream until
      it looks almost like a chocolate shake
      then he sees the coffee can.
      Oh, that's the coffee with
      the man in a dress, like a church man.
      ah-h, that's the one that does it for me.
      very good coffee.

I sit down again and he tells me
      some coffee has no kick but
      this one is the one.
      It does it good for me.

I pour us both a cup and
>   while we wait for my mother,
>   his eyes crinkle with the smile
>   and he says
>   yes, ah yes, this is the very one,
>   (putting in more cream and sugar.)

So I usually buy hills brothers coffee
>   once or sometimes twice a day
>   I drink a hot coffee and

>   it sure does it for me.

        —Luci Tapahonso

JB: Do you recall when you first started to write poetry or when it began to become an important force in your life?

TAPAHONSO: I don't remember writing poetry when I was a child, but I remember being fascinated with words and stories, books, at a really early age. I remember taking phrases that I really liked and just sort of memorizing them and repeating them to myself. So it was more a fascination with words than with poetry as a form of writing.

JB: At what time in your life did you make a connection between poetry and the possibility of your own writing?

TAPAHONSO: Not until really late. I was twenty-two or twenty-three. But I had been writing for years before that, since back in high school and I just had all this poetry. . . and I always say that I finally "came out of the closet." (laughter) When I first met Leslie and she taught a class, she was really excited about my poetry. It was really a step for me to show people because it was such a personal thing.

JB: A number of the younger American Indian writers have been influenced by older writers who have encouraged them. You say that Leslie Silko was a big influence in making you take your own work more seriously or making it public?

TAPAHONSO: Yes, yes. And then she helped me. My first short story was published, and it's true I would not have done much probably if I had not met her. I didn't take what I was doing to be something important to the general community.

JB: Memory seems to me to be very important in your work. Can you talk a bit about remembering and its relationship to your poems?

TAPAHONSO: A lot of my poems are memory poems—things that people have told me or memories from my own life, from my parents and from the stories they have told me. And I think that it is really important because the past determines what our present is or what our future will be. I don't think there is really a separation of the three. We have to have the past in order to go on and to survive to draw strength from. You know, a lot of times we think that we are in an awful situation or that this has never happened to someone before. Yet people will tell us of instances where something similar or even worse has happened to someone. Part of the whole thing about story-telling is that it is done in order to draw strength and in order to go on and see ourselves—not as separate from other people in terms of experience and problems and those sorts of things, but to see ourselves in a community and to see a unity with other people, our own family or our relatives, just the community at large.

JB: The idea of community also seems crucial to you as a writer and strikes me as being of great importance to most Native American writers. Yet I see a movement away from community on the part of the European American, a movement inward toward self and personal psychology while American Indian writers are moving in directions which seem to be toward others, their community, the Earth. Why—if you agree with me—is there such a difference between the European American and the Native American poet?

TAPAHONSO: I think that is true, though there are also people going into all kinds of encounter and self-help groups, going to all types of integration training and that sort of thing and that only happens because, maybe, they don't have a community and we're fortunate that we do. We don't see ourselves, I think, as separate. We don't see ourselves alone and, probably, non-Indian poets see themselves as that way—as by themselves—and so they're trying all sorts of things in order to feel secure. We have a whole past, our own history. You know, we *are* our own history, we *are* our own people. We don't see ourselves as separate from that. I think that we're very fortunate in that way because it helps us, it helps the way we think. It's real hard to explain to someone—this whole sense of community because, you know, it's a way of thinking, a way of feeling, actually, and that's hard to explain to someone who doesn't have that.

JB: American poetry—still talking about the European side—seems to be characterized very often by a longing and a loneliness, a sense of being on the edge of a kind of wilderness, a frontier, and trying to force that into a mold which you create on your own. That idea of changing the natural world, of changing everything around you to reflect your image, also

LUCI TAPAHONSO

seems to be counter to the vision of the American Indian writer. The title of your new book, *Seasonal Woman*, seems to indicate a strong relationship to natural rhythms. Am I correct in seeing it that way?

TAPAHONSO: Yes, you are. I also think that this loneliness, this clamoring for some sort of security, leads a lot of people to become "Wannabes," who suddenly decide that this is it, that they're going to be Indian and that sort of thing. That's always struck me as funny, but then it's sad in a way. I don't know, I can't imagine what it would be like to be in that position. To me, I think it would be like Hell, to be without family, to not know where you came from, not know who your relatives are, and to not be able to have a place and say, "This is, now this is who I am or this is where I came from." I think that it must be really scary.

JB: Geary Hobson told me the story of Adolf Hungrywolf visiting him when Geary was working at the Living Batch bookstore. Adolf Hungrywolf is a German who has been writing about the Blood people. He showed up at the bookstore wearing a huge choker, dressed in buckskins with his long dark hair in braids. I think it was dyed black and his skin was also dyed brown. He greeted Geary with a German accent. (laughter) There are cases like that of people who want to be something they're not. John A. Williams, who is a black American writer, said to me a few weeks ago that nobody in America seems to want to be who they are. Everybody wants to pretend to be somebody else. Yet it strikes me that you are correct—the American Indian writer doesn't want to be somebody else. They may be aware of the mixture of ancestry—a lot of people have both European and Indian ancestry. But I don't feel it is the kind of dividing force that it is for some people.

TAPAHONSO: I think that in Indian cultures when there was first contact with Europeans it was a hard thing to deal with. But then, through the generations, I think that it's become easier to deal with and people have accepted and adjusted. But then it's never really been in any Indian culture to disown one of their own because that's not the way we are. And yet you see that with a lot of Anglo families when the child is, maybe, half black. They can't deal with it. The love they might have for the person who is involved with this person of another race cannot overcome that sort of thing. And yet with Indian families, I think, the family overcomes any division that might occur. I think initially there's always sort of a shock, but that passes and people are accepted and the children, especially, cannot be held to any sort of disgrace because of something somebody else did.

JB: Wendy Rose has a series of poems she calls "Half-breed Chronicles." She sees it as a very complicated issue. That idea of disowning a person who was of mixed blood or calling them a "halfbreed," which is an insult, is very different from relating to them as one who knows something of two cultures and is able, therefore, to speak between and help people to relate to each other as human beings rather than as separate races. Is a more humane or human relationship to the person of mixed blood truer of the Indian way?

TAPAHONSO: I think so. I think also there's more toler-ance within one's tribe or one's family than with somebody of another tribe. So the antagonism Wendy Rose or somebody else has felt has probably come from someone of a different tribe. I think that people who are of mixed ancestry probably value their Indian ancestry more than somebody like me. It becomes dou-bly important. Sometimes, maybe, that sort of creates a conflict between people who are fullblood and people who are half of different tribes. . .

JB: Many of the people in the "first generation" of Amer-ican Indian writers in this part of the century who have become well known are people of mixed blood. But there is a new generation, a new wave of American Indian writers coming— let me take you as an example—who are not in that particular category, who are not people who have been pushed out into the world, divided between cultures, and then must work back toward that Indian culture. I wonder why it is that people such as Momaday, for example, who talks of his mixed ancestry in *The Names,* or Leslie Silko, or Wendy Rose have been some of the first out there to make those statements?

TAPAHONSO: I don't know. It's been said that it's a matter of identity. It's a matter of proving their identity. Leslie's book *Ceremony* can be looked at in that way—and in a lot of other ways—that it is a novel of finding one's identity and one's place. But I don't know. It's something that I'll probably have to think about—why that happened. I think that it's a good thing that that happened because it opened the way for the rest of us. I think that I would have been writing anyway because I was into journalism, investigative journalism. So I would have probably been doing a different kind of writing for a living and always doing poetry on the side because I wouldn't stop doing that. But I don't know if I would have ever taken my own poetry seriously.

JB: Then what happens to one person makes it possible for it to happen to another, opens the way?

TAPAHONSO: Yes, there's a whole circuit. There's not really any of that sort of competition.

JB: The idea of song seems central in your writing. Your poem "Listen," begins "Once in high school, a friend/told me: Don't marry a man who/can't sing. There's something/wrong if a man can't sing in Indian." Other poems in *Seasonal Woman* have song in them, for example "There Have Been Nights," and the last poem "A Prayer."

TAPAHONSO: With the first one, when she said "Don't. . ." it's like saying, you know there's a saying "Don't trust a man who doesn't like to drink." (laughter) Which is silly, but really being with a man seriously and him not singing is real unstable. It's very sort of crooked, sinister, you know? Because somebody who doesn't sing is, to me, sort of strange. In Navajo, you know it's very important. There's a song for everything. There are songs for nothing and there are songs for anything. I think it's just natural that it would work itself into the poetry because the poetry, too, is a song—in the sense that it stirs one's mind or that it creates a dance within a person's imagination. It creates movement, so that song is movement not only physical, but spiritually, emotionally. Good poetry is that, is motion and relates to the whole thing of dance and prayer because *they* are all one motion. They are all together. There is no separation.

The poetry is sort of a new extension, a contemporary extension of that sort of thing—for myself, because I'm here, and for my children because they're growing up very differently than I did. At first I used to sort of mourn that. But now I see that it's not really anything that's bad unless we see it that way. That is something I've come to terms with through my writing, I think. I can see how my daughters are growing and I can see how my poetry and the songs and the prayers and their everyday lives are affecting them and how they're changing and so it's a good thing.

JB: The poems in *Seasonal Woman* seem to be very much linked, to flow from one to the next, to form a sort of cycle. I'm interested in one character who shows up in several poems: Leona Grey. She's in "Her Daughter's Eyes," "Time Flies," and "No Particular Reason." For a time I thought of her as a person like "Noni Daylight" in Joy Harjo's poems who is sort of an extension of Joy herself, another persona. But I wonder about Leona Grey since, though there may perhaps be some paralleling of your own experience in hers, she also ends up being killed in "No Particular Reason."

TAPAHONSO: That's not for real. I killed her but she's back. I did that in frustration. But what she is, is not really my experience. It is my experience in terms of the way that I know her, but she's several different women that I've known and for a long time I was writing her down as always "she" or "her," giving her names, different names. But then I decided I would put her all together and have her be this real reckless but wise person. So I wanted to pick a name that was sort of real raunchy, so I thought Leona was a good name. I hope I never meet anyone with that name. That would be scary.

JB: And then "Grey?"

TAPAHONSO: "Grey" meaning. . . in terms of that color. Not necessarily something like being a dark person or a gloomy person, not anything like that. I liked that, "Grey." I don't have any particular reasons.

JB: Gray does turn up frequently in the colors of Navajo weaving as one of those transition colors—halfway between dark and light. So it seemed like a very good name for Leona. You say that she personifies a kind of reckless but wise woman? There seems to be a great deal of freedom in the ways women are presented in poems by Native American women as opposed to the ways women live and are presented in poems by many non-Native American women. Have you noticed that?

TAPAHONSO: In fact, gosh, I couldn't sleep last night and it's really strange you should ask me that because I was thinking last night that men are very restricted in our (Navajo) society. Men are very restricted and women aren't. You can do whatever you want and it's all okay because you're a woman and it's the opposite with men.

JB: I like the way you begin this book with the picture of your child, "Misty Dawn at Feeding Time." Was that poem written right after the birth of one of your children?

TAPAHONSO: Misty—that's Misty when she was a few months old, my younger daughter. I always begin my work, no matter what I'm doing, with something for my children. I think it's a good thing to do because I feel good about my children. They're not a hindrance to me and I feel really good about them, so beginning that way I think helps me. It's sort of like assurance that things will go well. So my readings, or whatever I do, I always begin with my children.

JB: Unlike the type of sexuality that occurs within a "typical" American poem, there is a sort of natural and often subtly funny relationship between the sexes. It occurs, for example, in "Raisin Eyes," or "Promise Me a Long Night," or "One More Shiprock Night" from your earlier book. Does that characterize your vision of the relationship between men and women?

TAPAHONSO: I think that it's important to see it for what it is, to be able to see it distinctly and see it aside from any emotions that come along with it. That is important, too, but to be able to see it for what's really going on. You know, people always say love is blind. I think that happens a lot of times.

People can't see the situation that they're in. But it's important to see things clearly, with a sense of *clarity* and in simple terms. I think as we grow older a lot of times we lose that perception. We tend to complicate things or read things in or just think that the way a person is looking at you—it means something else. You know, all that sort of thing. But if you can see it for what it is, what's really going on, then it is so much easier.

JB: In some of the poems of Joy Harjo, Leslie Silko, and yourself those events become myth; it becomes like an old story.

TAPAHONSO: Which it is. I think that we were raised with that. How do we know what people generations from now are going to be talking about? It could very well be us. I think that's true. What we are ties in with stories and the future. We are, you know. Who knows what we are probably repeating. . . and we are repeating what has happened over and over again, not only to us as people. Because people are no different than spiritual beings, I think, and that's the whole key—that we can see things on those different levels. So it ties in with the whole thing of "We are the Earth." At home I remember that people always say, "Oh, she's just being Changing Woman," referring to somebody who is just doing things that are really crazy, then being real serious and acting sane and being the way that this society wants us to function. . .

JB: Or the character of Coyote. Coyote turns up in Joy's poems or Simon Ortiz's poems. . . actually you could make a list as long as your arm. Almost all American Indian writers have a Coyote image or a Coyote story in their work.

TAPAHONSO: Um-humm. And they say things like, "They're just doing that because they're from this clan which is just this certain clan," or, as a joke, "Why, your grandfather was a Bear," and that sort of thing. So there's really not any distinction. I think it works well for us. In Navajo stories, a lot of stories I heard when I was growing up, the animals were people and they had done something, something that gave them their animal form. That ties in with not taking things for granted, not saying in a derogatory sense, "You are such an *animal*," or that sort of thing that other people do. Because who are we to say that we are any different?

JB: Violence comes up in a number of your poems. Why is it there?

TAPAHONSO: It goes back to being able to see things clearly or trying to see things clearly for what they are and not, maybe, giving any reasons for it or that sort of thing. It is all part of our everyday lives. We can't really say that it's not. I don't know. I don't know what I'm trying to say. I know what I want to say but I can't put it into words.

JB: There is another kind of conflict I see in some of your poems—between white and Indian. In your poem "Pay Up or Else" a young Indian man is killed because he doesn't pay the ninety-seven cents overdue on the gas he got. How do you relate to that climate of racism on the part of Anglos in the Southwest? What do you, as a poet or a person, do about it?

TAPAHONSO: I don't know how to answer that. I think that first it's important to see that it's here. I know I've experienced it and people close to me have experienced it, even people I don't know have experienced it. It is a familiar feeling to us. It's something that we deal with all the time. And being able to recognize it and to see that it's happened and not to let it frustrate you or let it upset you is important, I think. Maybe that's why I have to write about it because it's important to see things, you know, for what they are—not to mar them or not to cloud them over, to present them simply because it makes us what we are, it's a part of us. I don't know if that explains it.

JB: It seems as if more and more Indian people are reading the poems of American Indian writers and finding something there they need. Do you see your poetry as something of use, as a tool?

TAPAHONSO: I think so, because I consider it a real compliment when people come up to me and say, "I *know*," or "*That* happened to me! I *know* what you mean." So that it's a good thing because young Indian students can relate to literature *finally* and enjoy it and *laugh* and that's very hard to do. When I was going to school, we didn't have that sort of thing. So it's important for them to read this and to really like it and say, "Hey, that's really neat!" or "I could do *that*." It's just such a neat feeling. I have met people who have said that Simon's poems have really helped them deal with certain situations in their lives. So it is a source of strength and it's a source of being able to say, "Well, it's okay." Just being able to relate to poetry because it's *them*.

JB: Is there any poem in particular that you like better than any of the others in *Seasonal Woman?*

TAPAHONSO: No, they're all my babies. (laughter) You probably know how this feels—for a long time I had these poems and they were mine. And then it was finally out in print. Sometimes I think about it and it gets me a little bit depressed because I think a lot of people have this book, a lot of people I know—and I feel good about that—a lot of people I don't know—and so I don't know how my poems are. It's like my kids are running around someplace and I don't know who's taking care of them, something like that. And they're finally out, they're not mine anymore, and I'm sharing them with other people. So that's sort of what I went through with this and I'm still sort of in a slump after this came out. When it came out I was telling Earl, this is just like having a baby.

JB: The postpartum depression.

TAPAHONSO: Yeah. (laughter)

JB: I really like that poem "Hills Brothers Coffee."

TAPAHONSO: It's a translation, a direct translation from Navajo. So that gives it. . . a lot of the words are probably different than if I had written it only in English.

JB: Are any of these others in *Seasonal Woman* a direct translation from Navajo?

TAPAHONSO: I think this is the only one in here. Um-hum. (looks through book) I think that is the only one that's a direct translation.

JB: Have you written any poems in Navajo?

TAPAHONSO: I'm doing a lot of poetry in Navajo now. In fact, there's a lot of slang for which there's really no translation in English. And if you do translate it, it just sounds kind of flat. So I've been doing poems in Navajo and then not even bothering to translate them and it works really well—at home.

JB: Someone said to me they felt the native language is so important to keep because it is the heart of the people. Do you see the Navajo language as a sort of force for yourself and your poetry?

TAPAHONSO: That's true, I think. They always say at home . . . if you lose, if we lose the language, then we're really not anything anymore. So that is important.

Follow the Trickroutes

An Interview with
GERALD VIZENOR

Since his first publications, Gerald Vizenor has been recognized as a multifaceted writer. His books include collections of haiku poetry, short stories, a novel, reworkings of Anishinabe traditional tales, and several nonfiction works. A member of the White Earth Reservation, his teaching has taken him to the University of Minnesota, the University of California at Berkeley, the Southwest and, just prior to this interview, China.

The interview with Gerald Vizenor took place on one of those cool but sunny days which characterize Berkeley, California. There Vizenor and his wife, Laura Hall, were living while he taught for a semester at the University of California. Just back from mainland China, Vizenor and his wife were staying in a small apartment piled high with books—some on shelves, some as yet unpacked. As we drank tea and talked, I thought how much Vizenor is like his trickster heroes, a man always in motion, rooted and rootless, his eyes flashing with wry humor as he speaks.

Auras on the Interstate

follow the trickroutes
homewardbound in darkness

noise tired
from the interstates

trucks whine through our families
places of conception

governments raze
half the corners we have known

houses uprooted
sacred trees deposed
municipal machines
plow down our generation vines
tribal doorsteps

condominium cultures
foam low
stain the rivers overnight

thin auras
hold our space in dreams
cut the interstates
from the stoop
bedroom window ruins

noise tired
we are laced in dark arms
until morning

      —Gerald Vizenor

JB: I'm pleased you began with that poem. It leads into a question I feel is central to your work—migration and the sense of movement. There are references to motion, roads, travels, and even pilgrimages throughout your writing. Why is this so and what do those motions and migrations mean to you?

VIZENOR: Life is not static. Philosophically, I think we should break out of all the routes, all the boxes, break down the sides. A comic spirit demands that we break from formula, break out of program, and there are some familiar ways to do it and then some radical or unknown ways. I suppose I am preoc- cupied with this theme because the characters I admire in my own imagination and the characters I would like to make myself be break out of things. They break out of all restrictions. They even break out of their blood. They break out of the mixture in their blood. They break out of invented cultures and repres- sion. I think it's a spiritual quest in a way. I don't feel that it's transcendence—or escape as transcendence. That's not the theme I'm after, but I'm after an idea of the comic, that the adventures of living and the strategies of survival are chances. They're mysteries because they're left to chance. Life is a chance, all life is a chance. And that's a comic spirit. A tragic spirit is to trudge down the same trail, try to build a better path, make another fortune, build another monument and contrib- ute it to a museum and establish more institutions to disguise our mortality. I consider all of that a formula to control and oppress—not evil, not in an evil manner, but it does control. So, I feel this need to break out of the measures that people make.

JB: That's interesting to me because, when we were talk- ing earlier, you mentioned the importance of a sense of place. A sense of place is still meaningful despite the motion?

VIZENOR: Well, the place is in imagination, an imagi- native landscape. The place isn't really on the earth because it'll change. But I think you need a place to attach to in moments of fear and detachment and confusion, a place that's familiar, a dream place. I think it's an *oral traditional* place, which means that it's greater than reality and it's greater than a mate- rial place you would find on the earth—this is more than just an intersection. It's a universal place. If you turn your back on the earthbound place, it will change. The seasons will change it. And surely human beings are going to alter anything you ever want to remember as a sacred place. So we take it into imagination, and I don't ever expect any place I've ever been in a spiritual way will ever be the same except in my imagination. So I see the permanence of things in a kind of oral traditional visual place. Now, there is, I think, a spiritual and a political risk in this. It is very impractical. The bulldozers can come and if you're off imagining, you can ignore it. I don't carry this as a life philosophy, but in response to your question.

JB: You have to strike a balance between an actual physical connection to a physical life on this physical earth and the imaginative connection which, in some ways, sustains you even when the physical reality changes or breaks down—or is taken away by the bulldozer. What is the physical and emotional reality you proceed from and what is the place on earth you carry about with you now in your imagination?

VIZENOR: That's very nice. Let me get there slightly indirectly. My father moved from the reservation to Minneapolis. I went around to hang out for a few minutes at all the places I had ever lived in the city. When I went to do this, less than ten years ago, I found that the places I had lived up until I went to college at the University of Minnesota, more than half were under cement. They were interstates, they had been razed. I thought, "My God, my past doesn't exist." I don't exist with respect to a geographical place. I saw this in myself and I've also written about it in other people. Marleen American Horse, for example, a fictional name but a real person who comes from North Dakota. Her place is under the reservoir. She doesn't have a home place anymore. But they exist, our past intersections, in my imagination. And anyway, I say to myself, everything out there is like television. They'll change the channel and it will be a different place, they'll redesign it. I have to separate what is mine by way of connections to the earth and what is "television." Most of what I've seen in the world is television—I mean, the world is television.

In the most romantic sense, there's a small grove of cedar in the Chippewa National Forest in northern Minnesota that is a *very* special place. I can't tell you why. There's no particular genealogical or geographical significance to it other than the fact that cedar is significant to religion in the tribal sense. But I found that cedar on a walk, a lovely place. I think of it often and I am connected to it. Somebody may have cut it down, conceivably, but it may still be there. *Physically,* I haven't been there for two years. There's another place at White Earth Reservation. It's on a hill right outside of White Earth, the St. Benedict Catholic Cemetery. That's a genealogical connection, historical, tribal-historical, a family place. There are family members buried there, Vizenors and Beaulieus, and right at the top of the hill there's a plot with several Beaulieus. It's the end of rolling woodlands and the beginning of the plains. From that hill you can see infinity. That's a special place; it represents, obviously, the Catholic Church Mission, conflicts of culture, religion, blood, geographies, everything, and that tension is not debilitating. That kind of tension in blood and in history is a stimulation, a chance to survive and prevail in good humor. I'm not oppressed by that. I'm stimulated. And that's a special place. And most bodies of water, being on most bodies of water is a stimulation.

JB: Some questions have come to me as a result of reading your work and thinking about it for a number of years. The first has to do with certain words or phrases you've coined. I think of these as they show up in the titles of some of your books: "Tribal histories," "Wordarrows." What do you mean by terms such as these. Why do you coin them and how do they work?

VIZENOR: I like to imagine words, imagine metaphors not theories, so that the ideas and images are not stereotyped. The word *"indian,"* for example: I try to avoid it in almost all of my writing. Where I've used *indian,* I've identified it as a problem word in some writing or italicized it in others. I think it ought to be lower-case italicized everywhere. It is one of those troublesome words. It doesn't mean anything, it is a historical blunder, and has negative associations. So I try to avoid the word in writing by referring the reader to the tribal people or "tribal histories" rather than *indian* histories to try to avoid some of the problems. So, some of the words I imagine or invent or combine are ways to avoid the traps, the historical traps. "Word-

GERALD VIZENOR

arrows" is an obvious metaphor for the cultural and racial
tensions between tribal and European cultures and it's a verbal
device. "Socioacupuncture" is another one of my words, or
neologisms, as the critics might say. I'm rather pleased with
that, borrowing an Asian theme. That's the right pressure at the
right place at the right time and tricksters are marvelous at
that, especially tribal tricksters. You apply just the right humor
and the right pressure at the right moment to convince or per-
suade or to achieve something. I used that as a theme in my
filmscript *Harold of Orange*. He actually has a school of socioacupuncture. What they learn in that school is how to raise
foundation money and how to play it right to the foundations.
The problem is that, while I may be able to write about this,
I've been an absolute failure at getting any foundation money
myself. Perhaps what I've done is so advanced that foundation
people don't trust me and say, "Oh no, we're on to his game."
That's a good question. I like playing with words and I think
part of it is a mixed blood tribal effort at "deconstruction." I
want to break the language down, I want to re-imagine the
language. It's the same as breaking out of boxes. I still haven't
broken very far out of grammar. I've broken out of the philosophies of grammar, English language grammar, but I haven't
broken out of the standard grammatical structure. I guess I don't
feel a powerful need to do that and I also think that if I broke
that far I just wouldn't have any reading audience at all. I don't
have much as it is! The more unfamiliar it becomes, the less
possibility of finding a reader. But I do break out of the philosophy of the grammar by trying to avoid most modifiers. If the
noun or action is not clear in itself I won't modify it with "l-y's."
I also like to run on images when pursuing an idea with mythic associations. When there is action, most of my sentences are
short and direct. When a scene is associated with dream and
with transcendence, with a shift in time, something magical, or
mysterious, or mythic, or when I'm drawing upon traditional
sources, the sentences are compound, they're run on. I try to
dissolve all grammar, any interruptions in the imagistic flow.

JB: I had a sense of that in your work but I hadn't seen it
as clearly as you've just expressed it. The idea of the shaman,
the trickster, the medicine person, appears to be central to your

work. What is the place of the shaman-trickster-medicine man in your writing and how does that character work as a symbol of the writer?

VIZENOR: I think a number of people have pointed out before that the writer can be a shaman and trickster. I think that writers in general are tricksters in the broadest sense of disruption. I don't think it's worth writing, for myself, unless you can break up a little bit. I don't think it's worth the energy unless the formulas can be broken down, unless the expectations of the reader are disrupted, because I think writing is revolutionary, radical in behavior. It's radical in action, it's disruptive in the social and cultural values. That's a trickster's business. The tragic risks all humans run are associated with their terminal creeds. They focus too narrowly, they derive too much pleasure and comfort from simple verbal formulas, simple rituals of transportation and movement and direction. So, as a result, I believe people who control their lives in such terminal ways are vulnerable, highly vulnerable to oppression, to violence, to totalitarian and authoritarian systems, colonial administration, the Bureau of Indian Affairs. So, the tricksters in all my work, everywhere, and, in one character or another, disrupt the ambitions of people, contradict, unsettle, and unglue the creeds. No trickster I have ever written about is evil, no trickster I've written about has ever taken advantage of weakness; my imagined tricksters are compassionate and comic.

JB: When the Trickster confronts the Gambler, for example, and defeats him, it is not through becoming like him?

VIZENOR: No, he doesn't take anything from him, doesn't gain anything. It's not a competitive act. And I have tricksters who make fun of themselves. Now that's a little more complicated because that's a form of masturbation. How can you be controlled by something and then break it down yourself? That's probably the highest development of humans, when individuals see their own folly.

JB: Having just been in the Southwest, I think of the way sacred clowns make fun of themselves even as they act out an important role. I see that in your trickster characters—the clown crows, other central actors in the journeys which take place in your poems and stories.

VIZENOR: Let me borrow two ideas: in a tragic world-view people are rising above everything. And you can characterize Western patriarchal monotheistic manifest-destiny civilizations as tragic. It doesn't mean they're bad, but they're tragic because of acts of isolation, their heroic acts of conquering something, always overcoming adversity, doing *better than* whatever, proving something, being rewarded for it, facing the risks to do this and usually doing it alone and almost always at odds with nature. Part of that, of course, is the idea of the human being's divine creation as superior. The comic spirit is not an opposite, but it might as well be. You can't act in a comic way in isolation. You have to be included. There has to be a collective of some kind. You're never striving at anything that is greater than life itself. There's an acceptance of chance. Sometimes things *just happen* and when they happen, even though they may be dangerous or even life-threatening, there is some humor. Maybe not at the instant of the high risk, but there is some humor in it. And it's a positive, compassionate act of survival, it's getting along. Now there's good and bad philosophical and economic considerations to both points of view, but tribal cultures are *comic* or mostly comic. Yet they have been interpreted as tragic by social scientists; tribal cultures have been viewed as tragic cultures. Not tragic because they're "vanishing" or something like that, but tragic in their worldview—and they're *not* tragic in their worldview. Only a few writers among the social scientists have seen this, say Karl Kroeber and Denis Tedlock, people who understand stories real well, who understand the comedy, the play, the chance, the ritual and festive connections to things universally. So I make that distinction, that the trickster is in a comic world, surviving by his wits, prevailing in good humor. He's in a collective, hardly ever in isolation. When he is in isolation, he's almost always in trouble, in a life-threatening situation he has to get out of through ritual or symbolic acts. Through reversals he has to get back to connections to imagination, to people, to places.

JB: For example in the Anishinabe story when Manabozho is swallowed by the great fish and then helped by Chipmunk who chews the way out?

VIZENOR: Yes, you have to restore some connection. You can't just rise above that by yourself like the tragic hero would without any help.

JB: These days the tragic hero dies in the whale's belly after giving a great speech.

VIZENOR: That's it! (laughs)

JB: I like the way this conversation is flowing.

VIZENOR: It almost makes sense. We are at some risk here of actually making sense!

JB: What about the various animals which appear in your writing? It seems that in your poems and stories animals and people not only intercept each other and interact, but in some ways they are almost interchangeable.

VIZENOR: Yes. It is the obvious tribal connection. That animals are not lower in evolutionary status. In all the woodland stories animals are significant beings. A language is shared, some humans remember the language, especially shamans, and there are many stories about intermarriage or relationships between humans and animals. Notice what happens to the language: children, contemporary children, use metaphors about animals in a very affectionate and humanistic way. They're in the family, all kinds of animals, even imaginary ones. But as soon as they become *rational*, in school, when they're obligated in their intellectual growth and the emphasis upon a philosophy of grammar, cause and effect, time, logical and rational, they start using negative metaphors for animals. We all do that. "Bird-brain" and so on. Almost all the references to animals we have make it appear as if we must be incredibly self-conscious and insecure about our status as humans, that we must deride all other life. "Like a snake," "like a chicken," "like a pig," all these negative references.

The thing I'm getting at, in *Bearheart*, to choose an example, is seen in the woman who has sex with two boxers. Now some readers find that pornographic, extremely obscene and disgusting. Bestiality. Well, it is none of those. What I am doing is simply saying—though there is nothing simple about it— that there isn't anything wrong, is there, with a human being expressing some love of a physical and emotional kind for animals. There are tribal stories everywhere and I use some variations of those stories. Characters tell those stories within my writing about those relationships with animals.

Animals that are very important to me are bear, squirrel, dog, and several birds. Crow. Cedar Waxwing is a very special kind of totem. I have felt in my life a kind of communication with Cedar Waxwing and Crow and Squirrel and Bear and Dog. These are either animals that I have felt tremendous fear or tremendous love for and emotional attachment, involvement, conversation, at one time or another. In all of my writing you'll see that Bear appears.

JB: What does the bear mean to you? Does the bear fit into your work as a metaphor, or perhaps not as a metaphor but as the protean character of the person at the center of your vision, your imagination, as a sort of shape-shifter?

VIZENOR: Oh yes, it is the great interior darkness of everything. It is the greatest power. We must all want to be bears. If we could be anything it should be bears. I say that, too, intellectually, knowing as most tribal people did that bears are skeletally and in muscular structure more like humans. And they play like humans. They chatter and talk. They're unpredictable and quick-witted. They even masturbate. They're like us and they're in us *and we're in them*. We're in the bear. We're in the bear's maw. Galway Kinnell has this fantastic poem, "The Bear," where the persona crawls inside the bear to sleep and be warm as it freezes overnight.

JB: Certain other things turn up frequently in your work. One of those is cedar itself. What is the role of cedar for you? Why is it so important?

VIZENOR: It's a ceremonial, burning cedar. The center of the idea of cedar is that it purifies and protects, and the smoke will restore a balance. My experience with it comes through culture, linguistics, and practice. I can't answer scientifically about cedar smoke, but I have heard someone say that it has something to do with ionization, rather like standing near a waterfall where there is higher negative ionization so it is more relaxing. So there may be properties in the environment which are altered by it, but it has drawn us all to it. There's a power in the word and it's a good word. It works everywhere and I draw people together with it, use it as a sacred reference. It doesn't require any iconography. It requires no symbols. It requires nothing. You don't even have to *say* anything. You just burn a little of it and it'll do the rest. To be truly comical about it, it's the ultimate in deconstruction. (laughs) It's a little puff of smoke. You don't need any language about it. So, if I draw upon it between characters, you can explain a lot of things about people in the way they use it or abuse it. In Cedarfaire, for example, people have made a business out of it. But it doesn't make any difference. You can sell it as they do. They don't understand anything about it, but it still works. Unlike icons. Do you suppose it could be the same as a plastic crucifix, or a figure of Mary has equal power? These are symbols, they don't have any aromatic power. But it's close. You can market all that stuff and make a lot of money about it, even have it glow in the dark. But if you believe in it, it still works. It's irresistible. But the powerful part of it for me is that it can be a ceremonial without icons and language. There isn't very much else you can do. You can bleed yourself, you can have a vision. It's possible to sing without ceremony and words. Sound things, you can sound as animals. But there isn't very much else we can do that has such a powerful ceremonial connection to so many people in this country, tribal people. So you can't abuse it. It works without the language and the ritual and the icons.

JB: Lance Henson told me that burning cedar as the sun rises is the first ceremony a Cheyenne child is taught.

VIZENOR: Is that so? I was told a wonderful story by a woman while I was teaching classes at the John F. Kennedy University. They were very earnest and eager to be saved by somebody. One woman got very angry and told a story about Rolling Thunder organizing a sunrise ceremony in the Santa Cruz mountains. They all paid about fifteen or twenty bucks to go to this ceremony—in advance. They all got there before dawn in the dark and climbed up the mountain in the fog and the cold. They waited and waited and Rolling Thunder didn't show. And that was the end of her story. She had finally unburdened herself of this terrible thing that was done to them and she felt cheated. I said, "So?" She said, "He didn't show!" I said, "Well, did the sun rise?" She said, "Well, of course." And I said, "Well, it just goes to show that you didn't need him."

The same thing goes with cedar.

JB: That's a great trickster story. (laughter) Can you tell me a bit about your own Chippewa background, how your knowledge of Chippewa practices and beliefs has come into your writing?

VIZENOR: Mostly through stories. I've never, in any way, lived anything like a traditional life, whatever that might have been. My contact with that is through elders. The closest would be my great-uncle Clement Beaulieu, John Clement Beaulieu, and my grandmother who is a good storyteller. I wouldn't characterize her as being traditional, but she's a wonderful storyteller. Clem, or John Clement, was not only a fine storyteller with a trickster's imagination, but there was a calmness and a great generosity about him. He lived at many places, White Earth and Cass Lake, and he lived at Red Lake for a time. He had several little shacks at Bena. He would buy one, fix it up, and give it away—and go get another one. He would do this because people around him had greater need. He never talked about it. These are stories I heard around him. He didn't boast about it. Part of the way he looked at it was that he was getting bored with the place anyway. So it was just as well to give it away. He had more interesting things to do. Clem was an introduction to language, to an imaginative resolution between mixed blood. A rich imagination about everything—women, animals, conflict, governments. He served in the First World War in Europe. I would say that of any one person, I was more stimulated by the possibilities of imagining things in a certain way because of Clem. He directed me. . . no, I shouldn't say he directed me. I was directed by things he said to pursue some loose ends of things that he understood pretty well. As a result I met a lot of people and found out things. I found out things about shamanism—I'm not a shaman, but I understood the energy. I wasn't afraid of people and I think that was helpful because practically every healer I talked with was pleased that I wasn't. Although I am sure they also had great fun playing with people who were afraid, too. Those were ways in which I found things out. I must say I found out a tremendous amount of things about this tension from non-Indians who have lived with, been around, admired, hated, married, divorced, been with, about, and engaged directly with Indians. I don't know how to say how much I learned, but the picture would *never* be complete for me without their view.

I had another insight into that in reading some stories about a woman who is Rumanian, becomes an American citizen, a Yale Ph.D. in Chinese. She's one of the first scholars to be in China in the late '70s. She was talking about the indirect way you have to learn about China. You can't learn about it directly. You have to learn about it *partly* through the way non-Chinese respond to the Chinese. I see that has been an insight for me, too. I have learned a lot from the way people have responded to me. I still do. I think I may have tremendous insight into that. I think that part of my insight is a bit cruel because I turn it into kind of a counter ideology.

JB: What is storytelling itself?

VIZENOR: Well, there is storytelling without the pen, the book. That is probably easier to explain than storytelling. My own feeling is that sometimes it works and sometimes it doesn't. When it does, I notice that teller and listener-participant are either willing to be surprised—they have subscribed to a surprise, they are present and loyal participants ready to be surprised—or, knowing that the story will lead them nowhere, they accept it. They're not audience and that's important. The story doesn't work without a participant. There are a lot of people who walk around Berkeley and they're crazy. They haven't found a listener in ten or twenty years. And it's sad because there *are* stories, but those stories are now just floating loose. You bump into everybody and try to shed yourself of the stories because they're really burden stories. The humor is gone from them—they're desperate stories and you don't want to listen to that any more. So there has to be a participant and someone has to listen. I don't mean listening in the passive sense. You can even listen by contradiction. You can even listen by saying "Bullshit!" if that's in good humor and not in a negative sense. So that's really critical in storytelling. The storyteller's properties have to tie in metaphorically to some kind of experience. And now I have to borrow from Hymes and Tedlock in observing Zuni storytellers, and I really celebrate their work so much and praise them so highly for making the simple observation that the storyteller *is an artist*. Right? Not, as Tedlock says, just a conduit of tradition. And the stories vary—now who would have thought that? Of course all stories vary! There's not two stories alike and that's the tragic thing which has happened to stories. They have been published and appear standardized. So young people come to these stories, especially in tribal areas where there's not a rich and centered traditional life as there is in the Southwest. In most of the woodlands states there's little traditional connection and oral tradition left and there's a lot of mixed bloods. There a lot of young people are offered these published stories in classrooms through well-meaning teachers who want to do a good curriculum on Indians and to help their Indian students discover themselves and their traditions. But they do it through a kind of standardized liturgy, as if it were scripture.

JB: Static?

VIZENOR: Yes, there's no life in it. It's just memorization, it's no story at all—and I think that stuff kills imagination because it's leading to people believing if you depart from the stories you depart from the scripture. So they don't listen to you anymore, and they believe you're cheating them or you're dishonest or you have some ulterior motive or purpose that's not honorable. That's a shame because imagination is so rich there shouldn't be any story that's limited by the text. And even a published text is not a limited story. The healthiest way to read is to look upon this as a possibility of the story.

JB: You've pointed out something very interesting here—the spiritual nature of the story itself. By "spiritual" I mean a carrying of a kind of power so that a person can be burdened by a story when that story can't be told because the participant audience has disappeared. I think that's a very crucial point.

VIZENOR: I don't know where we find the audience now. Once in a while I find it as a teacher. When I'm around nonstudents, people I trust and I'm familiar with, we always exchange stories. You're just ready for it. And I say, give me your best story! *You* know that. People call *you* long-distance late at night just to tell you a story. You're a wonderful participant.

JB: Can you remember any particular stories your Uncle Clement told which were particularly significant to you?

VIZENOR: He had a lot of stories about priests and the way people responded to priests, the tricks they pulled on them. Feeding them wild game they wouldn't eat themselves. I'm a little reluctant to. . .

JB: I'm not asking you to retell a story here and now. Just asking about the sort of content and the context.

VIZENOR: Oh, I see! I was getting a little nervous about repeating one.

JB: I get nervous about such things, too. I should have asked the question a bit better.

VIZENOR: No, no, I understand it. Two general contents. One is the stories of magic and faith healing and how things just mysteriously happened, how people appeared and disappeared. He'd have lots of those. Stories about people going hunting who would disappear and reappear. There would be mythic events taking place in unusual circumstances. Severe weather, for example. Somehow people would do remarkable things in this. They would come through or appear in half the normal time and show no physical wear and tear.

JB: A seven-days' journey in a day or something like that?

VIZENOR: Exactly. Time would be dissolved. The dissolution of time and out-of-body possibilities. He didn't tell these, though, in emphasis of this being unusual. This was just built in as ordinary circumstance. It was just after the story you would have to ask a few questions. The other category was stories of resolution of tensions and the play between the colonists—and I would include the government and the Church—and Indians. Then, the tension also between fullbloods and mixed bloods. Though that tension was different. There was much more play, much harder play in the best sense of the word between mixed bloods and fullbloods.

JB: That rough sort of teasing?

VIZENOR: Tease and put down—which I would characterize as more affectionate. Whereas the tension between colonists and Indians, mixed blood or fullblood, didn't lack compassion, but it was manipulative. You wanted to outwit. That was the motivation in imagination. You wanted to outwit either restrictions and bureaucracies or impositions. Whereas with mixed blood and fullblood, it was a duel and had a different character. It was a duel in the tribal sense, a compassionate duel. It wasn't competitive to win or outwit, but it was duel. Actually it was a leveler in a sense.

JB: The competition was as important as who came out on top.

VIZENOR: Um-hmm. For example, there's a story—one of my favorites, which I recently retold in a different sense—about the young priest who would thrust his head into a rain barrel. People wondered about that. But some people understood that. You put your head under water and thump the sides and there's a tremendous sense of distance. You could stand up and look across the prairie, but you put your head in a rain barrel and you can go farther. You can thump your way all the way to Asia in a rain barrel. So some people were taking bets on how long the priest could hold his head under. It was related apparently to the priest's imagination and what he was thinking at the time. The point was that, if the priest was concentrating on some imaginative event while his head was under water, he didn't need as much oxygen. So they timed him and took bets, spread it out over a few days and got an average and then took bets on him.

JB: I think one of the reasons I wanted to have you describe the kinds of stories your Uncle Clem used was to get a description of the kind of stories you use. I see a very direct connection between his categories and yours. Miraculous journeys, conflicts between white and native, mixed blood and fullblood.

VIZENOR: That's true. That's true. I have to say something else, though. Sometimes the interactions and the connections between people tell their own stories. I'm thinking of a little community named Bena. It's a mixed community, Indian and white. It's on Lake Winnebigoshis. Clem lived there, and I spent a fair amount of time visiting him and made some other friends there. The most incredible things went on in that place. Even if you weren't a storyteller you would be made one if you paid attention. You would have to be an absolute idiot not to—if you weren't arrogant and just holding yourself above them. Crazy things that went on there. There was a deputy sheriff, for example, who lived in a house trailer. He was the only law enforcement person in this village and he wasn't Indian. When I visited him he had dogs around the place and a dozen broken-down machines from snowmobiles to tractors. I knocked on the door and he opened it and dogs rushed out. None of them were angry, they were all friendly lap dogs of various sizes. So I felt pretty good about this sheriff. I knew this was going to be an unusual sheriff. Nice looking, balding man with a half-ass smile as if he wasn't really there, as if he was already ready to tell you it was a joke. He invited me in and I swear to god there were hundreds of pounds of chicken bones everywhere. I crunched on them as I walked across the floor. That was his primary diet. I'm just leading up to one sentence which focuses on this man. I said, "Well, didn't they call you that I was coming?" And he said, "I don't have a phone." And I said, "But you're the sheriff, the law enforcement officer here, and you don't have a phone?" He said, "Naw, I tried one for a while. But I had all these people calling me up with domestic problems, and I couldn't do anything about people's personal problems. So I figured if I took the phone out I wouldn't be bothered. If somebody wants to drive way back here, crawl through the dogs and the chicken bones to talk to me about it, it's probably serious." He also said, "I don't make many arrests around here." Now you have to understand this area has the highest arrest rate in the state. They called it the "Little Chicago" of Minnesota. But he said, "I don't like to arrest people. Most of the people I'd have to arrest around here

304   GERALD VIZENOR

are drunk." He wasn't just referring to Indian, he meant Indian and white. And he said, "If I have to arrest them, I have to put them in the back of my car and then I have to drive them twenty miles to Cass Lake and half the time they throw up in the back seat and the county won't pay me anything to clean up my back seat. So I won't arrest anybody." My point is that the sheriff was a wonderful human being who had worked out his own comic trickster resolutions to life. He was a living story. You'd have to be totally blind not to see some of these stories.

JB: I like the term "living story." It relates strongly to what you do with your characters. There's a direct connection, in many cases, between your characters and real-life people. You draw people you know—people I know—into your stories. How did you come to that?

VIZENOR: Part of that is just the way I tell stories. You put each other down in that playful trickster way and that's mutual. The difference is that I'm a writer and most of my friends aren't. So I have a slight advantage. We exchange the same kind of subtle trickster put-downs, but I figure out a way to put it into print. Yes, there's satire, of course, name a work that doesn't have satire. Any work that's worth a shit has got to have some satire. If I was just getting even with somebody, I already was even in play. And *even* is a good thing. That's a problem, because people suggest getting even is not a good thing. But it's just part of the give and take in the play. It's part of breaking down the terminal beliefs, so I don't look upon "getting even" as a negative thing. I know the term has negative associations and I don't like to use it much, but "getting even" is really positive energy. It's an honest, direct, playful engagement. You can go ahead and get into print and knock me down if you want—but that's not what I'm about. I really celebrate people I love in what I write. I don't have enemies that I get even with in my work. Not in my imaginative work.

JB: I sense a lot of objectivity in your journalistic pieces. People are allowed to speak with their own voices, events are allowed to unfold without a lot of editorializing.

VIZENOR: Yes, I've done that with the AIM leaders, for example. Even though I've been very critical of some of them and been uneasy about a number of things, I let them speak for themselves and don't try to snooker it or hoodwink or trick in the worst sense of the word—manipulate things so I have the power and control.

JB: I think it's difficult to write with the sort of clarity you use. I notice, too, you have a way of layering images and experiences. Things keep building up, almost by accretion, like sediment. How did you come to that particular form?

VIZENOR: Hmm, let me think out loud about that. I think in writing, when I come to say it directly, usually the first noun or verb in this layered scene or image, the first reference to action or description, is usually the obvious or categorical one. Then, I think, I break it down by additions or expand on it. I make it broader, expand the possibilities of it or even contradict it, which, I believe, expands it. Rather than simply modifying it. I think then you reduce it. Ah, here I'm close—if I write something which is categorical there's clarity in that on the printed page. There's a clarity in that as a sentence, but it isn't clear, there's more to it. Now you could say in expository writing, "for example" or "on the other hand" there are exceptions. You could quote someone, you could line up other points of view. But in imaginative prose I think I want the mind to go visually, so there's a category, comma, then even a few phrases or words which are variations, contradictions, or expansions of the category. So that the image, the event, the action, or description is broader than what is grammatically allowed.

JB: I think it's exemplary of some of your best work. I also wonder, too, how much effect the writing of the Far East has had on you. I know you have written haiku and been published in major anthologies of haiku. I know some people think of you as one of the better haiku writers in the United States.

VIZENOR: Really? I'm pleased to hear that.

JB: How does haiku affect your sort of image?

VIZENOR: Oh, I see! The haiku is the subtlest image. No need to break down the doors here because the house is open to dreamscapes. I have a new book of haiku, *Matsushima*. I think it is some of my best in a long while, a few of the

images there are the best I've ever done. In it, for the first time,
I've written an introduction on what I think haiku is. It's the
first time I've ever done that, because I don't think we ought to
get critically involved in explaining haiku. Either it works or it
don't! But I've gone against that and decided to make my own
statement because I don't think I want to come back to think
like that again. In it I fool around with ideas from some deconstruction critics and structuralists. I say that haiku may be an
unusual form of deconstruction. You reduce it to the briefest
brush stroke and you don't conclude anything. Everything is
open. What happens, if it happens, is that the reader takes it in
and the words disappear. It becomes a visual event, which of
course is the heart of a storyteller. The power of a storyteller—
the words disappear in visual memory through metaphor, gestures, animals, birds, seasons, tropisms trip the visual memory
and your own imagination. The haiku does that, if the haiku
does that in one image and the listener-participant makes that a
personal experience-event from his or her own experience, it's
deconstructed. The words disappear.

JB: I think you've already answered the question I was
going to ask about why you came to haiku and what relation the
haiku has to your consciousness as a Native American poet.

VIZENOR: Yes. Well, I came to it physically in Japan
when I was in the Army. I was delighted with haiku. It wasn't
until I got back and was in the University of Minnesota that I
studied Asian Civilization and ultimately ended up in graduate
school in Asian Studies. I had a wonderful teacher, Edward
Copeland, at the University of Minnesota. I want to tell this
story because it is very brief and it was a remarkable experience
with a teacher. I'm sure everyone has had one lesson, one
sensitive profound experience with a teacher. I took his class on
Japanese Literature in translation. It was in the spring term
and the trees were budding outside the window. Obviously, the
trees and birds were more interesting than the subject, much as
I liked the subject. Copeland, about the third or fourth week
of class—a very sensitive and gentle scholar—wrote a note and
left it on my desk as he concluded class and walked out. I
opened it up and he'd written: "The past month during class

period you've been looking out the window. What do you see?"
I read this as a real criticism; obviously, he'd caught me day-
dreaming and we're in this business for grades and I liked the
subject and I liked him and I'd disappointed him. So I wrote
him a haiku, a very risky thing to do, though I didn't think of it
as that at first. But when I left it on his desk and walked out
the door and was halfway down the stairs, I was in terror. I was
totally vulnerable. I'd made a stupid error. Can you imagine
trusting a university teacher with a subtle poem? Aggh! I was so
disgusted with myself that I had done such a dumb thing. I
was embarrassed and humiliated and I wanted to grab it back,
but I didn't. I suffered through the weekend and next Monday
tried to be an attentive student to overcome this vulnerability.
He left a note on my desk and answered my poem *in a linking
haiku!* It brought tears to my eyes, this wonderful sensitive man.
I still love him and speak of him and see him. That trust and
loving relationship led not only to A's in class, but we put a
book together, my first publication in haiku. It had a preface of
seasonal Japanese poems translated by Copeland, and then my
original haiku. *Raising The Moon Vines* was the title of the book.

JB: Was that your first book?

VIZENOR: No, just a few months before that I had
worked as a social worker at the state reformatory and I published—they had a print shop—for about $35 two hundred
copies of a small saddle-stitched haiku book. *Two Wings The
Butterfly.* But *Raising The Moon Vines* was the first serious book
from a publisher, and it was reissued a couple of times.

JB: What do you see going on now in Native American
writing?

VIZENOR: In prose writing, I see there's much more so-
phistication in reference to traditional events and experiences.
By that I mean it's not drawn idealogically any more—although
that was not so in Momaday and Silko. I think now any theme
is open, any theme, any structure, any style, and it can still be
seen and felt as Indian literature. I've been developing some
other ideas and critical thinking about Indian literature. What is
Indian literature? How can you tell the difference? So what's

the difference that you can perceive with a critical theory and write about in some way that is Indian literature and that would suggest it is different from other literature? I'm calling it "mythic verism." Mythic truth. Not just myths. There are myths everywhere. But mythic verism. Here I'm talking about my own work, also. There is something alive in the work which gives it a truth. Now that is something which comes from a metaphorical use of traditional energy and references. Momaday has it. Silko has it. You can do it through symbols, you can do it allegorically, you can do it through dialogue, you can do it in all kinds of ways. There's no limit to the ways you can make reference to traditional events, tribal events. That doesn't make it, though. It is the attitude of the characters which gives it the mythic verism and that attitude is comic. That's my theme. It is something that is alive and that is what makes the myth a truth, the way time is handled and resolved, the tension in time, and the sense of comedy or comic spirit through imagination and a collective sense that people prevail and survive, get along, get by. They're not at war with the environment, they're not rising above, and there are no subtle references to manifest destiny, monotheistic superiority. All of that's very subtle, but it's there and I think you can find it and I think we can focus on it and I think we can make a theory of it. There are people who appear to be white but they aren't. You can see in their language and their own conflicts, the way they resolve their conflicts or *avoid* resolving them that there is a comic spirit. You won't find that in much other writing. You can find a comic spirit in other non-Indian literature, but it won't have the same characteristics.

JB: Where are you going with your own writing now?

VIZENOR: I'm just about finished with a novel bringing together the Woodland trickster whom I think I understand very well and the Chinese Monkey King whom we met in China. So I have a mixed-blood trickster character who's teaching in China and the only way the Chinese can understand him— because he is in conflict with the bureaucracy and everything— is that he is the Monkey King and they really celebrate this

Monkey King who disrupts everything. They love this character. The title is *Griever: An American Monkey King in China.*

JB: The Monkey is also one of the most effective of the styles in the martial arts.

VIZENOR: That's right! It's a trickster style. That's very good. I hadn't thought about that. So I draw together the ideas from Chinese opera in it and my character is in conflict and a number of good things come from this—but only because the Chinese can understand him in their own cultural terms as the Monkey King. So what it suggests is the universality of the trickster character. In the future I hope to work on more stories out of Minnesota, trickster things, a collection of stories. One will be in *New America* and one will be in the *North Dakota Quarterly*—the same issue you're going to be in?

JB: Yes.

VIZENOR: The character in the story in *New America* is a much wilder trickster. "Monsignor Missalwait's Interstate." The main character has bought up a section of an interstate on the reservation and he sets up toll booths.

JB: Roads—and again you're going forward by going backward.

VIZENOR: Yes. It begins with a quote. I was horrified when I read that Hawthorn Dairy near Chicago is printing photographs of lost and stolen children on their milk cartons. Now several are doing that, but I was just horrified at the whole idea. A civilization in which children are stolen, what awful energies. These people are so vacant in their connections to other human beings that they have to steal it! They're carrion crow, they're vultures, they don't have any connections left. It has to be the leading worst primary response to the worst experiences of materialism and capitalism. Anyway, I quote that and my Monsignor, a pretend Monsignor—the Tribe gave him that name because he has a vision and consecrated himself— Monsignor Missalwait says in response to this stolen children Hawthorn Dairy thing, "Listen, when milk cartons bear the pictures of stolen children, then civilization needs a better Trickster. Look, white people drink too much milk before they come out to play anyway." Listen and Look reversed.

I Just Kept My Eyes Open

An Interview with
JAMES WELCH

Born in 1940 in Browning, Montana, James Welch's first book was a collection of poems, *Riding The Earthboy 40*, published in 1971 by Sun. It quickly earned Welch a reputation as one of the strongest and most unsparingly honest voices among Native American writers, a reputation strengthened by his first novel *Winter in the Blood*, which was brought out in 1974 by Harper & Row, who reissued *Riding the Earthboy 40* in 1976. Since then, with his second novel, *The Death of Jim Loney*, Welch has established himself as a writer whose tough, spare diction in his novels seems as crafted as the poems which first introduced his voice to the reading public. Though he published only a few poems since his first collection of poetry, his relationship to that craft shows in all of his writing—perhaps nowhere more clearly than in his newest novel, *Fool's Crow*, which is set in the country of the Blackfeet in the 1870s. Its images, its diction, and its vision are those of a writer who knows and loves both language and his own people.

My first meeting with Jim Welch was more than a decade ago when we both took part in a Third World Writers' Conference in Ellensburg, Washington. I remember a walk we took up into the Cascades before sunrise when a Lakota friend picked up a meadowlark and released it just as the sun broke over the peaks. Though Jim moved slowly, his eyes were always looking everywhere, seemingly before anyone else's, and when he spoke in that high clear voice of his, he usually said—in a few well-chosen words—the things that most of us either thought or knew that we should have been thinking.

That same clarity of voice came through as I spoke to Jim about his writing in the following interview we conducted over the phone.

In My First Hard Springtime

Those red men you offended were my brothers.
Town drinkers, Buckles Pipe, Star Boy,
Billy Fox, were blood to bison. Albert Heavy
     Runner
was never civic. You are white and common.

Record trout in Willow Creek chose me
to deify. My horse, Centaur, part cayuse,
was fast and mad and black. Dandy in flat hat
and buckskin, I rode the town and called it mine.

A slow hot wind tumbled dust against my door.
Fed and fair, you mocked my philosophic nose,
my badger hair. I rolled your deference
in the hay and named it love and lasting.

Starved to visions, famous cronies top Mount
     Chief
for names to give respect to Blackfeet streets.
I could deny them in my first hard springtime,
but choose amazed to ride you down with
     hunger.

—James Welch

JB: I'm glad you chose that poem, Jim. It has a number of themes in it I see as central to your work.

WELCH: Yes? It was one of the first ones I wrote. In it I wrote about things which were important to me instead of just following the way others at the time were writing.

JB: Writing about things important to you seems to me characteristic of your writing, not writing to a particular audience but out of a need to express things.

WELCH: In a way, yes. I remember it was about 1967 when I wrote that poem. Up until then I was trying to write about various things I didn't know much about or feel much about. Then Dick Hugo told me, "Write about what you know. Where'd you grow up, what was your Indian heritage, what kind of landscape was there?" So that little bit of common-sense advice just opened my eyes to things which were valuable and important. Once I heard that, it just opened up a world to me.

JB: When did you first start writing poetry?

WELCH: I can remember that pretty exactly. It was, let's see, January 1966. Before that I'd written some prose, but I started taking a poetry course then.

JB: Who, in addition to Hugo, was important to you as a teacher?

WELCH: Well, Madeline DeFrees was important to me. Of course she had a little different approach to things than Hugo. But I gained a lot between the both of them, kind of coming from opposite ends. Then another important person, kind of in a different way, was Bill Kittredge for fiction. He read my first novel and offered all kinds of suggestions. His advice really opened my eyes.

JB: Looking again at "In My First Hard Spring Time," I see a number of references from your Blackfeet and Gros Ventre heritage. How has that heritage affected your writing?

WELCH: Kind of growing up around the reservations, I just kept my eyes open and my ears open, listened to a lot of stories. You might say my senses were really brought alive by that culture. I learned more about it than I really knew. It was only after I began writing about it that I realized what I had learned. I knew quite a bit, in certain ways, about the Blackfeet and Gros Ventre ways of life, even though I wasn't raised in a traditional way. It made sense to me and I tried hard to understand those small parts.

JB: What would you describe as characteristic of those ways of life you know?

WELCH: I would say just a superficial understanding of the ceremonial life, the things that were important to them, their understanding of the world and how they were able to express it through the ceremonies. Also, the family life is very strong there. Of course there's a lot of alcoholism now and there are some broken homes, but the families up there are extremely strong. I don't find any white families which are quite like that in this country, those strong families without any separation of the generations, the old people and the young people. So those are two things that I see. And I've tried to understand it better through reading about the Blackfeet and the Gros Ventre.

JB: It's interesting the similarity between what you were just saying and the way Louise Erdrich told me she came to write about her Chippewa heritage. She thought she really had to write about something else, but that Indian heritage sort of forced itself on her and she found out she knew more than she thought she did.

WELCH: Uh-huh. I imagine that would be common among Indian writers today. You are in a culture which is so sensually alive. Later on you go back to it and find out how much you know.

JB: I notice in your writing the combination of the old world and the new and the strength of that old world. Even in a poem like "Christmas Comes to Moccasin Flats" in the midst of that snow-covered world where "drunks are draining radiators for love" you have a character like Medicine Woman telling an old story. Is it part of your vision that you see, even in the midst of the despair and alcoholism, that strength of the old ways?

WELCH: Oh yes. The vision that comes to mind of course is winter in Browning, how bleak it is, the wind blowing down from the Arctic Circle and people bundled up. Then, of course, there are the bad parts, such as the people drinking and falling down. So, that's a part of it. But the other part—you know, there's an opposite—is those people trying real hard to make something out of their life and just to keep going as a family. It's very important. It's kind of the one thing that ties it all together. Everyone is important within that family. I was really thinking about certain houses around Browning, how there were old people there and a lot of children around. The kids are just racing around and the older people are very tolerant. So I've always felt that. And I knew that there was a lot of knowledge in the old folks and a logical sense. Yes, I've always balanced that contrast between the sense of modern desolation and desperation and the old ways.

JB: That Indian ability to include things may mean including things you don't always think of as Indian when you're a non-Indian coming onto a reservation. Television, for example.

WELCH: Yes, it was just coming in back then and you'd find families huddled around just watching the thing. Of course now there are satellite dishes and cables and all that stuff. Back then it was more the radio in every house. Yes, when you get into that sort of isolation like that, television can be an important link to learning more about what's going on in the world.

JB: But learning more doesn't mean being overpowered or acculturated by it?

WELCH: No, no, as a matter of fact that woman who spits at her television—in my mind I kind of think of that as the 5:00 news, what was it back then? Huntley-Brinkley. She's reacting very specifically to news which is bad, killing people somewhere, that kind of thing.

JB: Reacting very appropriately. I'd like to ask about one of your poems which is probably most anthologized, "The Man From Washington." How do you feel about its being such a touchstone for anthologies or discussions of contemporary American Indian writing?

WELCH: Uh-huh. I know why it is used. It is very simple, very accessible. A lot of my poems, some people have said, are kind of obscure. They think that some of the images, a person would have to know that world to be able to understand.

But "The Man From Washington" is a very simple and straightforward little story. Its rhythms are quite regular and it's easy to understand.

JB: One other thing about that poem, a sort of technical point about revisions. The first time it was published was by John Milton in the *South Dakota Quarterly*, and it ended "a world of wealth, promise, and fabulous disease." In *Riding The Earthboy 40* it became "a world of money, promise, and fabulous disease," and finally, in *Carriers of the Dream Wheel*, it became "a world of money, promise, and disease." I wonder if you recall how you came to make those revisions?

WELCH: Well (laughs) I do! "Money" and "wealth," I just thought "money" was clearer. But when it comes to leaving out "fabulous"? I was working with an editor on that, and at that time the word "fabulous" was very popular. You know, people would say "fabulous" for everything, "Oh, that's *fabulous!*" So there was a particular quality to the word at the time that he didn't think appropriate and he wanted me to cut it. I wasn't forced to do it, I was convinced. So I just left out that word. But now that the word is no longer such a slang term I'm almost tempted to bring it back. Because those diseases were like nothing else they had ever experienced, to them they *were* fabulous. So if I ever get that poem reprinted, I think I will put back "fabulous."

JB: It affected me that way, too. I think of the way Small Pox became an actual character in some later Indian stories, walking around, a sort of fabled character. It *is* "fabulous disease," isn't it?

WELCH: Yes, it was put in with some of their other characters, modified or mythized, whatever you want to call it.

JB: I see certain characters, "Earthboy," for example, from your poems turn up in your novels. I wonder about the continuance that you feel from your poems to your two published novels.

WELCH: Yes, I guess that I feel that I'm always writing from the same world in the poems and the novels. And many of the people who live in that world are real. I don't feel I have to change names. There *was* a family named Earthboy living on the farm next to us and working the land. I used to ride around on the Earthboy 40. That's how I got my title. A name conjures up all sorts of associations.

JB: A real name has a kind of magic, then?

WELCH: It does, it does. If I were to make up a name like, say "Old War Horse," it wouldn't mean much. But a name like "Bird Rattler," that's a real name here. I don't intend to do like Faulkner . . . but as long as I think I can use a name I'll use it.

JB: What's funny about that is that a name like "Old War Horse" sounds like a name a non-Indian writer would make up.

WELCH: Well, I just made that name up, but I know what you mean. It's not a real name.

JB: Do you think that may be one of the problems non-Indian writers have, that they're writing from an imagined world rather than from the experienced reality of that world?

WELCH: Yes, but there are a lot of white writers who have been around Indians and know that world quite well, like James Willard Schultz who wrote about the Blackfeet. . .

JB: I was curious how you felt about Schultz. I like his novels, which have just been reissued.

WELCH: As a matter of fact, for my historical novel I read a couple of his. While he kind of overemphasizes his own importance, a lot of times he'll tell a story as it was told to him by an old warrior and those stories are good. They're told in very simple language. Now when he talks about coming back from a hunting trip and bringing game when everyone is starving, making himself out to be a hero, that's different. It's in recording the stories and retelling them. . .

JB: When the ego takes over the writing loses authenticity.

WELCH: Yes, it does. It's when a writer retells a story as it was told to him, without that ego getting in the way. . .

JB: How do you feel about writers such as Adolf Hungry Wolf? The contemporary German writer who was adopted by the Bloods and lives "as an Indian."

WELCH: I don't know what to make of Adolph Hungry Wolf himself. I have read one book of his. I guess what I like is the way he does record the stories, the way he writes about various clans, and so on. That's very interesting. But where he writes about himself as some sort of coming prophet, I don't know about that. I guess I don't have a firm idea about him.

JB: I remember a long time ago, more than a decade now, in the jacket copy for *Winter in the Blood*, you made a statement which ended "whites have to adopt a stance, Indians already have one," thinking about works written about Indians by whites. How do you still feel about that?

WELCH: Well, I remember that very well because the last part of that quote was left out. What I meant was that whites have to adopt a stance to write about Indian material, whereas for Indian writers that material is much more natural. I think the Indian can tell the story in a much more objective way. The white writer is either for or against the Indian, and I think that colors his writing. It seems as if the white writer is either a bleeding heart liberal or is saying down with them!

JB: That makes that statement make much more sense.

WELCH: I know. The way it was worded it made it sound as if the white writer has to adopt a stance to write about anything, whereas the Indian is sort of all-knowing.

JB: Back when you made that statement there weren't too many books by Indian writers around. How do you feel about the current wave of Indian writing?

WELCH: I think there are a lot of good Indian writers, especially poets. A lot of them are having success. I'm not sure quite what it is, but they adopt the mechanics of Western verse and a way of talking. Some have really developed a style similar, I think, to the writing of the nineteenth-century Indians. It's in their thoughts. For example, I think of Ray Young Bear. He has a superb style. And there are others. I've watched Joy Harjo develop from her first rather hesitant writing to the point where she's one of the very best poets today. We no longer have to apologize for Indian writing. Scott Momaday did great things. *House Made of Dawn* winning the Pulitzer prize opened many doors. He was an encouragement to many young Indian writers.

JB: In that dust jacket statement I mentioned earlier, you also mentioned toughness and fairness. I see both of those as characteristic of your work. How do you stay tough and fair when you write? What are your guidelines to try to maintain that balance?

WELCH: In some ways I was very fortunate in growing up: I was not within the culture in some ways, but I was also not an outsider. . . So, in a way I guess, I've always been treading the line. Doing that you have to be very aware of keeping your balance. That's what I've always tried to be very conscious of doing, maintaining my balance. That's why writing. . . I don't want to have to be. . . I like to get inside the minds of my characters, white characters as well as Indian. . . One thing about it, sometimes I get outraged. I was writing in my new novel about a massacre, a real massacre in which 460 members of this band of Blackfeet were massacred. As I was writing that scene I was getting more and more outraged.

JB: In some cases the kind of resolve and courage shown by your characters who are determined to survive on their own terms leads to a sort of suicide in an ironic sense. I'm thinking of the conclusion to *The Death of Jim Loney* or such poems as "Harlem, Montana. . ." or "The Renegade Wants Words." Your characters are defiant and true to themselves, but it leads to confrontations they can't hope to win. How do you feel about that theme in your work?

WELCH: I recollect mention made of the fact that it was sort of the only alternative for certain young men, that it's the only way Jim Loney can make a positive decision about his own fate. There were a lot of young men like Jim Loney when I was growing up who had no positive way to go.

JB: That word "warrior" is an interesting word and one that lately has been rather popular. But there has been some controversy about it. How do you feel about that? Are there ways in which you can see the Indian writer taking some of the stances of the warrior?

WELCH: I really can't. I don't think that kind of writing . . . The black writers were very militant. But that kind of writing doesn't survive. . . I'm not really sure the writer should be active as a militant.

JB: I've seen very little poetry of yours published since the mid-'70s and those poems from Greece which were in *The*

American Poetry Review. What led to the decline in output of poetry on your part?

WELCH: A couple of things. One was that . . . I felt my poems were getting kind of constipated and repeating themselves and so on. So, that's why I started writing fiction. I'm hoping now to get back to poetry again and that by now I won't be quite so . . . in my poems.

JB: Is there anything further you wanted to say, Jim?

WELCH: I wanted to make some mention of my new novel, *Fools Crow*. It's a much larger landscape than the other two novels and it shows where some of the younger characters in the first two books are coming from.

JB: It provides a historical background?

WELCH: Yes, it does that.

JB: Is that why you chose the broader canvas of the historical novel?

WELCH: Yes.

JB: In addition to poetry, what other plans do you have for your writing?

WELCH: I've been interested in writing a novel about urban Indian life. Also, I've been on the Montana parole board for the last ten years and I'm interested in eventually getting a novel out of that experience.

JB: Well, that would be new ground.

WELCH: Yes, I expect that it won't be right away, but I will someday write about that. I can't really say what my next book will be.

JB: Whatever it is, I'm looking forward to reading it.

Massaging the Earth

An Interview with
ROBERTA HILL WHITEMAN

It was early spring in Eau Claire, Wisconsin. The ice was
beginning to go out on the river, just visible outside the window
of Roberta Hill Whiteman's office at the University of Wisconsin. Like most offices used by teachers of English and Native
American writing, her walls were lined with bookshelves. For
some reason, though, I noticed most of all a smooth red stone
which had been placed—carefully, it seemed—on the shelf of
that single window in the narrow room. The stone was either
sandstone or the remains of a brick shaped back by the seasons
into something that blended back into nature, the square edges
worn away.

A member of the Oneida tribe of Wisconsin, those Iroquois people whose New York land was sold out from beneath them after the American Revolution, Roberta Hill Whiteman is a striking woman, tall and slender with long hair. I could see her face in the powerful drawing done for the cover of her book by her Arapaho artist husband, Ernest Whiteman, whose paintings were propped up around her office. Although she has been recognized for more than ten years as one of the foremost Native American poets, at the time of our interview Roberta Hill Whiteman's first book, *Star Quilt*, had not yet been published—though the page proofs rested on the table in her office. Roberta Hill Whiteman is not a writer to be rushed, it seems, and, as she spoke carefully, slowly, in response to my questions, the exactness of her answers was a justification for her measured approach.

Star Quilt

These are notes to lightning in my bedroom.
A star forged from linen thread and patches.
Purple, yellow, red like diamond suckers, children

of the star gleam on sweaty nights. The quilt unfolds
against sheets, moving, warm clouds of Chinook.
It covers my cuts, my red birch clusters under pine.

Under it your mouth begins a legend,
and wide as the plain, I hope Wisconsin marshes
promise your caress. The candle locks

us in forest smells, your cheek tattered
by shadow. Sweetened by wings, my mothlike heart
flies nightly among geraniums.

We know of land that looks lonely,
but isn't, of beef with hides of velveteen,
of sorrow, an eddy in blood.

Star quilt, sewn from dawn light by fingers
of flint, take away those touches
meant for noisier skins.

anoint us with grass and twilight air,
so we may embrace, two bitter roots
pushing back into the dust.

> —Roberta Hill Whiteman

JB: Why did you choose that particular poem to be the title poem for your new book?

WHITEMAN: I've been working on this collection for years, probably eight or nine years, before it was accepted last summer and the collection's changed a lot. I've always had a real hard time with poetry. I always have wanted to write but it seems that, whenever I sat down to write something, I wanted to put my whole life into the poem. This poem was sort of a revelation for me. I wrote it in '72 or '73, I think, so it's a very old poem but it brought with it this idea of making something. I saw in it that the language of a poem doesn't have to carry the weight of an entire life in that brief moment. It can be thought of as making something—like a quilt, as a woman would make a quilt for her grandson within a certain amount of time and yet the quilt itself has a lot of ramifications in either direction. It can be a symbol for something, it can be used for something. It's kind of my own understanding of poetry—that the quilt made, for example, for a fast or a quest helps that person. It's a physical thing, helps that person. And so in making the book I've had to deal with a kind of struggle with my own desire and need to work with language and to limit that desire, to shape it in some way. In working with the book, putting the book together, I had the idea of thinking of six directions: the Earth, and the Four Directions and then the Sky. Whether that comes through anymore in the collection, because it's changed in the time I first thought of it and the way it is now. . . I think it does. So the poem ends by going back into the dirt. And then the collection itself is arranged in west, north, east, south, seasonal kinds of images, not as categories but where images kind of flow back and forth into each other. Then the final poem has the idea of expanse, an image of expanse, the sky, though it doesn't really say "the sky," but it has that feeling of expanse.

JB: I like "Star Quilt" also because it seems to contain the primary concerns and images I recognize as characteristic of your work, concerns and images which relate to your background as an Oneida person, to yourself as a woman and a Native American writer, and also as a person who feels close to and influenced by seasons, earth, and other human beings whose lives come close to yours.

WHITEMAN: Well, I have a very hard time—people ask me about my work—and I have a very hard time fitting it all in, to know what's going on in it. I know my methods have changed a lot. I do, though, feel this intense love for looking at things, earth and sky and people. I really enjoy doing that. And I think it does come through. I don't know if this poem actually has all of the images, that kind of relationship. I like moths. Moths come up again and again.

JB: I've noticed that.

WHITEMAN: I just love them.

JB: Many writers credit certain events in their childhood with making them aware of the magic and power of poetry. Some draw images from those childhood experiences. I wonder what your childhood was like.

WHITEMAN: I had a hard childhood. (laughs) It was really pretty tough. But I was happy part of the time and I was really sad part of the time. Childhood experiences. . . my grandmother liked to recite poetry and to tell stories and to read. I remember, I think in my very early childhood, sitting in her lap and listening to her tell stories. I think she was in a way a poet. She would just recite and recite and she had a wonderful memory. She was in her seventies or her late sixties, and she just liked to recite and to tell stories. Very much alive. I can remember her. She left us, my family, some of the very few books that we had and they were poetry, Wordsworth and Shakespeare, and they were these enormous leatherbound— they must have been expensive in their day—huge books. I can remember as a child that was my favorite pastime, sitting underneath the dining-room table and trying to wade through the books because they were so important to her and because I sensed that there were so many pictures in them. It was like a catalog. I didn't understand a lot of what was going on, but I liked hearing her voice and the way she would tell things. My father was a musician and a teacher and made us get very involved with music at an early age, so I like music. These things were, I'd say, forced upon us—we *had* to do them, so I really enjoy those things. I think they have a lot to do with my love of language and rhythm. And dancing, too. I wanted to be a dancer but I couldn't manage that. I guess when I look back at it my childhood was kind of complex. My mother died when I was very young, which led me to a real awareness of life. That kind of experience I think really shapes the consciousness. For years I couldn't talk about it and I didn't want to write about it. I didn't want to talk about it. It's taken me maybe thirty-five years to admit that I really grew up in the area that I did, around Green Bay. I never really wanted to admit that I lived there. My family went back and forth between Oneida and Green Bay and Oneida and Green Bay, and when I went back to Oneida in '76 I had this terrible panic that I would have to move back to Green Bay—which is only ten miles away—if I couldn't find housing in Oneida. I had this great fear of Green Bay and what it was like there. And part of it was my childhood, that I've come to accept, that I've started to write about a little bit at a time. But, as Dick Hugo often mentioned to me, you cannot always deal with things. There are some poems and some stories that just never get written.

JB: Yes.

WHITEMAN: I guess in some way that's what my writing has been, to try in some way to just look at life, to appreciate life, its mystery, how mysterious it is.

JB: Did you realize early on that you wanted to write? When did that moment come when you knew that writing would be a very important thing for you?

WHITEMAN: I've always written. I had journals when I was a child. I kept journals and I wrote poems. I wrote stories a lot when I was young. But my grandmother was a doctor and my father had decided that I would be the doctor in the family so I was pushed to the sciences—math and philosophy, political science and psychology. I was encouraged not to get into the arts (laughs) and to go into the sciences and become a physician. I carried that burden with me until about 1970, when my father died and I realized I just did not have the mathematical ability that it took to get through college chemistry.

(laughs) Try as I did for years, I never could make it. And there was then a lot of soul-searching as to what I would do. I ended up majoring in Creative Writing and Psychology, kind of a blending of the two. And then I went to Montana because I couldn't find a job anywhere and college was my only choice. And that was where Dick Hugo just gave me such an understanding of what it was I had been struggling with, trying to force myself into something that I just was not.

There was a reason why I couldn't get through college chemistry—maybe I didn't have any ability in it. (laughs) But I had ability in other places. I've always loved writing, but I'd never thought of being a writer. I never thought I'd be teaching English.

JB: Um-hum. That sounds so familiar. I had the same experience.

WHITEMAN: You did?

JB: I was a major in Wildlife Conservation for three years and then ended up getting a degree in English.

WHITEMAN: Just trying to be. . .

JB: Something I thought I was supposed to be as opposed to something my heart was telling me I should be.

WHITEMAN: Right, I loved, I just loved poetry and I love writing and I love fiction. But for years I thought it just wasn't—those years when I was in high school in the '60s, my exposure to contemporary poetry was very small. We read Wordsworth. But as I began to become aware that there were *living* poets and people would tell me these things were possible, I wanted to be involved in it.

JB: You received your M.A. at Montana in 1973 where you studied with Richard Hugo. Was Hugo a very crucial person in your development as a writer?

WHITEMAN: Yes. He was able to talk with someone, not just on the surface of things. He had a sense of what you were feeling spiritually sometimes. He was very uncanny at times to talk to, and he would do this in a workshop, look at you and say things. He would never actually direct you and tell you what was going on in your life, but he had such empathy with people that he could sense things. I feel that he helped me to accept a number of things that I probably wouldn't have noticed without him just pointing them out.

JB: Were any other writers influential or important to you at that time?

WHITEMAN: Oh, I read an awful lot. I don't know that there was any one I really patterned myself after at all. Talking with certain poets has really helped a lot. I remember, when I was in Montana, talking with Jim Welch about how poetry works, what he was trying to do and what he sensed I was trying to do. Talking with and meeting with people—there were just so many people that I would meet and have a chance to talk to for a while, like Lance Henson and Leslie Silko. Other Indian writers really helped, to sit and just be able to *talk* with them, see what they're doing and see insights into things. I like a lot of contemporary poets and at different periods of time I've really felt attached to different people, as I'm sure a lot of people do. H.D. was one that I really liked and I still do, but there was a time when I wanted to read everything that she had written. Contemporary people, W. S. Merwin, Derek Walcott, there are certain people I'm just very fond of. I'll go back and look at some of the things Louise Bogan wrote. But I don't know that I consciously pattern myself after anyone.

JB: You're a member of the Oneida Tribe of Wisconsin. Has that connection been important to you as a writer? How, for example, have you drawn on Oneida history and traditions in your work?

WHITEMAN: Well . . . it is very important to me. For most of my life I felt this sense of exile and alienation and a fear. A lot of prejudice, growing up in an area in which there is a lot of prejudice I think affects people in that way. But there is this sense of home and of completeness that I also feel. Somehow I think that part of the writing is to set the record straight—for myself, to explain things for myself as if I were still a child inside. And I question it and I have to get it right. I have this feeling too, that other people have this same sense. They want to understand, they want to set it straight. There is such a difference between where I grew up as a child and Oneida that I really just treasure Oneida and my relatives who are there and the people I've found, the wholeness and the sense of understanding that I've gained from being there. It's been very important. I haven't always been able to do what I'd like to do. In some ways, as I said before, there are some things I want to deal with and write about but I either lack the knowledge about them or I lack the time to do it or I lack just the emotional stuff to deal with it. Some of it, it just takes some time to pull it out of yourself. It's hard. My Uncle was a very dear person to me. He died last year. I just learned so much from him. But he wanted me to write a history of the Oneidas from New York to Wisconsin and I started on it, but it's a real long project.

JB: I should say so!

WHITEMAN: I haven't completed it and that's one thing I want to do. Then in my early years of writing poetry, in the '70s, when I decided to just do it and I was willing to just throw everything else away and do it, there was a lot of anger in a lot of the poems. But I think over the years I have really wanted to and have gotten rid of some of that anger and I want to show and develop other sides of that connection.

JB: Yes. I think of a poem of yours such as "In The Longhouse: Oneida Museum" which seems to be a poem which deals with that history of dispossession. . .

WHITEMAN: Yes!

JB: . . . which deals with the Oneida people who are now scattered between, what, two nations, four states, and two Canadian provinces?

WHITEMAN: Um-hum.

JB: It is so incredible. It must be hard to deal with and this is something which perhaps may affect Native American writers in general, that history of dispossession and that need to put things back together again?

WHITEMAN: Um-humm. I think that we sense this even as children, that we have an intuitive sense of our own exile. We know this. We know this emotionally and spiritually and we understand it. But it is never dealt with, there's no comment on it. You'd never find in the establishment of the Oneida School anyone telling children, "You know, there's a reason you feel this way." It's in history, it's a fact that you feel this way. It was never mentioned to me as a child, why I felt that way. My father would tell us the history, but we never really understood. I think it took the '60s for Indian people to start to say "I know now why!" The perspective of the '60s brought a lot of things to the awareness of Indian people across the country that my parents were just not aware of. They had, in a way, to suffer through a lot of things. Yes, I think that poem is one that tries to deal with that, to look at it positively. It hints at things, tries to make a positive relationship.

JB: Has the Oneida language affected you at all? I don't know if you speak Oneida at all. A number of contemporary Indian writers don't speak the language that maybe their parents or grandparents did, but were you aware at all of Oneida or Iroquoian languages?

WHITEMAN: As a child I wanted to learn it, but my father wouldn't teach me. He would tell us that there was no positive thing to be gained from learning the language and that people would make fun of you. When I was living in Oneida several years ago, I was involved in trying to learn it. Unfortunately I didn't get to stay there and I moved over here, so I haven't been able to learn it, but I would really like to find some way to do that. It's a very complex language, a very difficult language to learn. It's very different from English. I wish I did know more. That's all I can say about it. I don't think it's influenced me directly.

JB: Are there things you've consciously avoided writing about which come from Oneida traditions, Oneida stories. I know that some Indian writers, Ray Young Bear, for example, feel they have to censor what they talk about, approach things very delicately because they might offend the traditional people.

WHITEMAN: I just stay away from that. I don't write about certain things. I don't feel that writing about those things is really my responsibility.

JB: "Awakening in Mythic Time" is the title of a paper you gave at the Modern Language Association in 1982. I'm interested in that dimension of "mythic time" in your work and in Native American poetry in general. Do you feel a special relationship between the writing of contemporary Native Americans and that time of myth? How much does your own work draw on that source?

WHITEMAN: Well, it's a difficult kind of question. I sense that Indian people have an awareness of . . . a different sort of time and a different sort of space. I have a real hard time trying to put it into words right now, but some of the things that I said in the paper were that this connection of a moving, living, and alive time, an alive space, a sense of everything being alive is so much a part of what I know, what I sense, and I find it in a lot of Indian writers and a lot of Indian poets. This connection to the earth is found in myth. I have a great love of the stories that I read and that I heard as a child and that I sensed in other traditions, too. One of the things I mention in that paper, which is not that well supported because I haven't done as much research for it as I'd need to do, one of the connections that I sense is one which I find in a lot of the contemporary writing on physics—let me see if I can think of this source. There's a man by the name of Bell, Bell's theorem that just came out in 1965. What he says is that everything has a quantum interconnectedness. (laughs) Which is something that Indian people have been saying all along. That things are instantaneous. That things which are known are instantaneous. That space between stars is not just empty space, that there's really no such thing as empty space, that it's all filled with something, dust or energy or whatever you want to call it. Indian people have an awareness of this earth and of the universe. My sense is that this is something which will come more and more into focus over the next hundred years or so. People will see that the conception of reality is changing, that it's gotta change, things can't be pigeonholed and classified and separated and analyzed. Things that are done in Phoenix, Arizona, affect people in northern Wisconsin. I sense that in other Indian writers. We are, in a way, aware of these things. Hopefully, the awareness will continue to grow. That, I suppose, is one reason why people write and why people paint and why people share things with each other, dance, try to see these connections. Because we have an enormously complex system to deal with,

Massaging the Earth

which denies all that because it has a lot of energy to keep going that way. It gains a lot from that denial which leads to further repression. There were a number of things that I tried to bring out in that paper. I looked at several poets: Joy Harjo and Linda Hogan, women poets. And, using images, I tried to show that the mythic world is very much alive, alive in the sense that you can see the themes and the content actually within the poem. But if you look in terms of the awareness of space and time within the poem and the way the images focus on this awareness, you get the sense that it is mythic. It comes from the stories. It has a sense of growth or chaos or complexity.

JB: I also like the use of "awakening." That is what it is, isn't it?

WHITEMAN: Yes! I think that we, Indian people, have been aware of this and have known this, but as far as trying to resolve and . . . in terms of the human community. . . I can see it not just in terms of the Indian people of this continent, but worldwide. The same kind of colonialism that affected the Oneidas affects the Aborigines in Australia and affects the Mayans and affects everyone. We, as Indian people, are becoming more aware of it and are able to be more vocal about it. We were vocal about it before but it wasn't time. It wasn't time yet. It still might not be time for all of us, but I think we are becoming more and more aware of it. I just sense a whole change. I think a lot of people do. Simon does.

JB: Yes, Simon Ortiz, Leslie Silko. I think it interesting, mentioning women writers, that there are so many strong Indian women writers now.

WHITEMAN: Well, I don't know. I like to think that that's intended—for whatever you want to take intended to mean. Lance Henson said something one time. I think of it every now and then. It's just marvellous. We walk around and we wonder, where do these thoughts come from? Where in the world do your thoughts come from? And he said "They come from your feet. When you're walking on the earth they come up through your feet." Up, up, up into your head. And women, you know, in Oneida culture, in the traditional culture, have this close connection between their feet and the earth. This idea of being close to the earth. When you dance, you know, you're close to the earth. You don't jump around, you massage the earth. And I like to think of that connection, that the earth is telling us things.

Connected to the Past

An Interview with
RAY YOUNG BEAR

Raised near Tama, Iowa, on the ancestral lands of his Mesquakie people, Ray Young Bear's poetry has a dual quality of
powerful statement and mystery which seems to emanate from
the earth itself. Perhaps this is because he is so involved in that
Mesquakie community, long known for its closeness and its ties
to traditional native culture. When the Mesquakie people were
forced to sell their lands in 1845 and were removed to Kansas,
they did not accept their resettlement. Instead, with collected
gold currency, Ray's great-great-grandfather, Mamwiwaneke, as
traditional Chief, initiated the purchase of eighty acres of land
along the Iowa River in 1856. That is why, to this day, no
Mesquakie thinks of referring to their lands as a reservation.

When *Winter of the Salamander* was published by Harper & Row in 1980, the jacket copy rightly described it as poetry expressing, among other things, "the spirit of a people who are, above all, survivors."

The interview with Ray Young Bear took place in a hotel room on the Iowa State University campus. We were there for a Native American Writer's program and a powwow, at which Ray's Woodland Drum, one of three drumming groups from the Mesquakie settlement, would be playing later that night. Family is of deep importance to Ray, and his wife sat beside him as he answered the questions. Ray is a husky man of medium height. As he spoke he would pause at times, as if not only looking for the right words, but also looking for the right language in which to speak them.

grandmother

if i were to see
her shape from a mile away
i'd know so quickly
that it would be her.
the purple scarf
and the plastic
shopping bag.
if i felt
hands on my head
i'd know that those
were her hands
warm and damp
with the smell
of roots.
if i heard
a voice
coming from
a rock
i'd know
and her words
would flow inside me
like the light
of someone
stirring ashes
from a sleeping fire
at night.

—Ray Young Bear

Connected to the Past

YOUNG BEAR: That is one of the very first poems I wrote . . . in 1968. Since I lived with my grandmother for the first twelve years of my life I owe much of what I know of Indian culture, of Mesquakie culture, to her. I think that poem, more than all the other poems I've written over the past fourteen years, has been published and republished. So, I go back to it often.

JB: Ray, I'd like to ask you a couple of very simple questions. First, when did you start writing?

YOUNG BEAR: I think in 1964, to be exact. I was in seventh grade then, and we were given an assignment by the English teacher to compose an essay on our family lives or something to that effect. So, I went home and wrote my paper—or what I thought was a paper—and the next day I went back to class and handed it in to the teacher. I then found out that my essay wasn't among those to be read that day. It came back with a lot of red marks on it, and I got discouraged because this was my first year out from the Bureau of Indian Affairs day school. At that moment I realized just how far I had to go as far as trying to write the English language and write it well. From that day on in the seventh grade I tried to make it a point to learn the English language, write it, and think in it, while at the same time trying to present some aspects of Mesquakie culture—without dealing with sensitive material.

JB: It reminds me of a story about Ely Parker, a Seneca sachem of the last century who also achieved success in the white world, even becoming a General in the American Civil War. When he was a boy he acted as guide to a group of British soldiers who made jokes about his inability to speak English well. From then on in he vowed to learn it so well that no one could ever question his ability in that language again. As you have done, he ended up a person whose language was eloquent and clear and often much better than that of those who grew up with English as their first and only language.

The statement was made on the dust jacket of your book of poems, *Winter of the Salamander*, that you think your poems in Mesquakie and then translate them into English. Is it true that you use or used that method of composition?

YOUNG BEAR: I think that in the beginning when I was trying to write I started out first in the Mesquakie language. I found out that most of our language translated almost . . . backward. So I used that method for a while and found it to be very successful, especially when I compared my translated poems with those which were being written then, around 1969, the period of Robert Bly—who has been a great influence on my poems. I liked the type of poems being written in the late '60s. I thought that some of my translations had, in some form or another, a connection to what they were writing. So, I did think some of my poems out in Mesquakie in the beginning. Lately, though, I think they all come out in English. Which reminds me of something that happened recently, and I would like to share it since it has reference to translating. An interesting example, anyway. Not too long ago, I submitted what I thought was a very good poem, "The Language of Weather," to *Another Chicago Magazine*. It came back with small notations on it to the effect that it was "abstract." I forget the editor's name. I was a bit let down by this because this was the fifth or sixth time this poem had been sent out. I keep a very good record of where my poems go and I keep more or less a collage of rejections to keep myself aware of how literary-minded people look upon *real* Native American poetry: poetic/cultural injustice and so forth. Anyway, once I got this rejection sheet I sat down and said "What will they publish?" I thought ACM had once published Ortiz and Harjo, so I whimsically asked myself, "What am I doing wrong?" So I sat down one day and thought, "Well, I'm going to write a poem out in Mesquakie and see what happens." I started talking to myself and seeing how best a poem could be translated from Mesquakie. I wrote four little poems, probably about ten lines each, typed them out—I think I did this in an hour—sent them and in two weeks I got an acceptance from *Another Chicago Magazine*. But, I am wondering whether one has to do this all the time, whether one has to revert to what I read recently in *The American Book Review* called "Ugh talk."

JB: Robert Penn Warren did that in his Chief Joseph book, a book which I don't particularly like.

YOUNG BEAR: To me it is kind of a negative term, but it does make a little bit of sense because I just wrote it from the basics. Whatever—the point is, I didn't touch it up, use hard words, or surrealistic images. Just realistic images, simple ideas of how facets of tribal life are. But that really surprised the hell out of me when the poem got accepted so quickly.

JB: That makes me think of a number of things. One of them is my original second question. Where do you get the ideas for your poems? Where do your poems come from, both in the idea sense and the other sense of where poems come from?

YOUNG BEAR: I think that poems come from a series of complex and intertwining graphic images which, in one form or another, somehow resembles what is for me the poetic, free verse form. Let's take the most recent poem that I've had published, "The King Cobra as Political Assassin," written on May 30th, 1981, and published by *Triquarterly* this year. It was a poem written mostly out of frustration because that year I was having some difficulty trying to come up with ideas of how I should write a poem and where the inspiration was going to come from. I had this dream the day before Ronald Reagan was shot by Hinckley, so I started this poem called "The King Cobra as Political Assassin" based upon that dream. I think it wasn't necessarily the idea that I was prescient. I wasn't thinking I was that. I was just trying to find a subject to write about. So I connected that dream to the attempted assassination. What came out of it was something I really liked because in it I discussed the fact that in the dream I was somewhere else apart from the Mesquakie Settlement and in the dream these two serpents were fighting in land which I had assumed to be land purchased by my Ukimau (Sacred Chief) grandfather. So I valued this dream a lot, but as far as trying to connect it to the Reagan deal, the poem was in reality just a statement on real estate and the need for investments in land. (chuckles)

JB: I love that! You know, the story of the Mesquakie people regaining that part of their land where the settlement now is—having it taken away and then purchasing it back—is a great inspiration. They sold their horse herd, didn't they, to buy back their own land?

YOUNG BEAR: Yes, land was purchased but the "horse herd" story has been stretched out a bit; it was a cash transaction. Anyway, that's how that particular "King Cobra" poem came about. But I sort of tie in dreams, some of my own imagery and my thoughts and, on rare occasions, something I heard which my Grandmother said—how we are connected to the past. Once in a great while, whether I am socializing in a university or an Indian tavern with my friends, I sometimes find out that some of my friends are great bearers of poetic images, even though they don't realize it. So I listen with keen interest and, in a sense, I can see that everyone in an Indian community is a poet of sorts. That's where I get my images, my poems, from—from just about anything.

JB: Can I ask you a few questions about who your primary influences were, as far as poets go?

YOUNG BEAR: I think my primary influences developed in the summer of 1968, when I was in an Upward Bound program at Luther College in Decorah, Iowa, and at Bemidji, Minnesota, where they were having a midwestern poets' and writers' conference. There I met Robert Bly, David Ignatow, David Ray, and John Milton, and several other very important people. They were there and why I decided to go I don't know. The Upward Bound people and English Department people at Luther College decided that perhaps going to a writers' conference and being around literary people would be a good influence.

I was impressed by the talk about poetry, the reading of poetry, and the teaching of poetry, mostly through Robert Bly. At that time I think I was more involved with just trying to make proclamations as to who I was, trying to get my identity lined. I had a manuscript of some sorts—at about eighteen years of age I had about a twenty-page manuscript—and one night Robert Bly along with David Ray invited me to their room and I took my poems. They started looking at my poems and started crossing lines off and editing it on the spot. I had no idea what they were doing until they started telling me word for word exactly what was going on, saying things like "Don't use i-n-g all the time!" I said, "Okay." "Don't use hard words!" I said, "Okay." They told me a bunch of other things which I still use to this day.

JB: Yes. They did it to me, too! (laughter) The same two people!

YOUNG BEAR: So I left the conference with great enthusiasm for poetry. That fall I went out to college in California and, even though I didn't know many of the poets then, since I was very new to the field, I started going to various poetry readings sponsored by the school. Among those reading there whose works I looked upon with great interest and respect were Diane Wakoski, Seamus Heaney, and Galway Kinnell. They had quite an array of these people coming in—oh, and Charles Bukowski. I went to all their readings and tried to absorb some of what they were saying. But I discovered that they had limitations, such as the absence of one's roots—which Native Americans have. So I said, "Well, maybe I can say something else a little better than what they're trying to do," which was this aboriginal, primal sort of poetry. Those people were probably the first influence, but since 1969 or '70 I don't read too many people any more. I'm not trying in desperation to keep up with who won the Pulitzer Prize this year and so forth, even though I did go into a poetry class—for one day—with Donald Justice and found out that I didn't belong in workshops. Or vice versa. On that same level, with no offense to anyone, I don't read the work of my tribal contemporaries. Because of my cultural and geographic isolation, my access to anyone's work is limited to what comes in free via the U.S. mail.

JB: I'd like to ask you about your first real book of poetry, *Winter of the Salamander*. I believe that you signed a contract for it at least four or five years before it was actually published. Is that correct?

YOUNG BEAR: Yes.

JB: It was published by Harper & Row in 1980. How was it that it took such a considerable amount of time from the signing of the contract to the actual publication?

RAY YOUNG BEAR

YOUNG BEAR: Well, let's see. I called Douglas Lattimer in New York and asked him what my chances would be of signing on with the Native American Publishing Program at Harper & Row. He responded by saying that, since he liked my work, admired it, the chances would be very good that they would accept. So I told him that I would send him a manuscript that I had, which was only about fifty pages long. I sent it and told him that I had some more poems forthcoming. He accepted it and sent a contract and a small advance. So, at a time when a writer should be enthusiastic and celebrating the fact that they had just gotten a contract, I thought that I had just taken on a heavy load. I began to see my inadequacies with the English language and in terms of how poems should be written correctly. It was, more or less, a sense of underestimation which is, I think, a congenital thing. So I kept writing and pushed myself to get this manuscript off to him. Six months went by and I was still working on the first sixty pages I had sent him and another year went by and I was still working on them. Then another year went by . . . and another year went by. . . and I was still communicating with him and he was glad, at least, that I was still working on it. Finally, when the time came to send the whole manuscript, I found he was no longer involved with Harper & Row. He told me the program was being transferred to San Francisco and he gave me a new address. Then I started communicating with a whole series of new people who, I must say, were very, very patient with my work and still are. Finally, in the winter of 1979, I looked at the third or fourth galleys and thought, "I can no longer be a poet at this point, I can no longer be a critic from a tribal or a literary point of view." As an old English professor by the name of Loren Taylor at the University of Northern Iowa used to tell me, "Just get the stuff out. To hell with it." Meaning to hell with my insecurities. It took me five years, but that's how I actually felt in the last leg. A painful gestation for an ordinary, lackluster birth.

JB: How do you feel about the book now?

YOUNG BEAR: That's a good question because I was going over it the past few days before this reading at Iowa State

University and trying to pick out some poems I thought would be appropriate. I only read one poem, "Grandmother," which I take great pride in, and as for the rest, somehow, I consider the rest of the poems experimentation. I'm not too satisfied with my work. As I said, there's a sense of underestimation that prevails in each stage of my writing. I know that within the course of time I'll develop some sort of aim and I think *Winter of the Salamander* is merely a stepping-stone toward higher things and better experience.

JB: One of the poems in the book, "For the Rain in March," is a response to the poem "Pow-wow" by W. D. Snodgrass. An African writer named Chinua Achebe once said that he wrote his first novel, *Things Fall Apart*, because he read a book about his native Nigeria, *Mr. Johnson*, by the English writer Joyce Cary. Cary's book was such a terrible representation of his people and his culture that Achebe felt he had to set the record straight. It strikes me that "For the Rain in March" comes from a similar feeling on your part.

YOUNG BEAR: Iowa State University Press published one of my poems in an anthology of poets that have been around the Iowa region at one time or another and this poem by Snodgrass was, appropriately or inappropriately, placed right next to me. I took great offense to this poem. I believe, at least, that is where I first read it.

JB: It's also included in his second book *After Experience*. It's a pretty well-known poem.

YOUNG BEAR: Perhaps, then, it is in there. I think that is the motivation which started me writing the short segment on him. After reading the poem, I was just amazed at how someone could go to a powwow, pay the standard admission fee, and think that the whole world of the Mesquakie people was going to be revealed to him in one program, when the fact of the matter is that these dances performed by the Mesquakie people are just tribal celebration dances. Snodgrass thought he saw a lot more than he did—especially when he thought he could make it a poetic commentary about the singers, some of the children, the songs. To degrade a form of tribal entertainment was, to me, a great slap in the face to the Mesquakies. I knew that a lot of the Mesquakie people who were the subjects of this poem were not going to read it at all. So I thought I would do an "eye for an eye" sort of thing and write some negative commentary back to him and hopefully he would see it somewhere along the line and know that we weren't as simple-minded and savage, I guess, as he put it in his poem.

JB: I think that poem, "Grandmother," and most of the poems in the book, in fact, especially certain of the short clear poems such as "One Chip of Bone" reflect your consciousness of your identity as a Mesquakie person and your protectiveness about your people and your culture, your determination not to say the wrong things yourself and to present people with an image which is strong and honest.

YOUNG BEAR: Yes. There is another interesting aspect to this thing of dealing with Harper & Row. Right now I am involved with a second book contract with them which I was forced to accept out of financial reasons. I first proposed to Harper & Row that I do a book on Native American writers and singers and sent this idea to them. It took one long year for the publisher to respond and when he did he made a counter proposal to do a book on Native American folk tales. They sent me a book which was to be, I guess, something that I could follow. It was a book by Italo Calvino of Italian folk tales. I like folk tales, but I didn't like what was written in the preface by Calvino. He said his folk tales were not made with the help of "little old ladies" who knew stories; rather they were gathered from library material and previous publications. I used this point when I responded back to the publishers. I said that if I did a book on Native American folk stories we should leave library material out and try and go after stories from the original storytellers themselves which were unpublished. This was my original idea. They responded by saying, yes it's a good idea, we'll lay aside some money so you can go to these storytellers and try and get them to translate some stories. I soon discovered, after a year or so of trying to get these people to write back to me, to correspond with me, and tell me who the storytellers were in the Midwestern region, that nobody . . . well, nobody responded. Period. I took this as a sign that the whole concept of telling a story is still regarded with a lot of veneration among Native American tribes. Then I was sort of stuck because I didn't have any material and Harper & Row was very anxious to get something out. So I wrote back to them and told them the problems that I had encountered. Basically I told them there were a whole lot of Native American spiritual leaders throughout the United States who were becoming increasingly aware of people who were making profits out of Indian culture. So I decided to completely scrap the project, on my own. I told them I didn't want to look back twenty or thirty years later and be criticized by neighboring tribes for telling their stories. I figured that if I had to tell them some stories, they would be Mesquakie stories. That is as far as I have gone with Harper & Row to this day. Right now they're waiting for my word as to whether or not Mesquakie stories are possible. I have been consulting my Grandmother as well as other people, and I am afraid that it is simply impossible. The first and only stories we could have picked from Mesquakie people were published by William Jones, who was a protégé of Franz Boaz, in the early 1900s. I tried to tell my relatives that there had been previously published material on Mesquakie people by our forefathers. I thought it would still be possible to, at least, try and share some stories now before they are forgotten. But this idea of trying to keep a culture free of what would be called cultural contamination is still very prevalent among the Mesquakie. It would be easier just to forget the stories and not publish them at all. If one attempts to do that, they are risking their lives. As my grandmother told me, "I used to hear stories about William Jones being here on the Settlement when I was young. He must have gone around with a bag over his shoulder, collecting these stories. But what happened to him? He went overseas and was killed by the Philipines or some other tribe in those islands in the Pacific." She uses that as a reference and I think it is reference that must be heeded.

Resources and Credits

Bibliography

In putting together this bibliography I have not attempted to make a complete list of all the publications by each author. Instead, I have tried to cite works which represent not only that poet's individual voice but also a good selection of his or her strongest poems. If, as in the case of Maurice Kenny's newest volume, a recent book brings together work previously appearing in earlier collections I have not listed those earlier books. Though many of these writers—Momaday, Allen, Blue Cloud, Kenny, Erdrich, Ortiz, Welch, Vizenor—have important publications in fiction, I have limited this bibliography to their poetic works. In addition, I have listed a few general anthologies and critical volumes which will be helpful to any reader who wishes to further explore contemporary Native American poetry.

One of the sad things I have noted in putting together this list is that far too many of the books on it—those by Duane Niatum, for example—are out of print. Other major voices, Simon Ortiz for one, have an incredible volume of work published in scattered places and crying for a good volume of selected poems. There is no doubt in my mind that we are in need of more publishers with a serious commitment to publishing not just short-run chapbooks but major collections of poetry by our most significant Native American voices—collections which they will keep in print. One of the exciting things for me is that all of the authors interviewed have just completed or are now working on new poems which will make up a great many more future volumes. N. Scott Momaday, for example, whose work has always been a breaker of ground for Native American writing, has just completed a new volume of poems entitled *Earth Pray My Days*, which has not yet been placed with a publisher. Thus, in many ways, this list can be seen as a point of departure for not one, but innumerable journeys.

Allen, Paula Gunn. *Shadow Country*, UCLA Native American Series, Los Angeles, Calif., 1982.

Blue Cloud, Peter. *Turtle, Bear and Wolf*, Akwesasne Notes, Rooseveltown, N.Y., 1976.

———. *White Corn Sister*, Strawberry Press, Brooklyn, N.Y. 1979.

———. *Sketches in Winter with Crows*, Strawberry Press, Brooklyn, N.Y., 1984.

Burns, Diane. *Riding the One-Eyed Ford*, Contact II Publication, New York, N.Y., 1981.

Cook-Lynn, Elizabeth. *Then Badger Said This*, Ye Galleon Press, Fairfield, Wash., 1983.

———. *Seek the House of Relatives*, Blue Cloud Quarterly, Marvin, S.D., 1983.

Erdrich, Louise. *Jacklight*, Holt, Rinehart & Winston, New York, N.Y., 1984.

Harjo, Joy. *What Moon Drove Me to This?*, I. Reed Books, New York, N.Y., 1979.

———. *She Had Some Horses*, Thunder's Mouth Press, New York, N.Y., 1983.

Henson, Lance. *Selected Poems, 1970–1983*, The Greenfield Review Press, Greenfield Center, N.Y., 1985.

Hogan, Linda. *Calling Myself Home*, The Greenfield Review Press, Greenfield Center, N.Y., 1978.

———. *Eclipse*, UCLA Native American Series, Los Angeles, Calif., 1983.

———. *Seeing Through the Sun*, University of Massachusetts Press, Amherst, Mass., 1985.

Karoniaktatie. *Landscape*, Blue Cloud Quarterly, Marvin, S.D., 1984.

Kenny, Maurice. *Is Summer This Bear*, The Chauncy Press, Saranac Lake, N.Y., 1985.

———. *Between Two Rivers, Selected Poems 1956–1984*, White Pine Press, Fredonia, N.Y., 1987.

Littlebird, Harold. *On Mountains' Breath*, Tooth of Time Books, Santa Fe, N. Mex., 1982.

Momaday, N. Scott. *The Gourd Dancer*, Harper & Row, New York, N.Y., 1976.

Niatum, Duane. *Ascending Red Cedar Moon*, Harper & Row, New York, N.Y., 1973.

————. *Digging Out the Roots*, Harper & Row, New York, N.Y., 1977.

————. *Songs for the Harvester of Dreams*, University of Washington Press, Seattle, Wash., 1981.

————. *Raven and the Fear of Growing White*, Bridges Books, Amsterdam, The Netherlands, 1983.

Ortiz, Simon. *From Sand Creek*, Thunder's Mouth Press, New York, N.Y., 1981.

————. *A Good Journey*, University of Arizona Press, Tucson, Ariz., 1984 (reprint of a 1977 volume).

Revard, Carter. *Ponca War Dancers*, Point Riders Press, Norman, Okla., 1980.

Rose, Wendy. *Lost Copper*, Malki Museum Press, Banning, Calif., 1980.

————. *What Happened When the Hopi Hit New York*, Contact II Publications, New York, N.Y., 1982.

————. *The Halfbreed Chronicles*, West End Press, Los Angeles, Calif., 1985.

Tapahonso, Luci. *Seasonal Woman*, Tooth of Time Press, Santa Fe, N. Mex., 1982.

Vizenor, Gerald. *Seventeen Chirps*, The Nodin Press, Minneapolis, Minn., 1964.

————. *Matsushima*, The Nodin Press, Minneapolis, Minn., 1984.

Welch, James. *Riding the Earthboy 40*, Harper & Row, New York, N.Y., 1976. (reprint of a 1971 volume).

Whiteman, Roberta Hill. *Star Quilt*, Holy Cow! Press, Iowa City, Ia., 1984.

Young Bear, Ray. *Winter of the Salamander*, Harper & Row, New York, N.Y., 1980.

Anthologies

At present, though there have been numerous anthologies in the past of both Native American poets and poems about Native American themes, there are only a handful of books which I can recommend. Again, especially when one considers the many new

Native American writers just beginning to appear in print, these books can be seen as points of departure and there is a great deal of room for future volumes.

Bruchac, Joseph (editor). *Songs From This Earth on Turtle's Back,* The Greenfield Review Press, Greenfield Center, N.Y., 1983. (310 pages. Contains poems by 52 Native American poets)

Dodge, Robert, and McCullough, Joseph. *New and Old Voices of Wah'Kon Tah,* International Publishers, New York, N.Y., 1985. (Much improved from the earlier volume, *Voices of Wah'Kon Tah* which contained some non-Indian writers. 130 pages. 46 poets.)

Niatum, Duane. *The Harper's Anthology of 20th Century Native American Poetry,* Harper & Row, San Francisco, Ca. (This volume, which is to be published in late 1987 or early 1988, is a follow-up to Niatum's earlier excellent anthology from Harper & Row, *Carriers of the Dream Wheel.* It differs from the earlier volume in that it is meant to be more inclusive of major twentieth-century Native American voices, including some Canadian Indian poets and such pioneering and now deceased writers as Frank Pruwit.)

Critical Studies

This is an area which is still extremely thin. Thus far, though a number of writers have taken a stab at producing books on American Indian writing, I cannot recommend most of them because they either deal with the oral tradition (which is, indeed, a fertile area worthy of study) or they display real ignorance about the Native American cultures from which contemporary Native American writers draw so much of their energy and inspiration.

Allen, Paula Gunn. *Studies in American Indian Literature: Critical Essays and Course Designs,* Modern Language Association, New York, N.Y., 1983.

Lincoln, Kenneth, *Native American Renaissance,* University of California Press, Berkeley and Los Angeles, Calif., 1983.

The liveliest sources of information about contemporary Native American poetry remain the magazines devoted to Native American scholarship. These include *American Indian Culture and Research Journal* (UCLA), *The American Indian Quarterly* (Berkeley), and *Studies in American Indian Literatures* (Columbia). Also, in recent years, numerous literary magazines have devoted special issues to Native American poetry and Native American writing. These include *Pacific Moana Quarterly* (a special issue entitled *A Nation Within*, Volume 8, Number 1, 1983, edited by Ralph Salisbury), *The North Dakota Quarterly* (Volume 53, Number 2, Spring 1985), *Sinister Wisdom* (a North American Indian women's issue entitled *A Gathering of Spirit*, edited by Beth Brant, Numbers 22/23, 1983), and *The Phoenix* (*The Native American Today*, Volume VI, numbers i and ii, 1986).

Publication Credits

Interviews

Page 23, Peter Blue Cloud: Selections appeared in "Coyote Was Here," edited by Bo Scholer, *The Dolphin*, No. 9, April 1984, Aarhus, Denmark. A briefer version (edited by Alyce Sadonger) appeared in *Atlatl*, Vol. 2, No. 3, Fall 1986.

Page 71, Louise Erdrich: Appeared in *The Greenfield Review*, Vol. 14, Nos. 1 and 2, 1987.

Page 85, Joy Harjo: Appeared in *North Dakota Quarterly*, Vol. 53, No. 2, Spring 1985.

Page 101, Lance Henson: Appeared in *Puerto Del Sol*, Vol. 22, No. 2, Spring 1987.

Page 131, Karoniaktatie: Appeared in *Contact II*, #41/42/43, 1986.

Page 141, Maurice Kenny: Selections will appear in *I Tell You Now* (autobiographies of American Indian writers), edited by Brian Swann and Arnold Krupat, University of Nebraska Press, Lincoln.

Page 153, Harold Littlebird: Will appear in *Akwekon*, No. 6.

Page 169, N. Scott Momaday: Appeared in *American Poetry Review*, July/August 1984.

Page 187, Duane Niatum: Appeared in *North Dakota Quarterly*, Vol. 55, No. 1, 1987.

Page 205, Simon Ortiz: Appeared in *Puerto Del Sol*, Vol. 22, No. 3, Fall 1987.

Page 243, Wendy Rose: Appeared in *The Greenfield Review*, Vol. 12, Nos. 1 and 2, 1984.

Page 265, Luci Tapahonso: Appeared in *Melus*, Vol. 11, No. 4, 1984.

Page 317, Roberta Hill Whiteman: Appeared in *Contact II*, #32/33, 1984.

Poems

Page 3, "Recuerdo" by Paula Gunn Allen: Previously published in *Shadow Country*, Native American Series, UCLA, 1982, Los Angeles, CA., and in *The Greenfield Review*.

Page 25, "Alcatraz" by Peter Blue Cloud: Previously published in *Turtle, Bear & Wolf*. Akwesasne Notes. 1976, Rooseveltown, NY.

Page 45, "Big Fun" by Diane Burns: Previously published in *Riding the One-Eyed Ford*, Contact II Publications, 1981, New York, NY., and in *Songs From This Earth on Turtle's Back*, The Greenfield Review Press, 1983, Greenfield Center, NY.

Page 58, "At Dawn, Sitting in My Father's House" by Elizabeth Cook-Lynn: Previously published in *Seek the House of Relatives*, The Blue Cloud Quarterly, 1983, Marvin, SD.

Page 73, "Runaways" by Louise Erdrich: Previously published in *Jacklight*, Holt, Rinehart & Winston, 1984, New York, NY.

Page 86, "Anchorage" by Joy Harjo: Previously published in *She Had Some Horses*, Thunder's Mouth Press, 1983, New York, NY.

Page 116, "Man in the Moon" by Linda Hogan: Previously published in *Calling Myself Home*, The Greenfield Review Press, 1978, Greenfield Center, NY.

Page 143, "First Rule" by Maurice Kenny: Previously published in *Between Two Rivers: Selected Poems*, White Pine Press, 1987, Fredonia, NY.

Page 155, "Moonlight, Moon Bright" by Harold Littlebird: Previously published in *On Mountains' Breath*, Tooth of Time Press, 1982, Santa Fe, NM.

Page 171, "The Bear" by N. Scott Momaday: Previously published in *The Gourd Dancer*, Harper & Row, 1976, New York, NY.

Page 189, "The Novelty Shop" by Duane Niatum: Previously published in *After the Death of an Elder Klallam*, The Baleen Press, 1970, Phoenix, AZ.

Page 206, "At Tsaile Lake" by Simon J. Ortiz: Previously published in A *Poem Is A Journey*, Pteranadon Press, 1981, Bourbonais, IL.

Page 227, "Dancing with Dinosaurs" by Carter Revard: Previously published in *Ponca War Dancers*, Point Riders Press, 1980, Norman, OK.

Page 244, "Truganinny" by Wendy Rose: Previously published in *The Halfbreed Chronicles*, West End Press, 1985, Los Angeles, CA.

Page 267, "Hills Brothers Coffee" by Luci Tapahonso: Previously published in *Seasonal Woman*, Tooth of Time Press, 1982, Santa Fe, NM.

Page 283, "Auras on the Interstate" by Gerald Vizenor: Previously published in *Songs from This Earth on Turtle's Back*, The Greenfield Review Press, 1983, Greenfield Center, NY.

Page 305, "In My First Hard Springtime" by James Welch: Previously published in *Riding the Earthboy 40*, Harper & Row, 1976, New York, NY.

Page 319, "Star Quilt" by Roberta Hill Whiteman: Previously published in *Star Quilt*, Holy Cow! Press, 1984, Minneapolis, MN.

Page 333, "Grandmother" by Ray Young Bear: Previously published in *Winter of the Salamander*, Harper & Row, 1980, New York, NY.

Addresses of Publishers
Cited in the Bibliography

Akwesasne Notes, Mohawk Nation via Rooseveltown, NY 13683
Blue Cloud Quarterly, Blue Cloud Abbey, Marvin, SD 57251
The Chauncy Press, Turtle Pond Road, Saranac Lake, NY 12983
UCLA Native American Series, American Indian Studies Center,
    3220 Campbell Hall, UCLA, Los Angeles, CA 90024
Contact II Publications, P.O. Box 451, Bowling Green Station, New
    York, NY 10004
The Greenfield Review Press, R.D. 1, Box 80, Greenfield Center, NY
    12833
Holy Cow! Press, 5435 Old Highway 18, Stevens Point, WI 54481
The Nodin Press, 525 N. 3rd Street, Minneapolis, MN 55401
Point Riders Press, P.O. Box 2731, Norman, OK 73070
I. Reed Books, 1446 6th Street, Berkeley, CA 94710
Strawberry Press, P.O. Box 451, Bowling Green Station, New York,
    NY 10004
Thunder's Mouth Press, P.O. Box 780, New York, NY 10025
Tooth of Time Books, 634 Garcia, Santa Fe, NM 87501
West End Press, P.O. Box 27334, Albuquerque, NM 87125
White Pine Press, 76 Center Street, Fredonia, NY 14063

American Indian Culture and Research Journal, American Indian Studies Center, UCLA, Los Angeles, CA 90024

The American Indian Quarterly, Native American Studies, 3415 Dwinelle Hall, Berkeley, CA 94720

Studies in American Indian Literatures, 602 Philosophy Hall, Columbia University, New York, NY 10027

About the Author

Joseph Bruchac, whose anthology *Breaking Silence, Contemporary Asian Poets* won a 1984 American Book Award, is best known as a poet, storyteller, and authority on Native American writing. His 1983 anthology of contemporary American Indian poets, *Songs From This Earth on Turtle's Back,* has been described as the most comprehensive collection of its kind. His poems, stories, and critical articles on Native American writing have appeared in over 400 journals, and he is the author of 21 books of poetry, fiction, and retellings of American Indian folktales. Founding editor of *The Greenfield Review Press,* one of the leading publishers of contemporary American Indian poets, he is also on the editorial board of Studies in American Indian Literatures. In 1982 he was awarded a Rockefeller Foundation Humanities Fellowship to study "Themes of Continuance in Contemporary Native American Poetry." This fellowship helped make possible the interviews which constitute this volume.